Business
Technology and

This text reveals the enormous impact of modern information technology on business and society. It presupposes no previous study of information technology or of business, so represents an extremely readable introduction to the subject for both students of business as well as for students of information technology.

Business, Information Technology and Society emphasizes the worldwide impact of new trends described and draws upon examples from the USA, Europe, Japan and the newly industrialized countries of the Pacific Rim. The book highlights the differing use of information technology in a variety of organizations – including manufacturing, services, the public sector and not-for-profit organizations – and the way this is constrained by the wider society within which such organizations operate.

Modern information technology (IT) is the result of a convergence between modern digital computing and communication technologies. The importance of IT is as the core of an 'Information System' which consists of a series of interactions between people, data, hardware and software, organizations and their social environment.

The theme of this book is that the way in which computing technology develops and is applied is the result of social decision-making. Stephen D. Tansey emphasizes the need to make conscious choices both in society as a whole and within organizations using the technology to ensure that it is used to serve the public interest in society and the strategy of the organization concerned.

Stephen D. Tansey has taught introductory courses on the business and social implications of information technology for the past fourteen years. He is a member of the Information Systems Group of the Business School at Bournemouth University. He also teaches Politics, and is the author of the successful introductory textbook *Politics: the Basics* (also published by Routledge, now in its second edition).

Geoffrey Darnton and **John Wateridge** are also members of the Information Systems Group of Bournemouth University Business School. Geoffrey Darnton is co-author of several books, including *Information in the Enterprise: It's More Than Technology*; John Wateridge has contributed extensively to the *International Journal of Project Management*.

Business, Information Technology and Society

Stephen D. Tansey
with contributions by Geoffrey Darnton
and John Wateridge

PARK LEARNING CENTRE
UNIVERSITY OF GLOUCESTERSHIRE
P.O. Box 220, The Park
Cheltenham GL50 2RH
Tel: 01242 532721

London and New York

**To the memory of Alisha May Tansey
9 March 2001–1 October 2001**

First published 2003 by Routledge
11 New Fetter Lane, London EC4P 4EE

Simultaneously published in the USA and Canada
by Routledge
29 West 35th Street, New York, NY 10001

Routledge is an imprint of the Taylor & Francis Group

© 2003 Stephen D. Tansey, Geoffrey Darnton and John Wateridge

The right of Stephen D. Tansey, Geoffrey Darnton and John
Wateridge to be identified as the Authors of this Work has been
asserted by them in accordance with the Copyright, Designs and
Patents Act 1988

Typeset in Baskerville by Wearset Ltd, Boldon, Tyne and Wear
Printed and bound in Great Britain by MPG Books Ltd, Bodmin

British Library Cataloguing in Publication Data
A catalogue record for this book is available from the British Library

Library of Congress Cataloging in Publication Data
A catalog record for this book has been requested

ISBN 0-415-19213-7 (pbk)
ISBN 0-415-19212-9 (hbk)

Contents

Figures

Tables

Case studies

Boxes

Exercises

Introduction

This book is primarily intended as an undergraduate text that introduces students to the enormous impact of modern information technology on business. It presupposes no previous study of information technology or of business. Although written from a British perspective it emphasizes the worldwide impact of the trends described and draws upon examples from the USA, Europe, Japan and the newly industrialized countries of the Pacific rim.

The theme of this book is that the way in which computing technology develops and is applied is the result of social decision-making. There is a need to take conscious choices both within organizations and in society as a whole using the technology to ensure that it is used to serve the strategy of the organization concerned and the public interest.

The book focuses upon the use of information technology in organizations of all kinds – including manufacturing, services, the public sector and not-for-profit organizations – and the way this is constrained by the wider society within which such organizations operate.

Modern information technology (IT) is understood in this book to be the result of a convergence between modern digital computing and communication technologies. The importance of IT is as the core of an 'Information System' which consists of a series of interactions between people, data, hardware and software, organizations and their social environment.

Information and its associated technologies are now so vital to business success that information is frequently regarded as an independent factor of production on a par with capital, land and labour. In the twenty-first century every business manager must understand the role which information technology plays, not only in their organization but also in the wider society, within which their organization must compete.

A full understanding of information technology is impossible without considering its interaction with the social world in which it has developed. Computer professionals who are unaware of the social, political, and economic political dimension of their work are doomed to be the pawns of 'decision-makers' who are.

In the real world a frequent cause of the failure of IT projects is a neglect of the human (including managerial and organizational) factors at work. No business or computing professional can, therefore, ignore the 'softer' elements in Information Systems, which paradoxically, often prove the hardest to get right!

How to use this book

For first-year undergraduate and Higher Diploma Business students the book will serve to link together their more general business studies with any more-technical study of information systems or computing and form a basis for later studies of business strategy. They should experience no great difficulty on a technical level but may find it useful to consult the Introduction to Information Technology section in Chapter 1 (pp. 3–14) and the Glossary (see pp. 230–8). Some recommendations for books which introduce the technology in more detail are to be found in the recommended reading list for Chapter 1.

For those students with a more technical background – such as those on Information Systems, Business Information Technology or Computer Science courses – the book should prove invaluable as an introduction to the broader business, social, economic and political factors which mould information systems. The book seeks to emphasize for them the practical importance of human relations in the workplace and the broader social factors which will influence their careers in a key industry. They may well find some of the case study material (often found in boxes amongst the text) particularly useful as the basis for class discussion.

It is also hoped that the book will be of interest to undergraduate students of Social Sciences and Media Studies, and to the general reader. The book avoids technical jargon, but does illustrate some of the different ways in which systems thinking may be interpreted (see especially Chapters 1 and 5); gives a straightforward account of the business and technical basis of the new media industries which are developing (Chapters 1 and 3); and introduces some of the ways in which technical developments are moulding, and being moulded by, contemporary society (see especially Chapters 2 and 7).

The book is organized into three parts. The first seeks to emphasize the economic, social and political constraints which mould the use of information technology in the contemporary world: the rise of an information economy and society, the nature of the core industrial sector within it, and the ways in which the use of the technology is regulated. The second focuses on the use of IT in the workplace: its impact on organizations (especially businesses) and on the people who work in them. The third part seeks to give an overview of the social choices facing decision-makers in reacting to social change conditioned by the new technology.

A number of case studies, exercises and key theories are highlighted in the text in 'boxes' which denote an expectation that the reader will actively engage with the material within the box. Each chapter is accompanied by an annotated list of recommended reading, which suggests texts or other sources appropriate for first-year degree students. References are given in full in the Bibliography at the end of the volume, enabling detailed references to be made to the authors' sources. Also included is a brief guide to the use of sources on the Internet (see p. 239) which constitute a growing and important source of information on this topic in particular. Amongst these is a specific page on Business, IT and Society maintained by the principal author, which will offer updated resources and suggestions for lecturers.

Acknowledgements

The major debt, which the principal author of this book must acknowledge, is to his colleagues in the Information Systems Group of the Business School of Bournemouth University who enabled him to complete the planned manuscript when 'production' had stalled somewhat. In particular Geoffrey Darnton and John Wateridge were mainly responsible for the following sections (for which they, not the principal author, hold the copyright):

Information systems (Ch. 1)	Geoffrey Darnton
Systems thinking and Social systems (Ch. 1)	Geoffrey Darnton
Systems analysis (Ch. 1)	John Wateridge
The information economy (Ch. 2)	Geoffrey Darnton
Project management (Ch. 5)	John Wateridge
Systems analysis (Ch. 5)	John Wateridge

These colleagues were also kind enough to comment on other parts of the book.

A further debt in regard to this book is to another colleague at Bournemouth University, Jim Muir, with whom the principal author collaborated for many years in teaching a unit on the Social and Economic Factors in Information Technology on an HND in Business Information Technology course. Besides encouraging an interest in the subject, he has allowed us to adapt his original material, especially in parts of Chapter 4. We would also like to thank numerous students at Bournemouth University and its predecessor institutions on various HND, BSc, BA, MBA and MSc Business and Information Systems courses who have helped us to clarify our ideas in this area.

Thanks are due to the following who read and commented on parts of the book in manuscript: Michael Rendell (University of the Third Age), Gareth Tansey (Creative Sales Co. Ltd), Paul Blanchard (Oxford Brookes University), Lynn Snape (Anglia Polytechnic University), Steve Clarke (Luton Business School), Bruce Bluff, Mark Ridolfo and Karen Thompson (Bournemouth University Information Systems Group). Routledge editorial staff who helped to improve my original offerings include Stuart Hay, Michelle Gallagher, and Alan Fidler.

Thanks are due to all the above for the improvements their efforts brought about; errors and omissions remain my responsibility. The authors would especially like to hear from any readers with suggestions for the improvement of later editions (see On-line resources on p. 239 for email address).

A note of formal copyright authorizations are due for the following:

Figure 1.3 Basic Features of a Computer, Les Pettman formerly of Bournemouth University: Case Study 2.4 'A Publisher', reproduced with the permission of AltaVista Internet Operations Limited. All rights reserved.

Figure 2.1 Stages of Industry Growth and Table 2.2 'IT Industry Evolution 1964–2015', from *Waves of Power* by David Moschella. Copyright 1997 by American Management Association. Reprinted by permission of American Management Association via the Copyright Clearance Center.

Figure 2.3 International Growth in Information Employment, ICCP – Information Computer and Communications Policy – No 11. *Trends in the Information Economy*. Copyright OECD, 1986.

Figure 5.2 Nolan's Six-Stage Model of IT Growth, reprinted with permission of Harvard Business Review. Exhibit 1 from 'Managing the Crises in Data Processing' by R.L. Nolan, March–April, 1979.

Figure 5.3 Business Process Re-engineering, reprinted from *The Journal of Strategic Information Systems*, Volume 3, Michael J. Earl, 'The New and the Old of Business Process Redesign', pages 5–22, copyright 1994, with permission from Elsevier Science.

Figure 6.5 Alternative Typewriter Keyboards, from *Applied Ergonomics Handbook* by Ian Gater. Reprinted with permission of Butterworth-Heinemann.

I would also like to acknowledge the use of shorter quotations of copyright material and/or the use of non-copyright material or of information from the following: Axel Zerdick and Springer for the European Communication Council: Box 2.2 'Ten theses relating to the Internet economy'; Dell Computer Corporation: Case Study 2.1 'An original equipment manufacturer'; Borland Software Corporation: Case Study 2.2 'A software house'; Electronic Data Systems Corporation: Case Study 2.5 'Information services provider'; International Data Corporation: Table 2.1 'IT industry by value chain contribution'; *Washington Post*: Case Study 3.1 'Microsoft and the courts'; *Financial Times*: Case Study 3.2 'Singapore'; *The Observer*: Table 3.1 'Multinationals and countries compared'; The Information Commissioner and HMSO: Box 4.1 'Data protection rules'; Robert Block and Yourdon Press: Box 5.2 'Informal political tactics in organizations'; Health and Safety Commission and HMSO: Box 6.4 'Legislative guidelines for the use of VDU equipment'; Michael J. Earl and D.J. Skyrme and *The Journal of Information Systems*: Table 6.1 'Key competencies for hybrid managers'; Global Reach: Table 7.1 'Web users by language'; NUA Internet Surveys and Computerscope Ltd: Table 7.2 'Net users on-line by area'; Christopher Tansey and Cream Ltd: Box 7.1 'OnyerBikes: Fund-raising Through the Web'; Louise Proddow and Hodder & Stoughton: parts of the Glossary.

Part I

The environment of computing

1 The environment of computing

A systems approach

Topics

- Business and information technology
- Information systems
- Systems thinking
- Systems analysis
- Technical systems: hardware and software
- Social systems
- Technology and social systems

This chapter has three main themes. First, the nature of modern information technology (IT) and its impact on modern business. Next, the idea of how thinking in terms of systems of different sorts helps us to understand the nature of IT and its impact on society. Finally we focus upon theme of technology change and IT management.

For less technical readers the section on technical systems gives a brief explanation of how hardware and software systems operate and inter-relate.

Business and information technology

What is information technology?

Linking together definitions of 'information' and 'technology' from the *Shorter Oxford English Dictionary*, 'information technology' means 'the systematic study of the industrial arts relating to the communication of instructive knowledge'. This definition includes studying printing, or, for that matter, smoke signals. However the general usage today, followed in this book, is more like the definition employed by Flowers (1988, 284) 'the application of computers and telecommunications to the collection, processing, storage, and dissemination of voice, graphics, text, and numerical information'.

One notable development in recent years has been the convergence of communications and computer technology, with both becoming intensive users of data embodied in binary digital form and processed by microprocessors on silicon chips. In this book therefore 'IT' is normally used in the broad modern sense to encompass both computing and telecommunications technologies. In some books, IT is used more narrowly to refer principally to computing and 'ICTs' to refer to information and communication technologies more generally.

Industrial and commercial implications

If we consider the industrial and commercial implications of the employment of the new information technologies then we must take on board that the computer is a *general purpose* machine which mechanizes human brain-powered operations just as the Industrial Revolution mechanized human and animal muscle-powered operations. The impact of such a broadly applicable technology is inevitably widespread and far-reaching. Computers have become a *pervasive* technology applied in all sectors of life, including industry, commerce, government, education and leisure activities.

In succeeding chapters we shall see the impact of computers in the creation of new products and services, new methods of production, and in transforming information processing and communication. A brief summary of some of the obvious uses of information technology is given in Box 1.1 and will be elaborated upon in later chapters.

Information systems

For businesses, information technology is only a means to an end – which is the use of knowledge to make and implement commercial decisions. Efficient organizations require established systems to enable them to make the best possible decisions in the situations they are likely to meet. Thus an organizational information system should collect data, analyse

---

Box 1.1 **The uses of computers in business**

- Storage and easy retrieval of information: databases
- Analysing information: spreadsheets, accounts packages
- Internal communications (within business): networks
- External communications (with other businesses and customers): e-mail, booking systems, etc.
- Presentation of information: word processing and desktop publishing
- Computer-aided design (CAD)
- Computer-aided manufacture (CAM): robots, process control
- New and better products: video recorders, washing machines, etc.

and present this as useful information that can be retrieved as the basis of expert knowledge at the point of decision. Once decisions are made they must be passed on to those who implement them, carried out, and the success or failure of the operation monitored. Increasingly decisions can be automatically implemented using the technology, thus enabling organizational objectives to be achieved with maximum efficiency.

Information is a – perhaps *the* – major resource of modern businesses. Consider the importance of the sorts of business information listed in Box 1.2.

In many cases businesses could even profit from having their physical plant destroyed, but could never recover from losing their information resources. This was graphically illustrated in post-Second World War Germany/Japan when bombed industries recovered dramatically with new plant and inherited know-how.

Hence some economists argue that information is a fourth major factor of production (in addition to land, labour and capital), which is of increasing importance.

However, an important point not so far stressed, is that the business information we have been describing is not just a series of isolated lists but is all interrelated. If one piece of information alters (e.g. the specification of a product) then many other items will be affected (e.g. how to produce it, suppliers required, potential customers, etc.). In other words a business's information is a system and should be organized accordingly.

A related, but not identical, point is that it is misleading to think of business information as a static list of useful things to know; rather, it

---

Box 1.2 **Key types of business information**

- *Lists of customers:* actual or potential, their needs, financial status, etc. (Frequently bought and sold as 'good will', etc.)
- *Information on the business's products:* legal standards they must conform to, how to manufacture them, product designs, etc. – often protected by patents, registered trademarks, copyright, etc. Firms must often pay quite large licence fees to produce other manufacturers' products (for instance Coca-Cola!).
- *Information on potential and actual suppliers:* capabilities, financial status, etc.
- *Information on stocks and flows:* orders, stocks of materials in hand, production levels, finished goods in the warehouse, etc.
- *Accounting information:* production costs, money owed by customers, to suppliers, etc. (debts can be sold to factors, and if not pursued may become losses).
- *Information as a business product:* many businesses are selling information for a living – e.g. publishers, stockbrokers, schools and colleges, computer software houses, advertising agencies, etc.

should be considered as a dynamic flow. Thus information will be acquired by one department and used. This then creates new information, which is vital for a second department. Computer people usually talk in terms of 'data input', 'processing' and 'output', to describe what goes on within a department or part of the work process. In these terms what we are saying is that one man's output is the next woman's input!

Few, if any, existing information systems are completely automated – indeed, people normally play a key role at each stage of the process, collecting data, analysing and presenting information, and using knowledge to make decisions (see Figure 1.1). The behaviour of people in organizations is usually profoundly modified by the structures, incentives and 'culture' of the organization. Older forms of information technology such as paper files, newspapers and letters frequently are also employed.

The quality of an information system will thus depend not only upon the excellence of the hardware and the subtlety of the software employed, but also on the accuracy and relevance of the data collected, plus the quality of the human professionals who use the system, This, in turn depends upon the extent to which the organization succeeds in coordinating and motivating employees to achieve corporate objectives.

From all of this, and a measure of common sense, some preliminary principles of good information management may be suggested. The contribution which modern information technology (particularly through a

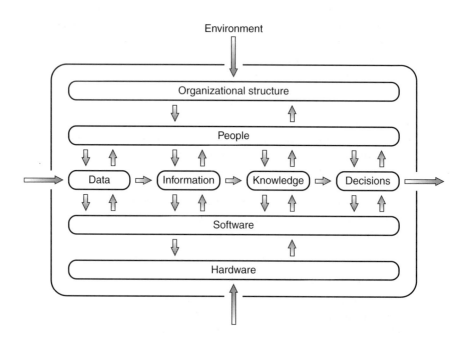

Figure 1.1 An organizational information system

Box 1.3 **Criteria for a good management information system**

Good information management will ensure that information available to decision makers is:

- Appropriate
- Accurate
- Timely
- Easily accessed

- Economically provided
- Consistent
- Safeguarded
- Of high quality

centralized database system or an Intranet) can make to this will be discussed in Chapter 5.

To understand the nature of information systems requires an understanding of terms such as 'information work', 'information technology' and 'information processes'.

'Information work' refers to any kind of work involving information (see Box 1.4). Within an enterprise it is likely that effort spent on information work is an order of magnitude greater than effort spent on computer-based information technology applications. For example, high IT spenders in the economy are enterprises such as financial institutions and government agencies. They may spend up to 8–9 per cent of total enterprise expenditure on computer-based IT applications. Such enterprises are likely to spend in the order of 70–80 per cent of total expenditure on information work. Examples of relatively low computer-based IT spenders are manufacturing and oil companies. They may spend 1–2 per cent on IT, and 35–40 per cent on information work. More information on this topic is available in Vincent (1990).

Usually the term 'information work' refers to formal activities with information. In an enterprise it is also likely that other kinds of information activities are performed, such as informal information work, or even 'information play'.

Formal information work is usually performed to carry out required procedures or produce the information component of required enterprise outputs. This includes results such as:

- the essential transactions carried out by the enterprise, such as purchases, sales or the provision of services, hiring employees or contractors, or handling calls within or to the enterprise

Box 1.4 **Examples of information work**

- Management
- Administration
- Planning

- Design
- Learning
- Problem-solving

- taking and implementing decisions
- monitoring and controlling activities
- deciding and implementing enterprise objectives and strategies
- designing products and services
- marketing and selling products and services
- training and development
- reporting activities, results and reviews
- handling calls, enquiries and problems
- contemplating alternatives.

Informal information work includes all information work that does not appear in any deliverable of the information work (but it may have been crucial in creating the deliverable), or it is work necessary to the deliverable but for one of various possible reasons cannot be written down. For example, in taking a decision various people may be consulted about alternatives and consequences, but what is eventually represented in a formal way is just the decision actually taken. An example of informal information work where the result may not be written down would be considering who might be good at doing a piece of work, and who might not be good at it. The formal result would just be the decision about who is to do the work.

Information play includes activities such as general discussion, watching television, listening to music, reading a newspaper, or some surfing of the web.

Information processes are the things that may be done to information. This can be analysed initially in terms of a life cycle of information:

- *Create:* information must be invented, brought into existence, created, or some such similar concept.
- *Use:* when information exists it will be used for one or more purposes (if information is never used to inform someone, or to affect a decision, it is useless and might as well not exist).
- *Maintain:* many pieces of information become out of date and must be corrected to take relevant changes into account.
- *Archive or retire:* many pieces of information become out of date or are used very rarely. In this case, the information is likely to be archived. Some information will be destroyed (such as old newspapers, or old commercial documents) when it is no longer needed, and some information will reside in archives such as libraries, micro-form, or electronic storage where it can be retrieved and used if desired.

This life cycle – create–use–maintain–retire – represents a minimum list of information processes. There are many more, most of which are examples of these four basic processes. Other such common processes are:

Collect	Send	Calculate
Analyse	Communicate	Report
Store	Correct	Consider
Read	Discover	

Technology is the study or science of the use of artefacts to help achieve an objective. Therefore 'information technology' is strictly the study or science of the use of artefacts to support purposeful information processes (Darnton and Giacoletto, 1992).

A very common bias in business literature today when discussing information technology is to restrict the discussion to computer-based information technology. However, this definition means that it is not appropriate to think of IT in terms of only computer-based artefacts. In fact, given these definitions, IT is several thousands of years old. Table 1.1 sets out a possible sequence of generations.

Today, as we shall see shortly, these second and third generations are intimately connected in most existing information systems. Examples of third-generation information systems that are purely information or communications technology are very rare.

We now have some of the key building blocks for a basic understanding of information systems.

A 'system' is usually considered as an ordered collection of components that interact together and behave as though the collection is pursuing one or more objectives. There are many possible formal characteristics of a system (for a more detailed discussion of the use of the terms 'system', 'technology', 'information', and so forth, related to information systems, see Darnton and Giacoletto, 1992). These include boundary, purpose, components, behaviour, possible states, extensive and intensive properties. This means that the idea of an information system is not straightforward. In common usage, the term often means a configuration of just a computer (or network of computers) along with all related hardware, software, and applications. However, by itself such a configuration would never do anything. The definition of a system requires the identification of one or more purposes. The people who use a computer configuration

Table 1.1 Generations of information and communication technology

Information generation	Information technology examples	Communications technology examples
First	Megaliths, microliths, symbols, simple accounting systems	Semaphores, signalling devices
Second	Writing, paper, printing	Telegraph, telephones
Third	Computers	Computer networks

usually provide these, or they are obtained from the reason why the configuration is used. Thus an information system usually needs a human context for its full definition.

This broad definition of an information system raises difficulties with reference to much literature about information systems. There is another serious bias in literature about information systems in that many authors treat such systems as though they are primarily concerned with computer-based IT. As we saw, expenditure on information work is an order of magnitude greater that expenditure on IT, so information systems are far more extensive than IT configurations. For this reason, information systems may take one of these three forms:

- *Substantial IT dependence:* a system which could not function effectively without the proper functioning of IT (for example, space travel).
- *Substantial second-generation IT:* a system that has extensive components such as paper, printing, and telephones (for example, enterprise marketing communications).
- *No IT:* an information system which makes little use of technology (for example, brainstorming or medical diagnosis).

Many cited examples of IT delivering substantial benefits or efficiencies are the result of the convergence between computing and communications technologies. For example, a modern supermarket certainly uses computers for pricing products at the checkout and performing related stock control, ordering, accounting and loyalty card tracking. However, the whole system involves the convergence of many technologies, including optics, lasers, materials handling, magnetics, communications and transportation. Take out any of these components and the system would need to be redesigned. Therefore we are likely to see an evolution from IT to ST (system technology). What is often referred to as an information system can be thought of as the brain and nervous system of a wider system of some kind.

Systems thinking

To describe all the information within a business organization as constituting a 'system', as has just been done, is a useful first step to understanding how such information may be employed more effectively and can help us to an understanding of its relationships with the rest of society. However, 'system' is a slippery term which requires some clear thinking if it is to be used to best advantage. Different writers and different academic disciplines use this term in overlapping but distinct and sometimes even contradictory fashions. It is important, therefore, to understand in what sense the term is being employed on each occasion it is used.

Systems thinking is usually contrasted with deterministic thinking or with structured thinking. Deterministic thinking is characterized simplistically as 'if A happens, then B will follow'. Structured thinking is characterized by approaching problems with a process of de-composing large 'things' into smaller 'things'. A system involves the interaction between many interacting components. In this sense a system is more than the sum of the whole.

A very common (perhaps the most common) way of characterizing a process is to use an input–process–output (IPO) model. The outputs of a process are some function of the inputs. That function is the processes performed on the inputs to generate the outputs. In fact, this IPO model is often so entrenched that it seems to have the status of, 'of course processes should be described as inputs–processes–outputs'.

For example, imagine a bank (or indeed any other institution). The bank has a capability to perform all kinds of processes involving people's money. The arrival of a customer triggers a process, which in turn may trigger something else, and so on until a whole 'process chain' has finished and the transactions required by the customer have been completed. This is, to many people, 'normal' thinking.

A very simple change to the IPO model implied by systems thinking is that not only are the outputs of a process a function of the inputs, they are also a function of the outputs of the same process in an earlier period of time. That is how things grow. Deposit some money in a bank, say £100. The rate of interest is 10 per cent per year. Output of the savings process is not just the rate of interest applied to the initial sum, if interest is retained in the account. The money in the account will experience compound growth as long as money is not withdrawn.

Another way to think of differences between systems thinking and structured thinking is to consider the problem of describing a large organization (or even something as large as a 'society'). Perhaps the most common way to approach this problem of description is to use a 'de-composition' technique; large things are de-composed into smaller things. Thus a large company may be described by an organization chart showing the major functions, or divisions of the company (say, sales, manufacturing, marketing, administration, planning, accounts, and so forth). The problem with such de-composition techniques is that a company is not just the sum of all the divisions or departments – *it is also the way in which those divisions or departments interact.* Where do the divisional or departmental interactions appear on an organization chart? Usually they do not.

For these kinds of reasons, systems thinking is fundamentally different from either deterministic or structured thinking.

Perhaps the first extensive and practical description of systems thinking applied to commercial organizations was that of Forrester's *Industrial Dynamics* (1961). He explains his theme as:

> Industrial dynamics is the study of the information-feedback characteristics of industrial activity to show how organizational structure, amplification (in policies), and time delays (in decisions and

actions) interact to influence the success of the enterprise. It treats the interactions between the flows of information, money, orders, materials, personnel, and capital equipment in a company, an industry, or a national economy.

(Forrester, 1961, 13)

For Forrester, the role of information is crucial in providing the feedback in a system that is such an important part of the interaction between system components.

Note that Forrester takes his systems thinking beyond the enterprise to that of a national economy (and presumably by implication to the international economy). He extended his systems thinking beyond industry in later work to look at urban systems (Forrester, 1969) and world systems (Forrester, 1971). Forrester's *World Dynamics* (1971) had a profound impact in the early stages of what is often called the environmental, or green, movements, which have one key goal of moving to sustainable human activity and a sustainable economy. This fundamental concept emerged from Forrester's models that show phenomena such as the unsustainable depletion of world resources in the absence of sufficient renewal or reuse. The *World Dynamics* model was used by the Club of Rome for its first major report, *The Limits to Growth* (Meadows *et al.*, 1972). The Club of Rome expressed the need for systems thinking about large-scale social issues when William Watts, in the Foreword to *The Limits to Growth*, states, 'the major problems facing mankind are of such complexity and are so interrelated that traditional institutions and policies are no longer able to cope with them, nor even to come to grips with their full content' (1972, 9–10).

Forrester has influenced systems thinking fundamentally. Prior to his work, the early contributions that were available to him, and are generally considered part of the discipline of systems thinking, are cybernetics and general systems theory. The term 'cybernetics' was used originally by the ancient Greeks (Plato) to refer to the science of steering ships. The first explicit relationship between cybernetics and society was the use of the term by Ampère (in the 1830s) for the science of the control of society. Its current use in systems thinking was initiated by Norbert Wiener (1948) who defines cybernetics as 'the science of control and communication in the animal and the machine'. Initially, cybernetics appeared to have a narrow focus, and was often applied in areas such as robots. However, the application to broader social issues, and society, was emergent from the beginning. Indeed Wiener himself produced *The Human Use of Human Beings: Cybernetics and Society* (1950). The difficulty in having the term accepted and used beyond mechanistic applications also prompted Stafford Beer to introduce the term 'managerial' cybernetics (Beer, 1985).

Beer's practical application of cybernetics was focused on the concept of a viable system, meaning in essence some organizational unit that has some sense of robust viability in its environment. Thus a practical system is a coherent collection of interacting components, pursuing one or more 'purposes' and structured to have a meaningful sense of viability in its environment. For example, when Digital Equipment Corporation decided to cease its management consulting business it was not possible to identify a coherent separate business that could either be sold or be bought out by management. This was due to the consulting operations never having been set up as a separate business, with all elements such as buildings, infrastructure, and organization dedicated primarily to the management consulting activities. Thus, management consulting was not, in the managerial cybernetic sense, 'viable'.

Another key work in the emergence of systems thinking is that of von Bertalanffy (1968). His view is 'systems theory is a broad view which far transcends technological problems and demands, a reorientation that has become necessary in science in general and in the gamut of disciplines from physics and biology to the behavioral and social sciences and to philosophy' (1968). He sets out to describe the key concepts of system and a wide range of applications of the idea.

An important idea in the concept of systems theory is that, in a mathematical sense, there may be abstract systems models that transcend specific systems. For example, mathematical models have been attempted to understand the occurrence of war (Richardson, 1960). Richardson's work represents a mathematical description of a system, but it was early enough not to have been influenced by the emerging explicit areas of cybernetics and general systems theory. There had also been attempts to develop mathematical theories of social behaviour and human relations.

An early work that applied systems thinking to society, but predated von Bertalanffy's seminal work, was Buckley's *Sociology and Modern Systems Theory* (1967). He contrasted several schools of sociology (mechanistic, organic, process, and Parsons-Homans) with 'The General Systems Perspective'. He did use some of von Bertalanffy's earlier work, but also identified some key concepts from de la Mettrie in the eighteenth century. Of course, much work in the field of sociology is concerned with social systems, but not explicitly with the application of systems thinking to social systems.

The application of systems thinking to social systems continues to expand into an ever-increasing range of systems. A useful summary of many concepts applied to management situations can be found in Yolles (1999). He gives a broad history of the emergence of systems thinking in management. He explains its fundamental purpose as 'This is a book about managing complexity, and within it we adopt a management systems approach to situations that we see as uncertain and complex, and that involve what many might refer to in the abstract as *purposeful adaptive activity systems*' (1999).

An important and practical approach to the use of systems thinking is found in Checkland's seminal work, *Systems Thinking, Systems Practice* (1981) – a work very much concerned with practical ways to take a complex area of concern and identify what can be done to produce some perceived improvement. The core of the work is an articulation of a soft systems methodology (SSM). Several years of experience and application are described by Checkland and Scholes (1990). The central role of information in systems thinking has been mentioned already, and it will be apparent on a deeper reading of systems-thinking literature. This leads to a serious problem in creating an operational definition of an 'information system' – it is easy to take the view that after a proper understanding of systems theory it is unlikely that there is any such thing as an information system, other than as part of some other larger viable system (in other words, an information system, *per se*, cannot be viable). Checkland and Holwell (1998) have started to address this conundrum.

Thus, systems thinking applied to social systems may be concerned with matters such as:

- handling the complexity of real-world systems (management, enterprise, industrial, social)
- understanding the components of complex systems, including the interactions between components
- recognizing that simplistic IPO models are generally inadequate for describing real-world processes and systems
- positioning feed-back and feed-forward in a system description
- appreciating the importance of purposes and objectives for understanding systems
- knowing that systems can be represented by many kinds of model and that the choice of a model type depends very much on the reasons for producing a system model
- identifying system boundaries in such a way that viable systems have been identified
- producing system models that are sufficiently general to have possible application beyond the original domain of system study
- agreeing the scope of a real-world situation of concern and agreeing a course of action to produce an improvement.

Systems analysis

Many organizations are dependent on information technology and information systems in running the business. These information systems are often very complex and very expensive to develop, therefore organizations need a way to develop such systems in order that they can realize the benefits expected of them. The information systems must deliver the requirements of the business plan or strategy. The early stages of development of an information system is called 'systems analysis'.

Box 1.5 **Benefits of the system life cycle approach**

- subdivision of a lengthy project into more manageable stages
- coordination of different facets of the project is helped by the fact that all these facets must reach the end of the stage together
- deliverables or products provide an input to the next stage
- decisions to proceed or cancel the project are constantly monitored
- expenditure on the project is closely controlled
- estimates and end dates tend to be more accurate with the smaller units of work

An information system development project is divided up into a number of different stages. This is called the system life cycle. The benefits of this type of approach are shown in Box 1.5. The stages are completed in sequence (although it is often iterative – going backwards and forwards – within stages) from problem identification through to an operational system and a review of the system. There are a number of different approaches to the development of computer-based information systems, but the principles behind each are similar. After a number of years in operation, business needs will have changed, so that there is a fundamental need for change and therefore the cycle will start again. By adopting this life cycle approach the project can be better managed.

The first four stages in Figure 1.2 are normally termed 'systems analysis'. The person carrying out this investigation is the systems analyst. The start of any IS project is the identification of a problem or an opportunity. This can come about in a number of ways. For example:

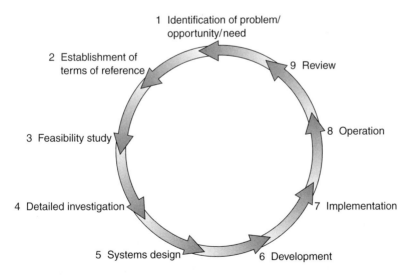

Figure 1.2 The systems development process

- a system cannot deal with the business requirements (e.g. bottlenecks, backlogs, excessive paperwork, excessive time taken to carry out processes)
- there is a requirement to become more efficient (e.g. achieve cost savings)
- demands for increased effectiveness (e.g. providing management reports)
- need for better customer service (e.g. enquiry services)
- as a result of changes in legislation (e.g. data protection, payroll tax changes).

After a problem or opportunity has been identified, the systems analyst, along with all the interested parties or stakeholders, will need to establish the terms of reference. The overall scope or boundaries of the investigation will need to be defined. This will identify what areas of the system the analyst will need to investigate. The 'stakeholders' (see Chapter 5) will also define their objectives for the new system. The terms of reference will often be drawn up by the project sponsor or by steering committee and it provides the basis for the feasibility study.

The feasibility study is concerned with a broad overview of proposed solutions to a particular problem. The report at the end of the study will inform the sponsor or steering committee whether any of the solutions would potentially be beneficial to the organization. It will provide estimates for each proposal on the costs and the benefits. The main reason for carrying out such a study is to identify at an early stage whether the project is viable. Large amounts of money could be spent on a project that will not realize any benefits. However, the feasibility study is not an in-depth investigation. Therefore, the figures are only a guide.

The systems analyst will address three main areas when undertaking the feasibility study: the economic, social, and technical viability of the proposal. Every project will incur costs and reap some benefits. There has to be some assessment of the relative costs and benefits to decide whether a project is viable. The systems analyst will examine a number of alternative ways in which the objectives can be met. Each of these options will have different costs and benefits. The sponsor or steering committee will need to examine these options and decide which (if any) is the most viable. Costs can involve:

- analysis, design, development and implementation
- software
- hardware
- operating
- redundancy.

Many of the costs will be incurred up to the implementation of the new system replacing the old, but there may be ongoing costs (such as maintenance costs/licence fees for hardware and software). The benefits are often much more difficult to estimate. They are categorized as tangible benefits (easily identifiable monetary benefits) or intangible benefits (benefits difficult to attribute monetary value to). Examples of tangible benefits are savings in labour costs and the reduction in input and data errors. Examples of intangible benefits are more effective decision-making and better customer service. It is difficult to give a monetary value to these. The benefits are associated with the system after implementation. Therefore the systems analyst will need to adopt a technique (such as discounted cash flow) to make due allowance for the value of money (i.e. £100 today is worth more than £100 in five years' time). However, the net present value calculated using discounted cash flow is only an indication of the viability of the project.

The systems analyst will need to examine the technical feasibility of the project to demonstrate the possibility of a computer solution to the problem. The issues that will be addressed here are response times of the computer system, accuracy and timeliness of information provision, the type of tasks (repetitive, complex) to be undertaken. The social feasibility addresses the human and organizational issues such as the likelihood of resistance to the change, the effect on personnel, the views of trade unions, the organizational structure in place to make most use of the change.

The feasibility study report will detail the various options available and the relative costs and benefits of each option. There will be a recommendation, along with the reasons for the recommendation. This will allow the sponsor or steering committee to make an informed decision on the way forward. After there has been a decision made on which each option is to be pursued, the project can proceed to detailed investigation.

First, the systems analyst will need to investigate the current system, its procedures and problems (if any). There will also be the necessity to record any new requirements of a new system. There are a number of ways in which a systems analyst can obtain the required information about the current system and the environment, including interviews, observation, questionnaires and examining current documentation.

The most important, and the most common, way that a systems analyst can obtain information is by interviewing all key personnel who either use the current system or have an interest in the outcome of the new system. The analyst must understand the objectives of each interview clearly, with thorough preparation on the questions to be asked and any particular terminology used by the interviewee. The advantage of the interview over other methods of collection is that the interviewer can explore details in greater depth and follow up answers with other questions not originally prepared. However, each interview should not be too long and rambling.

To supplement the information gained from the interviews, the analyst can observe the processes that are currently carried out within the system.

The analyst is able to see at first hand the functions of the system which are not apparent from interviews. The analyst is able to see any bottlenecks and problems in the system which may not be gained from interviewing members of staff. Unfortunately, this can be very time-consuming for the systems analyst and people tend to act differently when they are being observed. Questions could be asked of users during this observation process.

If there are a large number of users, spread over a wide geographical area, it may not be practical to interview each one. In this case a questionnaire will be the appropriate method for obtaining information. There is a low response rate for questionnaires, therefore questions must be simple and brief. The amount of useful information is limited. The systems analyst will also need to examine documentation about the system. This will include procedure manuals, input forms, job descriptions and publicity material. In many organizations collecting the documentation is a time-consuming exercise. Some documentation can be collected at interviews. Nevertheless, to get a full picture of the system documentation is invaluable.

After acquiring the necessary facts about the system, the analyst will need to convert the results into a diagrammatic form in order that all the procedures, data and data flows between functional areas are understood. There are a number of ways of showing such information. The analyst can use flow charts. However, the most common method is for the analyst to draw a data flow diagram (see Box 1.6). This diagram can first be used to show the existing system. In fact, a data flow diagram could be developed as part of an interview. At the very least it will be used as a way of confirming the analyst's understanding of the system. The data flow diagram can then be used to develop a logical view of the system, as opposed to a physical one, as a precursor to creating a new system.

Not all the processes will be shown on one diagram. In a large system this would involve a large diagram. The analyst will therefore decompose the diagram and create a number of 'levels' of the diagram, grouping processes together to ensure that none are omitted.

After developing the data flow diagrams to show the processes and flows, attention must be turned to the data within the data stores of the

---

Box 1.6 **Components of data flow diagrams**

- *Processes:* a description of a procedure carried out by the system, signified by an active verb.
- *Data store:* where data is held in a file for storage or retrieval.
- *Data flow:* a line showing the data that is being sent or received by a process.
- *External entity:* something or someone not part of the system providing data to or receiving information from the system.

Box 1.7 **Entity relationship modelling**

- *Entity:* something about which data can be held (e.g. an employee, department)
- *Attribute:* properties of an entity (e.g. for an employee, surname, date of birth, gender)
- *Relationship:* the linking of two or more entities (e.g. two entities, employee and department, are linked because employees work in departments)

system. The method used is entity relationship modelling to create a logical data structure. The key features are shown in Box 1.7.

The analyst will develop a logical data structure to show the relationships between data entities. This is fundamental in helping the eventual design of a database to store data on a computer.

The third view of the system data is the entity life history. This examines the entities from the perspective of what happens to the data over time, from when it is created to when it is deleted, taking account of all the changes to the data during this time.

An alternative approach to analysing and modelling systems, which does not require a separation of data and process, is linguistic. The leading tool developer for this was PSL/PSA. More information is available at www.pslpsa.com

Technical systems: hardware and software

For the benefit of less technically minded readers we shall start by looking at the basics of computer design ('hardware'), then move to the 'software' which is essential to operate it. A brief discussion of changes in communications technology will help to explain the idea of 'convergence' already referred to. But these technicalities are only of relevance to us as a basis for understanding the basic components of modern systems for meeting the information needs of business and other organizations and, indeed, individual human beings. This being, in turn, a preliminary to our main theme: the impact the technology is having on both business and society.

Computer hardware

Some basic description of the parts of a computer may help the reader to understand the logic of their use. A computer is a device to store and analyse data (the basic components of information). Logically, therefore, it can be broken down into four major parts: input, memory, processing and output. First, data must be fed into the system by another machine or a person (input); this data must be held in some form by the system (added

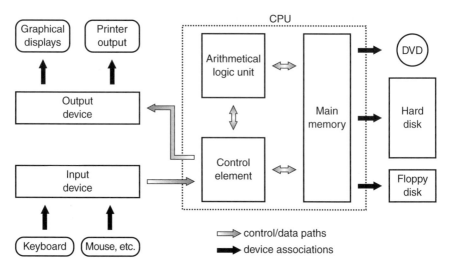

Figure 1.3 Basic features of a computer

to 'memory'), it is then 'processed' (e.g. added to, or subtracted from, some other data or merely retrieved from the 'memory'), and finally the data is transmitted outside the system to another machine or person ('output').

The computers with which most readers are familiar are electronic devices, and this preliminary explanation will focus upon these. Logically, however, computers can be of a variety of forms such as the purely mechanical devices used in previous centuries or, possibly in the future, devices using biological or laser technology.

Input

In contemporary computers the input device is typically a typewriter-like keyboard, plus a visual display unit (VDU) screen probably combined with a 'mouse', this latter enabling any part of the screen to be pointed to and selected. However, as you can see in more detail in Box 1.8, all sorts of other devices are employed to feed data into computers. One of the most important contemporary sources of data are the signals from other, perhaps far-distant, computers (e.g. e-mail). In such a case it is clear that a 'network' of connected computers is a set of potentially powerful communications devices.

Memory

The nature of the 'memory' of a computing device is directly related to the way in which data is represented by it. In Charles Babbage's

---

Box 1.8 **Input devices for computers**

Amongst the oldest input devices was a 'reader' which could sense the presence or absence of holes at fixed locations in a series of 'punched cards' not unlike postcards in size. This type of machine was invented by Hollerith in the nineteenth century to count the USA census returns mechanically. This was clearly a very awkward arrangement requiring the specification of how each standard card would be used and interpreted for each job, and human operators to punch the data onto the cards with considerable potential for error.

Any device which is being used as an auxiliary data storage for another similar computer can be transferred and used as input. Thus it was formerly very common to transport large reels of magnetic tape physically from one commercial computer to another.

Another important source of input to computers is instrument readings on machines to which the computer is linked – for instance, in a plane on automatic pilot, radar, compass, altimeter readings, etc. will be inputted directly from the instruments.

One input device of particular commercial importance is a scanner, which, in combination with appropriate software, can convert text or graphics on a written page to a text or graphics file on the computer. Similarly, a microphone may input sound which can be converted by appropriate software either into a recording or, if the sound is a human voice, into text. Such a conversion requires the use of extremely sophisticated software which can both recognize the sounds as speech, different pronunciations as equivalent, and interpret the speech as a particular language with all its peculiarities of spelling and punctuation.

---

nineteenth-century computer, data was represented by the position of a mechanical cog in the device. Each cog had ten teeth so that one cog represented units, the next (with which it meshed) represented tens, the next hundreds, and so on. Thus each part of the computer's memory may represent up to ten numbers; such a computer could be termed a mechanical decimal digital computer. Moving a unit cog one position clockwise might represent the addition of one unit, moving one position anticlockwise could represent subtraction, with the resultant position representing a 'remembered' total. Modern computers are in effect composed of electronic switches which are either 'on' or 'off', rather than cogs which can be in ten different positions. If we take 'off' to be zero ('0') and 'on' to be one ('1'), each switch or element of the memory (technically known as a 'bit' of memory) can represent one element of a 'binary' number. Most readers who have had the benefit of a modern mathematical education will know that any ordinary decimal number (say '8') can be equally well represented by a longer binary number (in this case '1,000'). Hence modern computers should perhaps strictly be described as 'electronic binary digital computers' – although this mouthful is often abbreviated to the shorter but less accurate 'digital computer'.

The next box (1.9) discusses computer memory in more detail but could well be omitted at first reading by totally non-technical readers.

An important point to grasp is that although all data is held in the computer in the form of binary numbers this is today no bar to virtually any kind of information being held by one computer or transmitted from one computer to another. Thus text is easily dealt with by assigning a number to each lower case letter, each capital letter, and to grammatical features like quotation marks and full stops. This is often done on a standardized basis using an agreed 'standard' known as ASCII (the American Standard

---

***Box 1.9* How electronic computers remember**

Almost all modern computers have at least two different ways of storing data. 'Main' memory is a silicon chip or chips which is closely connected to the central processor unit (CPU – see p. 24). This, in turn, is divided into two: the ROM ('read-only memory') section which permanently remembers a series of instructions for processing purposes and the RAM (random access memory) which temporarily stores the data the CPU is processing and some of the instructions required for this purpose.

Additional memory will frequently take the form of a built-in 'hard disk' of very large capacity which stores all the regularly used data and sets of instructions (programs) normally required by the user. Hard disks are electro-magnetic devices consisting of a rapidly spinning disk from which data can be 'read' extremely quickly. Magnetically recorded information can be altered by operating an electrical current, but is retained even when the electrical power to the device is switched off. In 'networked' systems a number of computers keep most of their information shared on a common hard disk (or similar device) on a 'server' machine.

Most machines also have a 'port' into which 'floppy' disks – smaller capacity, but similar electromagnetic memory disks – can be inserted. 'Floppy' disks are these days usually rigid (3.5 inch) affairs but used to be thinner, flexible (as much as 8 inch) objects – hence the name.

Most machines now also have a port into which CD-ROM (compact disk-read-only memory) disks can be inserted. Such disks use a different technology, being 'read' via laser technology and storing information via tiny indentations on their shiny surface rather than by magnetic variation. As the name suggests, these disks contain 'fixed' data so that they are, strictly speaking, input devices. However, similar devices which can be 'written to' by the CPU are now available and constitute very high capacity memory stores.

Numerous other memory devices are, or have been, in use and no doubt still more are under development. These include magnetic tape (cf. tape-recorders), a recent version of which is the very high capacity but removable 'zip' drive.

Code for Information Interchange). Pictures, even moving pictures, and sound can also be reduced to digital form in similar ways (see Box 1.10), the only problem being that a brief movie clip requires a huge amount of memory to record.

Finally, in relation to memory, it is worth grasping a few technicalities relating to how data is stored and measured. It is clear from what has gone before that any piece of information other than the digital numbers 0 and 1 will occupy more than one 'switch' or position in the memory. The practice, therefore, is to group positions together in 'words' which can represent at least a reasonable-sized number or (therefore) a letter. The earliest computers generally grouped such memory locations together in groups of eight, this being technically referred to as a 'byte'. Memory capacity is still quoted in bytes. An early computer might have had a total capacity of approximately 1,000 bytes (approximately 8,000 bits), this being referred

---

***Box 1.10* How binary numbers represent graphics (etc.)**

Several techniques have been developed by computer scientists to represent pictures and other images. The simplest of these is known as 'bit mapping'. A simple black and white diagram can be broken down into tiny squares (dots). Each square is either black or white. Thus each tiny square can be represented by either '1' for black or '0' for white. The location of each dot can be described in terms of its distance from the left-hand corner of the diagram. Say the diagram is 1,000 dots wide and 1,000 dots high, then (0, 0, 0) could represent a white dot in the bottom left hand corner; (1,000, 1,000, 1) a black dot in the upper right-hand corner; (500, 500, 1) a black dot in the centre, and so on. It can be seen that quite a small diagram would have a million (1,000 × 1,000) dots and require at least a million numbers to describe it. Thus graphics tend to eat up the memory of a computer. (This is still true even if we allow for all sorts of ingenious tricks which are used in practice to cut down the memory demands from the enormous figures suggested here.)

If it is desired to add colour or intensity then additional data will have to be stored and processed to describe this. Clearly, the more dots per inch (dpi) the better the quality of the picture produced. So high-quality colour pictures demand even more computer memory.

A moving picture will be constructed, as on film or television, from a succession of still pictures presented rapidly enough to fool the human eye into the illusion of movement. Each successive picture (or, more accurately, each change from the previous picture) will have to be 'labelled' to indicate at which fraction of a second from 'Go' it is to be presented, thus presenting further demands on data storage and processing.

All this gives an indication of why 'multi-media presentations' are a relatively recent feature on computers and how even the rapidly increasing memory capacities of contemporary machines can be so easily stretched by the demands of such applications.

to as a kilobyte (KB). More recently memory capacity has grown so markedly that units of approximately a million – a megabyte (MB) – and even approximately a billion (1,000 million) – a gigabyte (GB) – are common. For supercomputers and high-speed fibre-optic links, terabytes (TB) (1 trillion bytes) have now come into use.

Whilst early production computers had words of 8 bits in length, more recent computers have adopted longer words of 16, then 32 and now, increasingly, 64 bits. The location of each word in the memory is technically known as an address, and groups of addresses may be allocated to storing particular kinds of data.

Processing

Word length is also of significance in terms of how the computer processes data in that well-designed computers can process the entire contents of a 'word' simultaneously. Hence, other things being equal, a modern 64-bit machine should be able to process data at least eight times faster than an old 8-bit machine.

In practice, however, modern machines have a still greater advantage over older machines in that they now do each key operation much faster. This is described in terms of the 'clock speed' of the main microchip (central processor unit, or CPU) which performs all the key operations in the computer. This is measured in megahertz (MHz) each of which represents a somewhat incredible million operational cycles per second. This is all the more striking when it is realized that contemporary machines operate at several hundred megahertz.

The central processor unit consists of three main elements, the first of which is the main memory already described. The heart of a modern computer is the second element, the arithmetic logic unit section of the CPU which, as its name suggests, can perform a restricted number of arithmetical and logical operations incredibly fast. At a minimum, this must be able to add, subtract and compare the contents of two addresses in the main memory. In fact, strangely enough, some of the most sophisticated computers have the simplest CPUs because these can operate faster. From these very simple operations, and with the right set of instructions (the program), very sophisticated analyses can be carried out and complex screen displays and sound effects managed. The third part of the CPU is a control element which marshals the data in and out of the CPU and the memory.

As this is not intended to be a technical computer science text, the temptation to elaborate on the numerous subsidiary parts of a modern computer will be resisted. What should be emphasized, however, is that until recently virtually all computers were designed on the lines so far described with a single CPU responsible for almost all operations performed. (Common minor exceptions are additional chips for some complex mathematical operations – 'floating point arithmetic' – and to control video displays.) Technically this type of machine is described as having a 'Van Neumann' architecture.

The existence of a single CPU may seem quite difficult for the non-technical to believe when it is considered that computers often appear to be doing several things at the same time. A simple example would be that a modern machine can be seen apparently simultaneously controlling a printout of data, accepting the input of text into a spreadsheet in one window on the screen, and displaying a World Wide Web page in another window. However, it must be remembered that the human eye or ear would register two operations carried out within a thousandth of a second as simultaneous, whilst even a relatively slow (1 MHz) computer can carry out a thousand operations in that time.

A relatively new development is the development of a 'parallel processing' architecture in which a whole set (array) of microprocessors, often of very simple design (i.e. RISC – reduced instruction set chips), operate together. The problem with such machines is that the control element of the processing array then faces extremely difficult problems – for instance to prevent two processors simultaneously attempting different operations at the same memory address.

Output

Some input devices can also operate as an output device – notably a cable connection to another computer or the screen of a VDU. Many output devices, however, are dedicated to that function alone, for instance loudspeakers and printers. Without pausing to elaborate on the various printing technologies which can be employed – including daisy wheel, dot matrix, ink jet and laser – it is worth mentioning that most of these incorporate a microprocessor of their own and are, in fact, special-purpose computers in their own right.

Just as we saw that other machines can be directly linked to a computer for input purposes so a computer can output instructions to linked machines. In our previous example an automatic pilot is, of course, a computer which directly controls the rudder and aileron on an aircraft (taking into account instructions on heading, height, etc. previously inputted by the pilot). More generally computers control a variety of machines in automated production plants – for instance paint-spraying machines in vehicle assembly plants.

Computer software

We saw earlier that computers are inherently rather stupid (or, more politely, limited) machines. Without detailed instructions in the form of programs in binary form ('code' ultimately written by human beings), computers can do little more than add up and compare. Most programs are 'software' in that they must be fed into the machine in some way – for example as instructions from a keyboard, on magnetic tape, or CD-ROM – but some, we saw, are built into the machine's ROM. It may be helpful to outline some of the main types of software.

Operating system

A set of instructions has to exist to tell the computer how to work – for instance how to create video screen displays, how to perform routine (and sometimes quite complex) mathematical operations, to translate keyboard instructions expressed in letters and arabic numbers into binary digital instructions which can be implemented by the machine, and so on. This 'operating system' differs greatly from machine to machine so that some micros, like the BBC-type formerly used in UK schools, have a built in facility (in ROM) to understand BASIC programs. Apple Macs and most modern PCs, however, require a special program to be loaded into the machine from a disk before they can 'interpret' such programs.

A major area of variation is in the type of user 'interface' machines offer. Macintosh and modern 'Wintel' (Windows operating system plus Intel central processors) PCs operate via a 'WIMP'-style 'interface' (that is, using windows, icons, menus, pointers), but older IBM PC-type and 'BBC' machines had to be instructed by typed words or function keys. In contrast with stand-alone machines, network and mainframe operating systems have to cope with additional complexities like rationing and charging numbers of users, and keeping each user's files separate and secure.

Applications packages

Another type of software enables you (the user) to employ the computer for specific purposes without necessarily knowing how to instruct the computer directly. Almost every reader will have operated computer games, which are one form of applications package. Many readers will have used Word or another word-processing package. Increasingly, business use of computers consists in using standard commercially produced software for functions such as those listed in Box 1.1.

Programs

Traditionally most commercial users have (except for word processing) employed systems analysts and programmers who write 'bespoke' (tailor-made) programs specially designed to meet the needs of the employing organization. Such programs are at present usually written in so called third generation or 'high-level' languages such as C++, COBOL, BASIC or Pascal which require specialist knowledge and experience. This book does not attempt to turn readers into programmers, but will attempt to outline what programmers and systems analysts can, or cannot, do for managers. (Fourth generation languages are now much in use and are supposed to be usable by non-specialists – in effect they are similar to applications packages so that, in principle, the user only has to know what they want to achieve, not how computers work.)

Other files

Each of the previous types of program will be held in the computer memory in digital form. However, other files are created when these programs are implemented – e.g. a Word document is created using the Word applications package. Such files may either be the ultimate output the user intended to create (an output file) or merely intended as a working document to be drawn upon by other programs (a data file – e.g. a list of figures to be turned into statistics by a statistics package, which will in turn be displayed as graphs by the same or another package).

History of computing

Computing technology has developed to date with dizzying speed. This is often expressed in terms of 'generations' (occurring much more rapidly than human generations that are conventionally supposed to last for thirty years). It should help most readers to understand the current state of the technology by giving a brief outline of how it evolved.

The concept of a 'generation' and the table (Box 1.11) are intended as helpful simplifications of a complex story of technological development. Essentially it should be emphasized that the development of hardware (which included some revolutionary leaps forward) was accompanied by a somewhat more gradual evolution of software techniques which enabled improved use to be made of the machinery.

Box 1.11 Computing generations

Generation	Decade	Hardware	Software
0	Pre-1940s	Mechanical	Punched cards etc.
1	1940s and 1950s	Valves	Machine code
2	1960s	Transistors	Assembly language
3	1970s	Integrated circuits	High-level languages
4	1980s	VLSI	Application generators
5	1990s	Networks	Artificial intelligence
		Parallel processors	HTML

VLSI = very large-scale integration of circuits; HTML = HyperText Markup Language

As we have indicated, before the first generation of electrical digital computers there were a number of mechanical devices for mathematical calculation and for the sorting of complex data sets. On an experimental basis, Charles Babbage also developed a programmable computer in the nineteenth century. These are indicated in Box 1.11 as 'generation 0'. Before computing could become a reality the intellectual tools upon which programming is based also had to be developed. These included the ideas of mathematical logic. In the 1930s the pure mathematician Alan Turing developed the theoretical concepts of computing to the point at which he devised a test for the concept of a machine with 'artificial intelligence', despite the absence of practical computers to perform the required operations.

During and immediately after the Second World War the first electric computers were developed as experimental research devices (including research by British academics to crack German codes and US research to develop a nuclear arsenal). These computers were clumsy and unreliable devices relying on complex arrays of electric wires and valves (a device resembling a small light bulb in appearance), only programmable by the researchers who developed them and were familiar with their architecture. To do this they employed 'machine code' – that is, binary instructions to move data from a specific part of the memory to another.

As computers became mass-produced devices used by people who had not developed them, each manufacturer developed somewhat easier 'assembly languages' with which to instruct the machines how to operate. These still required some knowledge of the specific machine used and considerable training on the part of the specialist personnel who used them. Computers at this stage were still large and expensive mysteries locked away in air-conditioned back rooms.

The development of the transistor to replace the valve meant that machines became much smaller and more reliable. On the software side new third-generation programming languages, such as Fortran and COBOL, were developed and enabled programs to be written which were not specific to particular machines by personnel with months, rather than years, of training.

In fourth-generation machines the development of the microchip meant that the CPU became a tiny and highly reliable element of the complete machine with a very small manufacturing cost (as part of a manufacturing run of millions). Applications such as word processors and spreadsheets became accessible to millions of users after only days or even hours of training.

Contemporary (fifth generation) developments include the production of supercomputers with large arrays of parallel processors and experiments with laser technology. Machine-user interfaces such as touchscreens and voice recognition enable untrained users to use computers on a large scale. A major development in the 1990s has been the application of earlier technology on a global scale through the Internet and similar networks. The use of HTML (HyperText Markup Language) has enabled even untrained users to access global networks through the World Wide Web.

The development of artificial intelligence (AI) languages has enabled software to mimic the behaviour of human experts. Turing's test for artificial intelligence was that a human being interrogating a machine with this characteristic would not be able to distinguish its replies from those of a human expert. AI languages enable programs to be set up on computers which take a series of rules obtained from human experts (e.g. 'always invest in stocks and shares with a net asset value greater than their price'; 'always buy when prices are at least 10 per cent below peak value for the last twelve months', etc.), vet them for consistency and apply them to particular circumstances (e.g. should I buy, sell or hold stock in IBM?). The result is a decision or recommendation based on human best practice which often outperforms the average professional in the field concerned. Such software appears to meet Turing's test, but it does depend on human expertise in gathering in and evaluating appropriate rules for the program to use.

The chip as a technological breakthrough

Although the story of the development of computing is quite complex it can be summarized fairly easily in terms of a number of surprisingly consistent trends which have meant that the technology has been transformed in half a century of rapid development (Box 1.12). Thus a machine which could once with difficulty be accommodated in a single room has now been reduced to credit card size; that which once cost millions of pounds can be manufactured for pence; that which once accounted for an industrial size electricity bill can run on a solar-powered battery; that which broke down daily can now run for years unattended and unmaintained. In memory capacity and speed, increases in performance represent multiples of millions on the original experimental machines. Increased user-friendliness means that computers have progressed from research laboratories to primary schools.

Box 1.12 **Computing trends**

- Reducing cost
- Reducing energy use
- Reducing size
- Increased reliability
- Increased memory capacity
- Increased speed
- Increased user-friendliness

Types of machine and modes of processing

It may be helpful to sketch the different types of computer employed by businesses and, perhaps more importantly, to distinguish the different ways in which computer processing of information is related to the business processes of the organizations concerned.

The oldest type of computer and the earliest form of processing is the 'mainframe' computer, first engaged upon 'batch' processing of data. A mainframe computer is simply a powerful machine that constitutes one of the few major computing resources of the organization concerned. (What constitutes a 'powerful' computer has altered greatly over the years as we have seen.) In such an environment large amounts of data (batches) would be brought to the computer centre to be processed. In some cases the aim might be to bring the data to the centre at the normal close of business for one day and process it overnight ready for the beginning of business the next day. This would mean running an expensive nightshift, so the alternative for less urgent processing would be to run the data in the day. In this case all data coming back from the computer would be at least 24 hours out of date – probably more with weekends and the queuing of less urgent work.

Smaller, less powerful, computers are or have been described as minicomputers (these might run departmental rather than organizational information systems), still less powerful ones as microcomputers (which have often been also referred to as personal computers since they were originally designed for individual use). However, it should be noted there is no formal accepted definitions of these terms and the terminology has become grossly misleading over the years. One major reason for this is that processing power and memory capacity have improved so rapidly that a personal computer from 1999 would probably be more powerful than a microcomputer built in 1994, which in turn could well exceed in specification the mainframe from 1989, and so on. In practice the way a computer is used is more important than its technical description.

It was soon discovered that one (mainframe or mini) computer could easily cope with the work being inputted by several human operators at separate keyboards and VDUs (terminals). It was also found that the terminals could be situated at distant locations from the central computer. At first this was merely a convenience enabling data to be inputted from (say) every branch of an insurance company each day with all the data still being run through in a batch at intervals. However, it was soon seen that data from one terminal could be viewed at another so that the computer could be used as an 'electronic mail' (or e-mail) system. Similarly, as processing power increased it was seen that there was no need to wait for all the operators to add their data in before a batch 'run' was performed. As each new piece of data was added to the database it could be reanalysed as required. Instead of waiting hours or days for results each terminal could read the up-to-date results down the electronic line to the central computer. Thus 'on-line' processing of data became possible and is now a common feature of computerized information systems.

So far we have described here systems based upon one central computer feeding a network of terminals without computing power of their own – these are referred to as 'dumb terminals'. The advantage of such systems from an organizational point of view is that they can be planned and coordinated from the centre with every member of the organization having appropriate access to the same basic data. The snag from the organization's members' point of view is that the information planned for them may not be what they feel they require and that developing new information facilities depends upon the staff controlling the centralized facilities.

At the opposite extreme from these centralized systems would be an arrangement in which virtually every employee had their own independent personal computer on which he or she could keep whatever information they wanted, presenting it in the most convenient way for doing their own job. The difficulties of this include inconsistencies between the information different employees are using, failures to communicate potentially useful information, and lack of expertise in using computers by employees without enough training in computers. (The problems of 'end-user computing' are discussed in more detail in Chapter 5.)

Most organizations today, however, have moved away from either of these extremes to a more flexible arrangement in which, although key organizational information may be concentrated on one (or a number of key) powerful computers, these are linked to computers with independent processing capabilities which can 'download' appropriate data for further use and analysis as required. This is known as the 'distributed' processing of data. We shall discuss the considerable managerial problems of doing this well later in the book (see pp. 137–42).

Distributed processing can take a number of forms, including the creation of networks of networks. Each smaller network may be linked to a more powerful 'server' machine (or machines) which provide software resources, databases and/or communication 'hubs' for the network, while 'network computers' (NCs) may be provided as terminals which have more processing power than dumb terminals but less independent facilities than a stand-alone PC.

Communications technology

The attentive reader will already have noted that we have referred more than once to the possibility of using a computer or several computers as communications devices. We saw how output from one computer could become input for another and how a single mainframe with multiple terminals could act as an e-mail system. In discussing computer memory we showed how pictures or sound, as well as graphics, could be represented digitally.

If we turn to long-established methods of communication – books, newspapers, telephone, fax, and broadcasting – it will be seen that digital techniques and computer technology have become of overwhelming importance for these older methods of communication. This has presented important opportunities for the integration of what were previously independent products and industries.

Printed books and newspapers were, of course, originally produced using a rather laborious technique of arranging metal type in rows on a plate, inking the plate and then pressing pieces of paper against the plate. Until fairly recently newspaper printing technology still involved craftsmen mechanically 'typesetting' impression cylinders which inked the paper passed at high speed through the press. This had little in common with computing technology. However, modern printing techniques have basically adopted a similar technology to that of a computer with a laser printer. So much so that this book, in common with most others, was submitted to the publisher in the shape of a computer disk which was then modified for printing purposes. Similarly, newspapers are now designed on computer screens and largely use information contributed from portable computers in digital form via the telephone lines.

Telephone technology (like the fax) was developed in the nineteenth century, pre-dating the electronic computer and employing an 'analogue' mode of transmission which depended on electric signals mimicking the sound waves normally used in speech, rather than a digital signal. Hence it is still usually necessary when sending computer signals down ordinary (copper two-strand) telephone lines to 'translate' signals from a binary format into an analogue format using a 'modem' on transmission and back again on reception. However, in order to operate telephone exchanges on an automatic basis and to maximize the number and quality of messages that can be sent down long-distance telephone lines it was found to be desirable to translate analogue signals into digital ones. Most long-distance links between exchanges are now fibre-optic 'cables' which allow thousands of digital laser signals to pass along strands little thicker than human hairs. Exchanges are heavily computerized with messages routed from one destination to another by complex computer programs which take into account congested routes, breakdowns and other factors. When the entire system is converted to ISDN (Integrated Services Digital Network – see Chapter 4) then high-quality picture and data, as well as voice services, will be available to all subscribers.

Similarly, broadcasting technology has moved from a purely analogue wave technology, as found in early radio broadcasts, towards increasing reliance on digital signals. In Britain, in 2002, both satellite and terrestrial television and radio are now available in digital form. A television picture, being based upon pixels (squares of a certain colour, shade, etc.), is obviously akin to the bit-mapping technique referred to earlier. As with telephone signals, the main advantage of digital signals over analogue ones is that more messages can be transmitted over the same transmission media, thus allowing much greater choice of channel for the potential audience. The quality of reception should also be improved since digital signals are less susceptible to interference than analogue ones.

The commercial significance of this convergence of technologies is worth outlining here and will be returned to in more depth in Chapter 3. Any media product produced with digital technology can be converted fairly easily from one media to another. Thus an illustrated book (e.g. an encyclopaedia) can be converted into a CD-ROM for use on PCs. This might be illustrated with clips from videos made for television transmission by the same publisher. One digital media (e.g. a newspaper such as the *Sun*) can publicize another owned by the same publisher (e.g. BSkyB satellite television). Programmes made for one television station can be transferred by satellite data-link to another station elsewhere in the world and seamlessly re-edited. A television cartoon can be used as a publicity device for a computer game produced with similar software by the same media group. The economies of scale and the opportunities for cross-fertilization open to a global digital media group are rapidly becoming more obvious – and to some eyes sinister.

Social systems

Earlier we defined a system as an ordered collection of components that interact together and behave as though the collection is pursuing one or more objectives. We have considered technological systems and seen that they can be part of an information system. It is clear that an information system is, in turn, normally a part of an organization. System theorists, and a broader range of social scientists, would all regard organizations as social systems.

Clearly the members of organizations tend to interact more closely with each other than with outsiders, have some common objectives, and generally behave towards outside organizations and people (customers, suppliers, etc.) as if they are members of one entity. There is a vast literature about the behaviour of people in organizations (e.g. Pugh, 1997; Pugh and Hickson, 1996; Huczynski, 2001), which we will refer to in more detail in Chapter 6. But we can mention here their propensity to develop common ways of looking at and behaving and feeling towards the rest of the world and themselves. This is termed 'the development of organizational culture' by sociologists and helps to explain the many aspects of social behaviour which we shall be looking at. At the same time it is clear that within organizations there are structures of authority and conflicts between sub-groups within the organization which one might describe as political (Tansey, 2000, Ch. 1 and References). Most of the organizations we shall come across in this book have as one of their major objectives an economic goal – the production of goods and services usually for profit. They usually have some sort of legal status too – companies, for instance, being legal entities recognized by law with the capacity to sue and be sued.

Organizations, too, are clearly parts of wider social systems – local, regional, national and, indeed, global societies. These wider social systems from the point of view of the lower levels are part of the environment, which constrains their behaviour but can also be influenced by them. Like organizations, local, regional, national and global societies have economic, legal, political and social aspects and so can be analysed as economic, legal, political and sociological systems.

Much of this book will be concerned to show how important a knowledge of the wider economic, political and social factors is for an understanding of how information systems work. It is also worth pointing out that often information systems themselves are attempting to accumulate data on their environment to enable their associated decision-makers to influence and control the outside world.

Social systems, then, are of crucial importance and have a real influence in the business world – but they are very difficult to describe on a theoretical level. For instance, people talk about the economy or the political system as if they are real objects, yet a moment's serious thought will convince most people that they are merely aspects of reality, convenient for purposes of analysis to separate out. When a rich businessman bribes a politician to misrepresent his poor electors and spend taxes on subsidizing the industry in which the businessman has an interest, is that politics or economics?

As we have seen, systems theorists like Forrester and Beer are quite eager to apply concepts like feedback and information flow to the analysis both of organizations and of larger societies. Some social scientists, however, whilst still talking of 'social systems', are more ready or even anxious to stress the degree of conflict between groups such as classes and ethnic groups which scarcely figure in the vocabulary of many system theorists (Dahrendorf, 1959).

Technology and social systems

It is important to realize that the various types of system described in this chapter are not independent from each other. In particular it is clear that technological and social systems interact in some vital ways.

We can illustrate the impact of social systems on technology by an examination of the literature on industrial innovation. Three (overlapping) main types of this kind of analysis can be distinguished: those following in the tradition of Rogers (1983) who are mostly concerned with the diffusion of relatively simple product innovations among relatively small 'businesses' such as farmers and doctors (see also Jones, 1975;

Foxall, 1984, Ch. 6), who for convenience will be referred to as 'diffusionists'; those mainly concerned with the conditions for technological innovation within firms starting with the classic work of Burns and Stalker (1966) but continuing with rather different emphases through those of Freeman (1982) and Twiss (1986), referred to here as 'technologists'; and those more concerned with the organizational impact of change such as Gross *et al.* (1971), Drucker (1985) and the CBI (1985) whom we may refer to as 'managers'.

The 'diffusionists' suggest that firms vary greatly in how fast they are prepared to adopt new innovations. Entrepreneurs' reactions to new developments are a product of their industrial environment, with early innovators having markedly different characteristics to the majority adopting an innovation at a later stage in terms of educational background of managers, size of organization and the like.

'Technologists' suggest that larger firms with specialized professional staff may be in a better position to innovate (Freeman, 1982, Ch. 6). Burns and Stalker (1966) also point to the importance of management style (an aspect of what we earlier termed 'organizational culture') in relation to capacity to innovate ('organic' flexible systems being preferred to bureaucratic or 'mechanistic' ones).

'Managers' have emphasized the need for successful firms to organize for change, to have 'intelligence systems' capable of grasping external opportunities, and training staff to cope with proposed organizational and technical changes (see Chapters 5 and 6).

Thus the likelihood of firms adopting new technology, or indeed inventing it, is related to the social characteristics of the organization. Societies as a whole, too, differ greatly in the extent to which they encourage technological innovation. The German sociologist Max Weber, for instance, compares the way that the Chinese Empire lasted for centuries without capitalizing on inventions such as gunpowder and printing that were discovered under its rule, whilst Protestant Europe made such inventions the linchpin of a new social and economic order (Gerth and Mills, 1948).

Similarly, the type of society and economy prevalent will clearly mould the technological innovations which are sought, found and exploited. In time of war extraordinary innovations are sometimes made in very short times – rocketry, computing and atomic fission during the Second World War for instance. More recently, in a time of (capitalist) peace, innovations have focused upon consumer electronics goods.

Conversely technology has affected social systems from the earliest times. Wittfogel (1957, 17–18, 26–7) showed how the need to control the flooding of the Nile profoundly influenced the development of the Egypt of the Pharaohs. We shall discuss in Chapter 2 how changes in technology (especially information technology) have moulded the development of the modern world.

On a day-to-day practical level, technologists and managers need to understand that in an era of rapid change the impact of changes in technology on organizations can often be extreme. Careful planning, not only of the technical side of information technology projects but still more of the human aspects, is required if the desired benefits are to be achieved. These themes will be explored in greater depth in Chapters 5 and 6.

Recommended reading

Checkland, P. and Holwell, S. (1998) *Information, Systems, and Information Systems,* Chichester, John Wiley & Sons. An excellent overview of basic information system concepts co-written by the guru of the 'soft' systems approach.

Dennis, A. and Wixom, B.H. (2000) *Systems Analysis and Design: An Applied Approach,* New York, John Wiley & Sons. Useful introduction to systems analysis.

Stalling, W. (2000) *Computer Organization and Architecture* (4th edn), Upper Saddle River, N.J., Prentice-Hall. Very good standard text which explains in some detail how modern computers work at the operating system and hardware levels.

Winston, B. (1998) *Media, Technology and Society. A History: From the Telegraph to the Internet,* London, Routledge. An excellent description of the development of modern means of computing and communication.

2 The IT industry and the information economy

Topics

- A complex industry
- The global information matrix
- Information economics
- A new industrial revolution?
- Defining and measuring the information economy
- IT and employment

This chapter considers the nature of the IT industry today, including the role of producers of hardware (computing and telecommunications) and software, publishers of information, retailers and consultants. This discussion is illustrated by a number of case studies of different IT firms, mostly in the words of the organizations themselves.

The chapter introduces the importance of two kinds of complex global networks. The first is the physical network of electronic communications which links computer systems across the world and enables multi-media connections between people and organizations of all sorts. The growth of this network is considered here; the social and political implications of this development are considered further in later chapters. The second is an economic network or global marketplace. The global IT industry has contributed to the first and is a part of the second. We consider the role of multinational industries and the interdependence between information technology in more detail in the next chapter.

Finally, this chapter considers the importance of information technology in contemporary society as a whole – examining the idea that information and its technology is the dominating characteristic of the age. We examine in more detail the nature of the 'information economy' and its implications for levels of employment.

A complex industry

IT firms

From our discussion in Chapter 1 it can be seen that the modern information and communication industry is a perhaps uniquely complex one. A preliminary distinction may be drawn between the producers of different types of communication goods and services, but in practice there is an increasing trend towards the integration of firms across categories. Each of these categories will be considered in turn, before the issues raised by the structural changes occurring at lightning pace within the industry are looked at.

The role of hardware suppliers seems, on the face of it, a straightforward one which has, seemingly, much in common with old-fashioned nineteenth-century industrial manufacturing operations. Raw materials may be presumed to come in the gates at one end of the works to emerge from the production line some time later as goods to be sold to consumers, the price of the goods reflecting the high cost of the sophisticated labour, machinery and materials employed. These assumptions are, however, largely false.

So called original equipment manufacturers (OEMs) of, say, personal computers are largely assemblers of components such as silicon chips, hard drives, equipment cases, cathode ray tubes, etc. The components will commonly have come from numerous countries and several continents. Some components will be from other manufacturers who may be thought of as being within the industry; others may come from general engineering or plastic moulding suppliers, for example. The value of the product often has little relation to the cost of materials, labour or even what may be colossally expensive machinery. Instead the value of the product will frequently depend upon the originality of its design and its

---

Box 2.1 **Different types of communications producers**

- *Hardware suppliers:* producers of engineered manufactured goods such as computers and telephone handsets
- *Software suppliers:* producers of application programs enabling sophisticated hardware to be controlled and used
- *Infrastructure operators:* supplying physical network connections between and within commercial sites and their customers
- *Publishers:* suppliers of information content to consumers and other firms
- *Information services providers:* coordinating information systems on behalf of others
- *Intensive information users:* large-scale users of information systems

usefulness to the buyer, who may well be another manufacturer or a supplier of information services.

It is worth highlighting that the technology – and hence the manufacturing techniques – employed is constantly changing so that, for instance, the manufacturing of televisions, telephones, and computers, which once were clearly separate products, is now clearly an overlapping set of processes sharing components, suppliers and customers.

The category of software suppliers is obviously a much newer one than that of hardware manufacturer. It too can be easily misinterpreted. It may evoke the image of a small group of millionaire teenage 'geeks' overdosing on Coca-Cola in an air-conditioned 'campus' in Silicon Valley, California, producing computer games for PC fanatics across the world. Such operations do exist, but most software houses differ from this in several respects. For instance, many software houses are now in India, which has

---

Case Study 2.1 An original equipment manufacturer: Dell

Dell, founded in 1984 by Michael Dell, with its headquarters in Austin, Texas, became the world's largest seller of PCs in the third quarter of 2001. It had a turnover of $31.8 billion in 2000/1. It employs 34,000 'team-members' worldwide. Although best known for PC manufacture, Dell is a major producer of powerful servers, and also offers consulting and on-line services and sells third-party software and peripherals.

Dell pioneered a direct sales strategy for selling computers, being the first company to record $1 million per day in on-line sales (in 1997), and now conducts the majority of its sales through its website. The site handles 650 million page requests per quarter in 21 languages and 40 currencies. Customers can obtain information about the progress of their own orders, and suppliers can share detailed information about Dell's product quality and inventory on-line through a secure site.

Dell prides itself on minimizing its inventory by the use of Just-in-Time manufacturing to order (see Chapter 5 for details of JIT). In 2000 it cut its average inventory (stock) holdings from six days' supply in the previous year to four. Production is concentrated in six regional plants (including two in the USA and one in China), with the one in Limerick, Republic of Ireland, serving Europe, the Middle East and Africa.

The company has proved financially extremely successful, with one share bought on 22 June 1988 for $8.50, when stock was first offered publicly, being worth $2,392 at 2 November 2001. (This is a decline on the 5 March 1999 price of $4,131.)

Source: www.dell.com

Case Study 2.2 A software house: Borland International

Borland is a leading provider of high performance e-business implementation solutions. Borland is the vendor of choice for professional e-business solution providers who demand a vendor-independent implementation platform that supports rapid time to market, high productivity, performance and availability.

Founded in 1983, Borland is headquartered in Scotts Valley, California, with operations worldwide. Borland provides customers with e-business implementation platforms designed to increase developer productivity and reduce time to market for enterprise software projects. These platforms consist of software products that help businesses to excel in all phases of the implementation process: development, deployment, and management of e-business applications.

For development, we offer JBuilder, C++Builder, Delphi, and Kylix. Our deployment products include InterBase, Borland AppServer, and VisiBroker. To manage these systems, we offer AppCenter, a visual distributed application management solution.

Borland is committed to all major computing platforms as well as to the open standards of the Internet. Further, through the online developer community and an e-commerce site, community.borland.com, we provide service and support for software developers around the world. This resource site supports the developer community with a range of technical information, value-added services, and third-party products.

In addition to our products, we offer a wide range of consulting, training and support services to customers.

The process of developing new high technology products and solutions is inherently complex and uncertain. It requires, among other things, innovation and accurate anticipation of customers' changing needs and emerging technological trends. Without the introduction of new products, services and enhancements, our products and services can rapidly become technologically obsolete, in which case revenues could be materially and adversely affected. Furthermore, there can be no assurance that such new products and services, if and when introduced, will achieve market acceptance.

We are recognized for providing high-quality, innovative software tools for customers seeking greater productivity and performance. We believe that our ability to develop innovative and successful products depends in large part upon successfully executing product planning strategies, research and development activities and our ability to attract, hire and retain highly qualified engineers and product management personnel.

We plan to continue to invest in the area of research and development in the coming year. Research and development expenses for the year ended December 31, 2000, were $42.5 million.

In November 2000, we completed the acquisition of Bedouin, Inc., a Chicago-based software company. The acquisition is expected to accelerate our entry into the market for hosted development services (HDS). Borland intends to deliver a platform for developers to build, deploy and manage applications via the Internet. As presently contemplated, hosted development services would be available on the Internet to developers at the individual, project and enterprise levels.

A primary focus during the year ending December 31, 2001 is the growth of our direct sales organization. In the year ended December 31, 2000, more than a quarter of our revenue was derived from this direct sales organization. In addition, we market and distribute products worldwide through our own e-commerce Internet site, independent distributors, dealers, value-added resellers and independent software vendors.

We sell our products to a broad customer base, which includes businesses, educational institutions, government bodies and individual software developers. As we generally ship products upon receipt of orders, backlog is neither significant nor should it be detrimental to our future revenues.

We conduct operations and sell products outside the U.S. and maintain overseas offices in Australia, Brazil, Canada, France, Germany, Hong Kong, Japan, Netherlands, Singapore, Taiwan, Sweden and the United Kingdom, and, as part of our continuing global expansion, are in the process of opening offices in the People's Republic of China, South Korea and India. In addition to our research and development facilities in Scotts Valley, California, San Mateo, California and Chicago, Illinois, we also maintain research and development facilities in Australia, Japan and Singapore.

International net revenues (excluding exports from the U.S.) accounted for approximately 55% of our net revenues in our fiscal year ending December 31, 2000.

We contract with third parties for replication of CD-ROM discs, printing and production of packaging materials and assembly of final product packages for shipment to customers. Our products are principally sold in CD-ROM form together with user manuals. Some of our products are delivered directly by Borland via electronic download from the Internet.

The computer software industry is an intensely competitive industry. Rapid change, new and emerging technologies and fierce competition characterize the industry. The pace of change has accelerated due to the emergence of the Internet and corporate Intranets and new programming languages. We face intense competition in the development and marketing of our software products and services.

To the extent that we are unable to obtain information regarding existing and future operating systems from the developers of (operating) systems, the release of our products for such systems may be delayed or may not be competitive. For example, Microsoft Corporation, a significant competitor to our Delphi and C++Builder products, is the developer of the Windows operating environments. Microsoft Corporation has announced that it intends to include increased middleware functionality in future versions of its Windows 2000 operating system. Microsoft Corporation has also introduced a product that includes certain basic application server functionality. The bundling of competing functionality in versions of Windows products requires us to compete with Microsoft Corporation in the Windows marketplace where Microsoft Corporation has certain inherent advantages due to its substantially greater financial, technical, marketing and other resources, greater name recognition, a larger installed base and the integration of its middleware functionality with Windows.

We rely on a combination of patent, copyright, trademark, trade secret laws, non-disclosure agreements and other intellectual property protection methods to protect our intellectual property. Despite our efforts to protect our intellectual property rights, it may be possible for an unauthorized third party to copy certain portions of our products or to reverse-engineer or obtain and use technology or other information that we regard as proprietary. In addition, the laws of certain foreign countries do not protect rights in intellectual property to the same extent as do the laws of the United States.

As of March 2, 2001, we employed approximately 934 employees, approximately 483 in the United States and 451 overseas. None of our U.S. employees are represented by a labor union.

Source: Extract from the Borland Annual Report for 2000
(www.borland.com)

produced few e-commerce millionaires. Many software operations are now tied commercially to hardware manufacturers – e.g. games producers may be tied to console manufacturers, or operating system developers to specific OEMs. Other software operations may be serving the needs of a specific industry and have close links to them. Thus an aircraft manufacturer may take over a supplier of aircraft simulation software. Many software suppliers are engaged in the development of 'bespoke' software for specific firms to meet specific needs. For example the British firm, Sage, specializes in the production of accounting software.

The most obvious and long-established infrastructure operators are the public telecommunications operators (PTOs). In most of Europe, until recently, this meant a publicly owned subsidiary of the Post Office, with a monopoly over the supply of telephone lines. Government policies of privatization, and the development of alternative telephone technologies such as broadband cable systems and mobile phones using broadcasting, have generated much competition in recent years. In the USA the Bell telephone system was broken up in an anti-monopoly action much earlier, whilst many Third World countries retain public monopoly systems. Other infrastructure operators include conventional broadcasting organizations, suppliers of out-sourced organizational networks and the operators of communication satellites.

The term 'publisher' may suggest a faded gentleman with inky fingers proudly clutching a dusty hardback novel. It does still encompass the producers of enormous quantities of print materials – including newspapers, magazines, trade catalogues and advertising flyers. The new IT has made possible the production of more paper rather than replaced it! All printers now make intensive use of information technology to prepare and produce their materials. In this context publishing also includes all those who use IT to produce communications commercially. This would include broadcasters on radio and television, film studios, the sellers and distributors of videos, CD-ROMs of all descriptions, and the designers and operators of websites.

Each of these activities is a complicated commercial operation and is frequently carried out by a series of separate enterprises. Most academic books, for instance, are still written on a freelance (self-employed) basis by authors who draw upon the information resources of a university. Proof correction, and the supply of illustrations, may well also be carried out by other contractors to the publisher. Most publishers contract out the printing and binding of books to independent firms. Many also employ public relations, advertising, legal and accounting firms. Virtually all sell through wholesalers, bookshops and via the web. Other activities such as film production, or TV broadcasting, may well employ many more firms working together through contracts.

However, it is clear that there are many advantages to be gained by publishing across several media simultaneously. A good example being where

Case Study 2.3 An infrastructure operator: AT&T Corp

The AT&T Corp. is the US equivalent of British Telecom. Formerly known as the American Telephone and Telegraph Company, it is a leading provider of global communications services, and the largest telecommunications company in the United States. Its main services include AT&T Wireless, AT&T WorldNet®, AT&T Solutions consulting, the AT&T Universal Card and the long-distance services.

Up to 1984, AT&T was the parent company of the Bell System, the privately owned, but government regulated, enterprise that formerly provided most telecommunications services in the United States. From then until 1996, AT&T was an integrated provider of communications services and products, network equipment and computer systems.

AT&T was originally founded in New York as a wholly owned subsidiary of the American Bell Telephone Company in 1885. At first, it managed and expanded the long-distance business of American Bell and its licensees. It remained the 'long-distance company' until 1899 when, in a corporate reorganization, it took over the business and property of American Bell and became the parent company of the Bell System.

AT&T has often been a pioneer: in 1927 the company began the first commercial transatlantic telephone service to London using two-way radio. In 1950, AT&T opened its first microwave relay system between New York and Chicago, and subsequently added considerable microwave capacity to its nationwide long-distance network. In 1956, the first transatlantic submarine telephone cable, TAT-1, service to Europe began. In 1962, AT&T placed Telstar I, the first commercial communications satellite, in orbit.

AT&T and the Bell System were, in effect, a legally sanctioned but regulated monopoly. AT&T president Theodore Vail argued as early as 1907 that telephone technology would operate most efficiently as a monopoly providing universal service. Government regulation, 'provided it is independent, intelligent, considerate, thorough and just', could be a reasonable substitute for the workings of competition.

In 1949, an 'anti-trust' suit was filed which led in 1956 to a 'consent decree' agreed by AT&T and the Department of Justice, by which the company agreed to limit its activities to the regulated business of the national telephone system and government work. Another anti-trust suit by the US government began in 1974 and led to the January 1982 settlement in which AT&T agreed to divest itself of the wholly owned

Bell operating companies that provided local exchange service. The US Department of Justice agreed to lift the constraints of the 1956 decree in return. Divestiture took place on January 1, 1984, and the new AT&T and seven regional telephone holding companies replaced the Bell system.

On January 1, 1984 AT&T started as a new company with only $34 billion of its former $149.5 billion in assets. Only 373,000 of its former 1,009,000 employees remained. Even the famous Bell logo and name was lost to the regional telephone companies – excepting for the name's use in Bell Labs. The new logo was a stylized globe accompanied by the monogram 'AT&T'.

This was seen by the company as releasing it from its former legal shackles, and from the increasing difficulty of working in old ways in a new information age. The technology developed at AT&T Bell Laboratories could now be used freely to compete in world markets.

Success in the new environment required a drastic change in corporate culture. The Bell System's culture stressed service, technological innovation, excellence, and reliability, and within a non-competitive framework of taking however much time and money it took to get things done right. The new company had to become a much more customer-focused organization. A task which proved far more complex and difficult than anyone imagined at the time.

Optimists within AT&T point out that the competition of over 400 rivals has greatly reduced the cost of telecommunications products and services by 60 per cent since 1984 whilst improving quality overall. AT&T's revenues have continued to grow and its financial resources have remained strong despite a rapidly changing environment. This has helped finance continued growth and improvement, including a multi-billion-dollar digitalization of the entire network, a continued move into the international market and major acquisitions and mergers. Mergers with major computing and cellular telephone companies (NCR and McCaw Cellullar) in the early 1990s helped the company acquire expertise and resources in these areas.

However, in 1995 AT&T announced a split into three more specialized companies: today's AT&T, which specializes in communication services; Lucent Technologies, a systems and technology company, which provides communications products rather than services; and NCR Corp., which is mainly a computer business. Lucent and NCR were hived off during 1996.

Source: 'Company History' by Sheldon Hochheiser, at www.att.com

Case Study 2.4 A 'publisher': AltaVista

The AltaVista Company in its own words:

AltaVista is the Internet's premier search network that integrates unique technology and services to deliver relevant results faster for both individuals and Web-based businesses. The AltaVista Network enables you to unlock the unlimited potential of the Internet, by providing you with the most relevant and immediate results from a wealth of Internet resources.

Since our inception in 1995, AltaVista has taken a deliberate course of action to provide Web enthusiasts with a broad range of Internet search services and, through our proven technology, has succeeded in delivering relevant and useful information faster. Today, AltaVista delivers the ultimate Internet experience through the utilisation of cutting edge technology, numerous international and regional Web indexes as well as a multitude of search related features all designed to give users the best possible search experience on the Internet.

AltaVista's search technology has consistently been a performance leader since it was pioneered by the company as one of the first search services ever available, measured both by users and objective outside sources. AltaVista continues to revolutionise how users and partners find the most relevant content, information, products, and services available through the Internet.

AltaVista is committed to delivering best-of-breed Web results to our key users, by integrating content and functionality from both within the AltaVista Network and through external partners. Our primary focus is serving our users across the globe. Capitalising on our broad and distinctive offerings of innovative features and services, AltaVista delivers the ultimate Internet experience through (an) international network of (19) search oriented sites.

AltaVista's Business to Business Software and Services Division is a global leader in providing cutting edge search technology to e-commerce firms, portals and global enterprises.

AltaVista's focused approach is to continually build upon our proven foundation of technology leadership and results orientation. The company's overriding promise is to offer unmatched search services to the Web community through the integration of internally developed offerings, best of breed relationships and strategic acquisitions. Through our personalized local search services, we have created a global constellation of Web destinations to give users the best in relevant local search resources.

Good ideas, lightning fast and powerful hardware equipment, and a strange fascination with keeping track of email brought AltaVista out of DEC's Research lab and onto the Internet. In the spring of 1995, three DEC employees began talking about Digital's new Alpha 8400 (nicknamed TurboLaser) computers over lunch. TurboLasers promised to run database software 100 times faster than the competition. Somewhere between bites of lunch, the idea of using TurboLasers to host a searchable full-text database of the Web was born.

Due to the lab's unusual fascination with keeping track of old email, a researcher had created a very precise email index to track bulletin board conversations posted over the past 10 years. The index was good at finding specific bits of information in the volumes of stored email. The researchers used this tool to settle fierce technical debates. This full-text search framework became the foundation of AltaVista – and one of the first search engines that continues to help people find specific information within the ever-expanding boundaries of the World Wide Web.

The idea for the name AltaVista originally came from a white board that hadn't been erased properly. The word Alto (of Palo Alto) was placed beside the word Vista and someone yelled out, 'How about Alto-Vista!' It then became AltaVista, meaning 'The view from above.'

Since the early days, other notable inventions to the engine include the first-ever multi-lingual searches on the Internet. We are also proud of Babel Fish – the Web's first Internet translation service that translates words, phrases, and entire Web sites online in Spanish, French, German, Portuguese and Italian. More recently, we launched Photo Finder, an image search technology. Other improvements include phrase detection, spell check, and natural language capabilities.

In January 1999, we became a wholly owned subsidiary of Compaq Computer Corporation (NYSE: CPQ). Compaq purchased Shopping.com in March. In August 1999, CMGI, Inc. (Nasdaq: CMGI) acquired 83% of our outstanding stock from Compaq, and Shopping.com and Zip2 became a wholly owned subsidiary. With this combination, we now have a broad range of commerce and media content under the AltaVista domain. We have also introduced multimedia search capabilities and added a variety of customisable features to Microsoft Internet Explorer 5.

Today, we are rapidly expanding our global search services even further through the integration of each of our platforms and the constant introduction of new features and services. We remain committed to providing our users with the best search experience on the Web from a single source. As we develop new and better ways to reach our objectives and fulfill our users' needs, our 'view from above' promises to keep looking better and better.

Source: Verbatim extracts from www.altavista.com

a novel can be serialized in newspapers or magazines, translated for foreign markets, adapted for television, film and video, and even turned into an interactive computer game – not to mention being the basis for T-shirts and toys. Consequently many media firms have amalgamated into large, often multinational, cross-media groups which can cooperate in translating one product idea into numerous media.

Information services providers constitute a new and varied group. It could be argued that the oldest established members of this category are the libraries, which are still key organizations in modern societies. But if we concentrate on the idea of the coordination of modern information systems for other organizations as being characteristic of this group, then it still covers some interesting and varied enterprises.

Perhaps the longest-established type of firm are those which concentrate on developing bespoke (tailor-made) information systems for (mostly large) individual firms. Traditionally they are composed of systems analysts and programmers who first analysed customer needs, then helped specify the hardware to be bought, next wrote the code to be used, and finally supervised the installation and early operation of the new processes. The Yourdon consultancy in the USA would be a good example of this sort of operation.

With the development of relatively standardized PCs and sophisticated fourth-generation applications programs, such an approach is increasingly rare and often redundant. New firms have arisen and often focus on customizing a range of specialist software – perhaps a database product such as Oracle, or accounting or telesales products. In many cases hardware manufacturers such as IBM or software houses may run their own sales operations offering 'total solutions' to clients' problems. For the client, the choice of adviser may be a difficult one. An independent consultant may be able to save money by suggesting combinations of products from different sources, but may be reluctant to accept responsibility if a part of the system is not actually supplied by them. An adviser tied to a particular hardware or software product may be 'free' and wholly responsible for its success or failure, but his or her solution may well be unnecessarily expensive and elaborate.

A relatively recently offered solution to this dilemma is that of the outsourcer who provides and operates a complete system at a defined cost for the client. The oldest established members of this group are perhaps those offering specialist services such as payroll operations and security back-up. By amalgamating operations and developing specialist expertise, out-sourcers may well be able to provide services at much less cost than an 'in-house' group. From a client perspective, however, as we shall see, there are drawbacks such as the need to define in advance the level of service required and a strategic dependence on a third party outside their control.

Case Study 2.5 Information services provider: EDS

EDS sees itself as the world's leading information technology services company. In the year 2000 its global turnover was $19.2 billion from 9,000 client organisations in 58 countries.

EDS supports 2.2 million desktops and 40,000 servers, and hosts websites for 750 clients. It processes 2.5 million ATM transactions a day and claims to be responsible for processing 11 billion daily transactions – equivalent to two transactions for everyone on earth.

Founded in 1962 as Electronic Data Systems, its early operations involved a handful of people processing clients' data by tapping into the idle time – usually at night – on other companies' mainframes. It now has 140,000 employees.

Its portfolio of services include Business Process Management, E solutions, Information Solutions and Management Consultancy. It stresses four themes in its relationships with customers:

- Collaborate in new ways: strategic alliances with customers and suppliers
- Continuous improvement: 'digitalise everything'
- Eliminate boundaries: operating anytime, anywhere
- Establish trust: 'gain customer intimacy, build digital wisdom and provide security and privacy'

An example of an EDS operation is Nova Scotia, Canada where EDS took over the mainframe computing operations of both the provincial government and the largest local telecommunications provider, MT&T, in a seven-year contract from 1992. Its data centre handles 350,000 interactive transactions per day in addition to 40,000 batch-processing jobs a month. All capital costs were met by EDS, which claims better service and lower costs have resulted.

Source: www.eds.com

Case Study 2.6 An intensive information user: HSBC bank

The following information, largely derived from HSBC's Annual Report, stresses the growing importance of IT for an intensive information user:

HSBC (formerly the Hong Kong and Shanghai Banking Corporation) can fairly claim to be one of the largest banking and financial services organizations in the world. It is the successor to a merger between a Hong Kong-based bank and one of the largest UK banks – the Midland. HSBC had total assets of US$674 billion and shareholders' equity of US$46 billion by the end of 2000. With a headquarters in London, HSBC operates through long-established businesses in five regions: North America, Latin America, Europe, Hong Kong, and the rest of Asia-Pacific, including the Middle East and Africa. A world network of about 6,500 offices in 79 countries and territories clearly requires a sophisticated communications system. The group provides a wide range of financial services to personal and commercial clients.

HSBC sees the Internet as one of several exciting new media, to be incorporated as an integral part of its working. The bank has concluded that e-commerce will change the fabric of the financial services sector and sees it as a way of finding new customers all over the world and improving its services to existing customers. It intends to use e-commerce to reorganize the business so as to provide higher-quality customer services more efficiently.

HSBC will be able to link its customers to the full range of international services and manage their processing wherever it chooses, which the bank sees as a considerable competitive advantage.

HSBC has adopted a 'clicks and mortar' strategy. This requires that customer Internet offerings must meet three criteria: customer needs and preferences come first; they must fit HSBC's existing distribution channels; and they must be multinational in scope.

Recently the group has been reorganizing its work for the e-age and putting in place some major components of such a strategy. In 2000, over US$2 billion was spent on technology, including a significant proportion on dot.com initiatives. HSBC aspires to be one of the first to provide customers with facilities through the Internet on a multi-geographical, multi-product, basis.

IBM is developing an Interactive Financial Services (IFS) system for the bank which links in with the full range of customers' own technology: the Internet, interactive TV, mobile phones and other wireless modes of data transmission. IFS is designed to give HSBC's customers the freedom to access their finances where and when they wish. HSBC launched the UK's first nationally available TV banking service digital satellite provided by Sky in 1999. This has already attracted over 126,000 customers.

During 2000, HSBC has developed 'hsbc.com' as a brand name and a portal for its consumer services. By the end of 2000, Internet banking was available to HSBC customers in eleven of its businesses, including the United Kingdom, Brazil, Canada, the Hong Kong SAR, Singapore and the United States. Operations based in the Channel Islands serve Internet customers in 150 countries and territories. In 2000, in Brazil and France, HSBC began banking by mobile phone using WAP technology.

HSBC is a major supplier of collection, payment, account services and liquidity management throughout the world, so corporate customers and financial institutions can manage their cash efficiently on a worldwide basis. A key part of HSBC's strong market position in cash management is the flexibility of electronic delivery using Internet-enabled, file transfer or personal computers, as best suits the client concerned.

As long ago as 1989, HSBC's UK arm launched First Direct, the country's first complete 24/365 banking service by telephone. Despite the growth in competition, First Direct has continued to attract more customers. An Internet version of the service 'firstdirect.com', already has 270,000 clients.

Source: HSBC plc Annual Report 2000

Large-scale commercial and public sector users of information systems – intensive information users – cannot easily be distinguished from operations which are clearly part of the IT industry. Thus when the UK Department of Social Security out-sourced the operation of several of its major computer centres in a multi-million pound contract, the employees of these centres, now employees of EDS, were clearly part of the IT industry. It seems paradoxical to claim that they were not so before the out-sourcing, since their jobs were largely unchanged! Many parts of the financial services industry and the public sector, for instance, are now almost exclusively involved in the processing of information using modern technology. They provide a major part of the career opportunities for IT graduates and are major investors in hardware and software. Similarly, as we have seen, many engineering manufacturing operations not only involve massive use of IT in their production processes but may also produce products – from cars to washing machines – with special purpose chips built into them.

Table 2.1 IT industry by value chain contribution, 1992

Industry sector	%
Vendor support and professional services	36
Distribution channels	11
Packaged software	16
Peripherals	12
Processors	14
Semi-conductors	11
Total	100

Source: Moschella (1997, 32)

The International Data Corporation has produced some interesting (if presumably very approximate) figures for the relative contribution of different types of firm to the economic value created by the IT; these give some idea of the relative financial importance of each (see Table 2.1).

The structure of the IT industry

It will already be evident from the discussion of types of firm, and the individual case studies accompanying them, that IT firms are closely related to each other. The question considered here is the sort of overall structure these relationships constitute and whether the industry structure is sufficiently competitive to safeguard the interests of consumers.

Moschella (1997) offers a useful and interesting overview of the past and likely future of the IT industry, summarized in Figure 2.1 and Table 2.2. Figure 2.1 suggests that industrial evolution can be seen in terms of

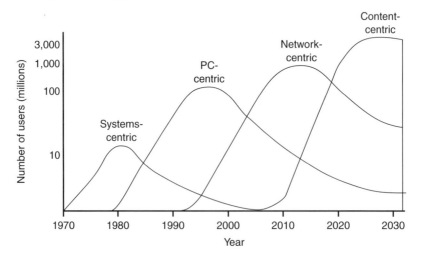

Figure 2.1 Stages of industry growth

Source: Moschella (1997: viii)

Table 2.2 IT industry evolution, 1964–2015

	Systems-centric, 1964–81	PC-centric, 1981–94	Network-centric, 1994–2005	Content-centric, 2005–15
Key audience	Corporate	Professional	Consumer	Individual
Key technology	Transistor	Microprocessor	Communications bandwidth	Software
Governing principle	Grosch's Law	Moore's Law	Metcalfe's Law	Law of transformation
Vendor offerings	Proprietary systems	Standard products	Value-added services	Custom services
Channel	Direct	Indirect	On-line	Customer pull
Network focus	Data centre	Internal LANs	Public networks	Transparency
User focus	Efficiency	Productivity	Customer service	Virtualization
Supplier structure	Vertical integration	Horizontal computer value chain	Unified computers and communications chain	Embedded
Supplier leadership	US systems	US components	National carriers	Content providers
Number of users at end of period	10 million	100 million	1 billion	Universal
End of period market size	$20 billion	$460 billion	$3 trillion	Too embedded to be measurable

Source: Moschella (1997, ix)

four waves of innovation, two of which have already happened, a third which is taking place now, the fourth being predicted by Moschella.

The first era of widespread commercial computing is, of course, that dominated by mainframe computers operated on behalf of corporate clients. From an industrial point of view it was an era in which, in the USA, IBM dominated the entire industry by supplying complete systems for the majority of large firms. It was said that 'no one ever got fired for buying IBM' in this period. In the US market there were, in fact, another seven fairly substantial system suppliers, whilst in some other countries, Britain being one, home-grown firms such as ICL achieved an almost comparable position to IBM in the USA. At this stage major firms frequently designed software to suit their own hardware and often sold or leased direct to major customers, offering consultancy services in addition. Smaller firms were often in a position of extreme dependency in offering a limited set of components or services to the major firms who sold 'bespoke' packages to large corporate customers. Customers were frequently boxed into a relationship with a supplier, from which they could only escape with great expense and difficulty. This 'vertically integrated' market structure is characteristic of the early stages of new technologically innovatory products.

The first upset to this rather uncompetitive picture came with the development of mini-computer firms, a number of which developed relatively cheaper machines to run Unix operating systems thus offering buyers the possibility of changing machines without abandoning software or vice versa.

However, the massive change came with the development of the personal computer and the decision of IBM to out-source the supply of central processor units from Intel and an operating system (MS-DOS) from Microsoft. The availability of these key features of the IBM design to other 'original equipment manufacturers' (OEMs) was crucial to the emergence of a new industry structure. The competitive mass marketing of PCs to individuals, as well as to firms, has meant that IT provision has become much more a commodity sale rather than the provision of a bespoke service. The industry thus became horizontally divided into a series of markets, each dominated by different suppliers. Thus microprocessors were dominated by Intel, operating systems by Microsoft, local area networks by Novell, printers by Hewlett Packard, database management systems by Oracle, disks by Seagate, and so on.

A third wave of transformation in the industry has now clearly begun, with the increasing importance of networked computers – particularly through the operation of the Internet and private intranets. How this has happened is discussed in more detail later in this chapter, but from the point of view of industrial structure it clearly involves more, extremely powerful, corporate players. In particular three new types of firm must now compete, or form strategic alliances with, conventional computer firms. The first type of player is the telecommunications infrastructure provider, particularly the PTOs discussed earlier, but also cable television firms and the like. The second are the manufacturers of consumer electronics products, which from mobile phones, through electronic games to digital televisions are increasingly overlapping in technology, function and markets with conventional PCs. Third are the multinational entertainment and news providers like the Murdoch empire, Disney, and so on. Moschella suggests that at first, in the network-centric era telecom giants will dominate, but in the long run the providers of content will prevail. The interested reader is referred to Moschella's book for more details of his thesis and for further explanation of Table 2.2. The 'governing principle' row in Table 2.2 is well worth some further immediate discussion here, however.

Herb Grosch's Law dates back to the 1940s and states that computer power increases as the square of the cost. This seems to favour the provision of bigger and more expensive (mainframe) machines since one computer that is twice as expensive as another will yield four times the processing power. It was this logic which prevailed in the 1960s and 1970s.

However, Gordon Moore, the founder of Intel, propounded the idea that semi-conductor performance would double every two years. This is a proposition that seems to have been confirmed by experience since the 1970s. The practical implications of this are the opposite of Grosch's Law because small 'commodity' machines are now developed much faster than mainframes on the basis of the latest high-power chips. Therefore it is often possible to replace an old expensive machine with a cheaper, more modern, one.

In addition, a series of PCs can often be networked together to form a 'virtual' larger machine at lower cost. This idea may be linked to the law associated with the name of Bob Metcalfe, the inventor of the Ethernet and founder of 3Com. He argued that whilst the cost of a network is linear (each extra machine costs roughly the same to add), the benefits are exponential (each extra machine brings in many more connections to the network – the larger the network the more connections). Thus the cost of an extra machine on a three-machine network is (say) £1,000 and creates three extra communication links between existing machines and the newcomer – cost per extra link being £333.33. The cost of an extra machine on a 1,000-machine network is still £1,000 but creates 1,000 extra links at a cost of £1 per connection. This logic is clearly driving the creation of innumerable in-house and, still more, Internet links. The Internet clearly becomes more valuable the more potential customers are connected to it, but the cost of connection to it is static or declining as the technology becomes more established and demand increases.

What Moschella proposes as 'the Law of Transformation' is based on the observation of Professor Negroponte that there is a large contrast in the extent to which industries are based on 'atoms' or 'bits'. More physically based industries such as manufacturing might be thought to be less likely to be affected by changes in IT than information-based industries such as banking or government. However, in the three early stages of evolution in the information industries, somewhat surprisingly, this contrast has not been particularly apparent. Moschella argues that in the forth-coming content-centric stage of evolution, however, this contrast will be magnified. He proposes a formula that suggests industries will be trans-formed in proportion to the square of the percentage of the value added by the industry, which is accounted for by bit-based information process-ing activities (1997, 223–5, 263–5).

Although Moschella's mathematical formulation of the law of trans-formation has an air of spurious precision, it does seem likely that some information-based activities like education and government have barely begun to be transformed to a fraction of their potential (see Chapters 3 and 7 in this volume).

The European Communications Council has recently published a stim-ulating report on the development of the Internet economy as a strategic challenge for business (Zerdick, 2000). The ten theses of this report give a good sense of fundamental changes that the Internet is helping to bring about (see Box 2.2).

Box 2.2 **Ten theses relating to the Internet economy**

1   *The digitalization of value as a strategic challenge*
    A global marketplace for digital bits is replacing more and more national industrial sectors.

2   *Critical mass as a key factor in the network economy*
    Instead of rarity leading to value, a position of global market domi-nance (surplus) is the key factor.

3   *Cannibalize yourself before someone else does it to you!*

4   *Giving products away as a recipe for success*

5   *Competition and cooperation through value networks*
    Firms must increasingly stick to their core competencies and form stra-tegic alliances with others in order to meet customer needs.

6   *Simultaneous price cuts and increased differentiation*
    Extreme specialization combined with very low cost becomes the winning strategy.

7   *Product differentiation through versioning*
    The same product can be sold to multiple markets in many different forms.

8   *Individualization of mass markets*
    Powerful databases, interactive links with customers and capacity to individualize goods and services enable mass marketing of personalized products.

9   *Traditional regulatory models become obsolete*

10 *Main challenges to future regulation*
    Globalization and the convergence of communications and media markets disrupt current means of regulation.

Source: Zerdick *et al.* (2000, 17–21)

A final recent development in terms of the economics of the IT industry which cannot be overlooked is the e-commerce 'dot.com' boom and crash which took place in the later years of the 1990s and burst in June 2000. This stock market speculative boom and bust was the latest in a series of speculations that have often related to new technology. Previous speculations include ones centring around exploring the South Seas, developing new breeds of tulips in Amsterdam, and the development of the railways in nineteenth-century Britain. The common thread is that investment in what might be a useful if risky new area is over-hyped by speculators who benefit from selling on a rising market and naïve commentators carried away by the undoubted long-term prospects for the industry. People are drawn into investing in stocks in the hope of making profits, not from the venture (these being long-term) but from capital appreciation in the stocks rising in anticipation of profits not yet made. Thus numbers of 'dot.com millionaires' were created whose companies were still trading at enormous losses. Many – probably most – of these entrepreneurs, of course, sincerely believed their new ventures would be immensely profitable in the long run and some were amazed at their new-found instant wealth.

The scale of the investments and losses involved is difficult to document, but an article in the *Washington Post* estimates that US venture capitalists invested a total of $13 billion in telecommunications, Internet and software firms from January 1997 to September 2001 (Johnston and McCarthy, 2001). Companies such as EqualFooting.com Inc, Zona-Financiera.com Inc and Varsity-Books.com lost sums ranging from $30 to 69 million invested in them. Companies such as SciQuest – a company operating an on-line market in laboratory supplies – which did survive have found their share prices falling from a high of $80 to a price of around $1 in November 2001.

In Britain the *Guardian* estimated that the top 50 Internet entrepreneurs had accumulated personal fortunes of £1.3 billion over roughly the four years preceding October 1999 (Teather and Cassy, 1999). Many of these 'fortunes' represented the value of shares in companies whose price subsequently collapsed, but a follow-up article two years later (Teather and Cassy, 2001) revealed that most of them remained millionaires – if slightly poorer ones! The richest UK entrepreneur, Paul Sykes, had announced his intention of deserting the net scene in October 1999, did so, and consequently was still worth £425 million.

Unfortunately the e-commerce crash, when it came, affected more than just the companies whose only real assets were a handful of more or less skilled personnel, an Internet server and a marketing plan. The crash also hit companies with real and expensive assets (e.g. telephone cables, factories with state of the art technology) and thousands of ordinary professional and skilled employees, which needed to raise more capital for investment purposes.

A global industry

Information technology is now one of the most international of all industries. This is especially true of the production of PCs, as an examination of any PC assembled by an 'original equipment manufacturer' from any country will show. The operating system will almost certainly be American (from Microsoft). The microprocessor may well be from an American firm, but it may not necessarily be manufactured in the USA. CD-ROM drive and memory chips (DRAMs) may well come from Japan or Korea. The disk drive may originate from Singapore, monitor, keyboard and mouse from Taiwan.

As we saw earlier, however, by no means most of value added by the IT industry is from the manufacture of hardware. Distribution channels will frequently have a major local element. Telecommunications are normally dominated by national PTOs. Consultancy advice, out-sourcing and writing of specialist software will usually be provided by the local economy. British firms often write games software for Japanese consumer electronics manufacturers, and so on.

As content becomes more important then British publishers and Hollywood production firms may come to have a larger share in the predominantly English language market – although the dominance of English cannot be guaranteed as Chinese- and Spanish-speaking populations become richer and more involved in the global communications market.

The largest consumer market by far is the USA, followed by Japan and, if treated as a whole, Europe. Although Singapore, Taiwan and Korea and similar NICs (newly industrialized countries) have been able to compete in some specialist areas they lack large domestic markets for their products. Although Europe is an affluent market for IT products it has so far been unsuccessful in developing dominance in any one specialist area – except perhaps mobile phones (with the Finnish firm Nokia).

The economy and the IT industry

The IT industry's performance cannot be detached from the rest of industry, although, for much of the last 50 years, consumer electronics, television, video recorders and computers have helped to lead the growth of the world economy. In 2000/2001, conversely, a slump in computers and telecommunications has helped to generate a slowdown or recession in the world economy.

The industry depends on its customers and suppliers outside of the industry itself. It shares the same environment – e.g. trade unions, investment climate and resources, human resources, transport and communication facilities, wage rates. Porter (1990) argues that a crucial aspect of the competitiveness of national industries is precisely the availability of skilled labour, capital and relevant services (e.g. efficient telephone and electricity supplies); the presence of a competitive supplier structure, a sophisticated domestic demand for the goods or services in question and a strong domestic competitive market within the industry.

The success of other industries is crucially dependent on adoption of IT by them. Equally, investment in IT is *capital investment* by those other industries, and this is particularly sensitive to fluctuations in the economy.

The global information matrix

Press reports increasingly speak of the 'information superhighway' as a dominant force in the modern world. Although an imprecise term, it does draw attention to the public availability of channels for the exchange of information across large parts of the globe through digital electronic networks. Increasingly this is being achieved by broadband technologies that permit multi-media exchanges involving voice and moving images, as well as the older-established use of text and graphics.

This should be distinguished from longer-established technologies such as the one-way broadcasting of information to mass audiences (of which satellite broadcasting is the latest example) and, less easily, from the use of older non-digital, narrow-band, electric communications technology such as (pre-ISDN) telephones, faxes and telexes.

Some writers speak of the 'wired society', but this may place too much emphasis on a technology that is already partially outdated by the development of private broadcast links and may be replaced by (e.g.) laser transmissions without cables. At present, however, the key technological expression of this is the development of fibre-optic cable links (although 'filaments' is perhaps a more accurate expression of their physical size).

With the development of ISDN (Integrated Services Digital Network) standards most of the advantages of broadband technology can be obtained via telephone cables. However, the cabling at present being installed mainly for TV entertainment purposes in many parts of the world does offer a broader-band link which might be used for other purposes – e.g. reading gas, electricity and water meters, security links to police stations, controls for area heating systems. In short, almost any number of WAN (wide area network) connections to computers elsewhere.

Technically the most impressive development in this direction so far is the development of the Internet. More capital has, however, been invested, so far, in converting the world's telephone networks to ISDN and to cabling for domestic entertainment purposes.

In addition, numerous private global networks have been set up by multinational corporations and military alliances. Some of these are largely physically separate from public telephone/data networks and use their own dedicated satellite links and lines – 'superhighways' might be the most appropriate term.

The growth of the Internet

The Internet originated in the first experimental network of three computers financed by the US Department of Defense (*c.*1966). This developed into the ARPANET (first publicly demonstrated in 1972) and then the DARPANET which linked the major university research centres which had research contracts with the US Department of Defense (DoD).

Although financed by the DoD, the Internet was developed for the first decade or more almost entirely by university civilian researchers (mainly postgraduate students) as a 'pure' research project.

None the less, expenditure was justified as potentially allowing defence installations to be linked in case of enemy missile attack. The architecture of the Net, which has multiple connections and allows the network to continue even if individual lines or computers are down, reflects this. A separate defence network (MILNET) was hived off from the ARPANET in the early 1980s, which became the remote ancestor of the 'Star Wars' project to set up a computerized anti-missile–missile system.

As academic interest in the ARPANET grew, it was taken over by the National Science Foundation and used to link most major US universities (NSFNET). Overseas links were developed early – with University College London being a very early member of the ARPANET and researchers from it playing a part in defining its protocols. Other electronic networks, such as USENET, BITNET and, in the UK, JANET (the Joint Academic Network), have also developed with gateways allowing degrees of reciprocal access.

A distinction can be drawn between the Internet – a group of interconnecting networks running on IP/TCP (Internet protocols/transmission control protocols) – and the 'matrix', which is the sum total of WANs which largely interconnect to some extent and include many using commercial protocols such as IBM's SNA (System Network Architecture). A distinction should also be made between the Internet and intranets. The Internet is a publicly available series of interconnected networks, whilst intranets are private networks using the same protocols. Other protocols in use include, of course, OSI, favoured by European authorities and, nominally, the US government, and the X.25 etc. standards reflecting CCITT (telephone providers) requirements.

The growth of the matrix/Internet has undoubtedly been enormous, but is difficult to measure because of difficulties of definition, the decentralization of the matrix, and security devices that cloak the number of users of many nets. Gilster (1994) quotes estimates of 100 networks in 1985, 500 by 1989, 2,218 in 1990, 4,000 in 1991 and 16,000 plus by 1994. User numbers have been estimated at 25 million worldwide in 1994, with an estimated 419 million by December 2000 (NUA Internet Surveys, 2001).

Speeds have increased enormously to cope with increased traffic, with

Box 2.3 **Main facilities offered on the Internet**

- *Remote log-on (Telnet):* users on distant computers have similar access to those on site.
- *File transfer (FTP):* whole files can be transferred from one computer to another.
- *Electronic mail (e-mail):* a special case of the above.
- *Bulletin boards/mailing lists:* enable interactive discussions among groups of users.
- *World Wide Web (WWW):* the provision of publicly available information through multimedia interactive displays.

the original NSFNET backbone consisting of 6 nodes operating at 56 k-bits per second. By 1988 13 nodes were operating at 1.5 M-bits per second. By 1992 Advanced Network Services Ltd (alias IBM, plus two other companies) were operating a 45 M-bit per second service (i.e. 7,000 times faster than the original network) on behalf of NSFNET as well as a commercial version of the Internet (ANS CO+RE).

In fact the original networks were originally designed with remote log-on chiefly in mind so that researchers at different universities could share expensive facilities. The potential for using the file transfer facility to develop a substitute for the post was only slowly appreciated. The most recent development – the World Wide Web – is an extension of the earlier idea of Bulletin Boards, which put files up for public access. With the development of graphic, video and sound file production and reception facilities, the distinction between viewing a computer file on a remote computer and viewing a television programme has been blurred. The distinctive feature of the WWW, however, is its *interactivity* – which means that a WWW site can be designed to respond to choices by the 'viewer' in a way impossible for conventional terrestrial television.

Tools such as gophers and the World Wide Web browsers enable information on almost any topic to be retrieved from a variety of sources worldwide. The development of the WWW and of user-friendly WIMP interfaces such as Windows has meant that the Internet has ceased to be a device accessible to a small, mainly academic, minority and has become a media available for mass communication. Millions of ordinary PC owners have gained access to the net in recent years. A new stage in the development of the web is its availability on much less expensive and more multipurpose devices such as mobile telephones and televisions. This is likely to lead over the next few years to affluent Western societies having a norm of at least one such device per household. The implications of this will be considered in later chapters.

Information economics

Much is discussed today about advanced economies moving towards being an 'information economy'. The normal discussion presents a series of economic stages or eras, such as:

- Hunter-gatherer
- Agricultural
- Industrial
- Service or information.

The fundamental concept seems to be that, in terms of dominant activity (that is, the greatest part of the economy according to measures such as value of output, or number of people employed), there is an historical trend that progresses through these stages. Simple economies are in early stages, and advanced economies are in later stages. Each stage is characterized in part by the application of fundamentally new technology and human organization.

For example, Ward and Griffiths (1996) look at very recent history culminating in a Strategic Information Systems era. Skyrme (1999) discusses the 'networked knowledge economy'. Drucker (1993) discusses recent evolution from capitalism to a knowledge society.

The notion of the information economy is a part of the broader question of the relationship between information and economy, so we shall first consider this question in terms of three fundamental areas of consideration:

1 Economic theory.
2 Macro-economic perspectives.
3 Micro-economic perspectives.

We shall then return to the definition of an 'information economy' and to the social and political implications of the concept, including the employment consequences of the widespread use of IT.

Economic theory

Classical economic theory in the West generally recognizes at least three factors of production: land, labour and capital. The key difference compared with Marxist economics lies in recognizing any factor other than labour (for example, is revenue from the sale of mineral resources to be treated as a return on the use of land as a factor of production, or is it to be treated as a return on the use of the labour used to extract and process the mineral?). A problem then lies in dealing with profit: is profit just a higher return to land, labour, or capital, or is it a return to some other factor of production such as enterprise or organization? This question is discussed in many well-known textbooks, such as Samuelson (1973).

There has been some recent speculation that information should be treated as a factor of production for several reasons (see Box 2.4).

A central theme of economic theory is the concept of perfect competition. In perfect competition it is argued that economic resources are allocated in an optimum way amongst the various members of the community through the market mechanism. An essential prerequisite for perfect competition is perfect knowledge of markets by buyers and sellers. Some writers (for example, Phlips, 1988) use the term *perfectly symmetric information* to describe a situation of all players in a market having equal knowledge. In game theory and information economics there is an important distinction between *imperfect information* and *incomplete information.* In markets, imperfect information exists when the behaviour of some market participants is not known. Incomplete information arises when all relevant factors are not known. The difference between imperfect and incomplete information is subtle but important. A company, particularly in a competitive market, is not likely to know everything about other players in the market. Some information may be kept secret by some players, or misleading information may be made available. This leads to imperfect information. On the other hand, a company may not know all the factors relevant to a market. For example, an airline may think that other airlines are the principal competitors for business class travel. Perhaps some competition is really coming from electronic communications and the airline does not know how much electronic communication is a factor in deciding airline travel. In this case information is incomplete.

It is not often that the value of information is obtained just by transferring the ownership information (in other words, if it is moved from one company's database to another company's database). The value of information is realized by propagating it so that it can be used to affect some behaviour. Information by itself has no intrinsic value. The real value of information arises from changes arising from the information.

There is an important link here with strategic planning. Some critics

---

Box 2.4 **Is information a factor of production?**

- It is used as an input resource by many processes that result in products or services.
- In some cases, information (knowledge) is the product in its own right.
- Many processes can be described as primarily information work.
- Information may act as a primary catalyst in using other factors of production in a particular way (is this enterprise and organization?).
- Some information may be an intangible asset in its own right.

argue that there is insufficient empirical evidence that having an articulated strategy is really useful to a firm. (We shall be discussing the idea that all firms need an information strategy in Chapter 5.) Information economics adds to that debate with a more sophisticated proposition that the usefulness of a business strategy is positively associated with the degree of information asymmetry in the market situation of the firm.

For these several reasons, there are important links between information and economics (see Box 2.5).

Macro-economics

A macro-economic perspective concentrates on the relationships across economies as a whole. Some key macro-economic issues relating to information include:

- Employment: the proportion of the workforce involved in information or knowledge work.
- Output: how much of an economy's output can be defined as information or knowledge?
- Long-term relationships between information, economy, and underlying social normative drivers of economic activity.
- Relations between technology and economy as far as information and knowledge are concerned.

Figure 2.2 shows a long-term breakdown of the proportion of the US population involved in principal classifications of economic activity (agricultural, manufacturing, service and information). This kind of diagram is often used to justify an assertion that modern advanced economies are becoming information and knowledge economies. There are some potential fallacies in this line of thinking. People still eat and drink. There are

---

Box 2.5 Information has special economic properties

- It is the product of intellectual labour.
- It is a non-material good.
- Its value can only be derived from the ultimate value of behavioural changes.
- Its use is usually by propagation, not by transfer.
- The cost of creating information is usually independent of the extent of its use.
- The more information is used, the greater its value.
- Generally, the value of information cannot be assessed at the moment of use.
- Depreciation of information depends on the progress of knowledge.

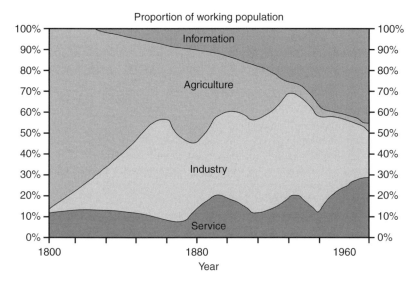

Figure 2.2 Segments of the US economy
Source: Adapted from Stone (1991)

more people. Therefore macro-economic output of the agricultural sector continues to rise. Fewer people are employed in agriculture now than in, say, the early twentieth century. These results have been achieved primarily through the application of technology in agriculture and the use of processes that require less labour. Easier access to food and drink is also facilitated by the extensive deployment of transportation technology. People acquire and consume more material goods. There are more people. Therefore macro-economic output of the manufacturing sector continues to rise. As with agriculture, many parts of manufacturing have seen substantial productivity increases through the deployment of technology. So both agriculture and manufacturing remain enormously important sectors of the economy even if information is 'dominant'.

Some of the expansion of the information-work part of the economy has arisen not because there is more of that kind of work, but increasing 'out-sourcing' of services can give the illusion of a fundamental macro-economic shift. For example, a manufacturing company that does all work such as accounting, design, marketing, finance, and law, in-house (such as a 'typical' nineteenth-century firm), will probably have all output and use of labour classified as manufacturing (if the primary output is manufactured goods). Out-sourcing work such as accounting, marketing and public relations does not alter the amount of different kinds of work done. But if new firms of accountants and marketing and PR consultants arise as a result, there is the illusion that in macro-economic terms there is less manufacturing work and more information work.

Box 2.6 **Summary of macro-economic relationships between activity and technology**

- In the main classifications of the economic sector (agriculture, manufacturing, knowledge), there has been long-term increasing total output.
- Labour productivity has increased in terms of output per unit of labour.
- Capital to labour ratios have been increasing.
- Eventually there is a decline in the increase in capital productivity expressed in terms of the output per unit of capital input.
- The impact of IT change is essentially independent of whether it is directed to be labour or capital replacing; it depends more on the relationship between price and demand for the products or services outputs of the industries introducing the technology.

There are therefore long-term relationships between the pattern of employment and the deployment of technology. In simple terms, the Industrial Revolution would not have been possible if there had not been a sufficiently large available workforce freed by the deployment of agricultural technology and innovation. Similarly, increases in productivity in manufacturing have freed a large number of people to be available for services and information or knowledge work. Thus automation may have a short-term effect of increasing unemployment, but in the long term new activity acts to reduce the level of unemployment (OECD, 1987).

What we want, and what we believe, are results influenced to a very great extent by the information to which we have been subjected. Thus there are long-term relationships between information and norms about lifestyle. Lifestyle norms have a significant effect on demand for goods and services. Some people pursue more and more material goods as a matter of habit and desire; some have limits to their wants. Some macro-economic activity is driven by needs. Most is driven by wants. Wants are often the result of information and information processing. This long-term relationship between information, technology and normative economic drivers is discussed in Darnton and Giacoletto (1992).

Micro-economics

Micro-economics looks at problems at the level of the firm, or individual enterprise. Here there are different concerns about the interaction between information and economy. The key issues are:

- *production functions:* for most goods and services the output can be generated in a variety of ways using different combinations of different factor inputs (land, labour, capital, organization, information);

- *costs* of the different factors of production;
- *whether information assets* exist in the sense of having value or being able to support a future stream of income;
- how can the *benefits* of IT be evaluated? (What is the return on investment?)

Information is an important ingredient in establishing prices and revenue. Demand for factors of production is demand derived ultimately from what customers want, and decisions those in enterprises take about production functions. As far as information is concerned, the special economic properties listed earlier indicate that it is a very difficult factor to replace. However, information and IT are used in many cases to replace other factors of production. IT has clearly automated many kinds of information work, thus replacing labour. IT, when embedded with other technologies, has been able to replace much capital (for example, computer-supported numerical controlled machines can reduce the need for a larger number of dedicated machines). The use of IT to relocate information work, or to disperse it, enables the substitution of expensive real estate by less expensive real estate.

Choices between factors of production may be made purely on cost grounds, but they may also be taken on the premise of having greater control over processes. Thus the use of IT in some cases may be more expensive than the equivalent labour costs, but greater control can be exercised over machines than over people. Computers do not react against an authoritarian management style; but people might. On a more positive note, more IT may result in more flexible processes.

The value of information assets *per se* can be judged from various perspectives.

The value of an enterprise is greater with the information assets than without. The earliest example of this, recognized widely, is the valuation of an enterprise in terms of its tangible assets, plus an additional sum for 'goodwill' – this is generally the willingness of customers to return to the enterprise and knowledge of customers and their behaviour.

Information assets may be deployed to produce a future stream of income. For example, a lawyer familiar with legal principles and practice can use that knowledge to generate an income even though the knowledge in the lawyer's head may have no other extrinsic value. In other cases, a specific information asset, such as copyright or licence rights in computer programs, may have extrinsic capital value and in addition, the enterprise may be able to use it to generate income from (say) licence fees.

In non-monetary terms information and knowledge may be valued because the individual concerned has high regard for that kind of information. For example, a book collector may place a high value on a rare book. (Rarity is a function of how many other people want the item in question, compared with what is available.)

There has been great difficulty in establishing clear, unambiguous methods for evaluating the returns available from many IT investments. Where this can be done is usually where there is a clearly defined project of factor replacement when all costs and outputs are identifiable. For example, it may be possible to estimate the return on investment of replacing a set of manual typewriters by a computer-based word-processing system. In many cases, IT investments take on the nature of infrastructure investments and these are notoriously difficult to evaluate in terms of return on investment. Thus some writers have focused on the difficulty of making simple general associations between IT investment and enterprise performance (for example, Strassmann 1990, 1997), while others have focused on the need to consider the evaluation of benefits in much broader terms than purely financial (for example, Remenyi *et al.*, 1997).

Information is an essential ingredient to support more sophisticated approaches to pricing. Perhaps the most traditional approach to pricing is cost-plus, where the costs of production at a certain level of output are cal-culated, and something is added for profit. Beyond that, there are other possible approaches, all dependent on the availability of the right information:

- *opportunity cost:* pricing is determined by alternative opportunities for revenue generation which have been foregone;
- *market value:* prices are determined by 'what the market will stand';
- *value pricing:* prices are determined by the value of the goods or ser-vices to the buyer (ideally, in economic theory, the greatest profit will be achieved if every price is set individually between each buyer and seller).

A new industrial revolution?

As was briefly discussed earlier, human societies can be seen as having gone through four stages: hunter-gatherer, agricultural, industrial and service or information (or post-industrial). These will now be considered in more detail in terms of the dominant method of production, styles of living, distribution of power and their associated information technol-ogies.

Economists frequently describe sectors of the economy in terms of primary (extractive), secondary (manufacturing), tertiary (services) or quaternary (information). Clearly all economies, even the simplest 'tribal' economies, include all four types of activity, but the tendency over time is for activities to become more specialized and the balance between them to shift from primary up the scale to first, secondary, then to tertiary and perhaps finally to quaternary activities. Thus in both hunter-gatherer and agrarian economies the main economic activities – first of all, gathering wild plant products, hunting wild animals and fishing, then farming planted crops and domestic animals – are mainly concerned with extracting raw materials from the earth. In the industrial era the craft skills used for manufacturing on a small scale in domestic establishments are replaced by factory mass production systems which come to employ the bulk of the labour force and produce most of the wealth in the economy. In the information era, although farming and industrial manufacturing continue to be major economic activities, research, education, design, finance and marketing activities employ more personnel and are seen as the crucial activities 'adding value' in the supply chain.

Clearly, as economies shift from hunter-gatherer to post-industrial the standard of living will rise from conditions in which people exist on the margins of existence, through subsistence farming, to an increasing affluence as industrial economies develop. In information economies the optimistic prediction is made that everyone will achieve a high and stable standard of living with increasing amounts of leisure for all.

Some geographical contrasts between these historical eras are worth remarking upon. In hunter-gatherer societies tiny populations are nomadic – shifting with the availability of edible foodstuffs. In small settled and rural communities of agricultural economies there is relatively little mobility – though some long-distance trade may occur in luxury goods. There is no distinction between home and workplace, with farmer and labourers, or craftsman and apprentices, living and working together. In industrial economies, large urban populations work in one place and commute daily to work. There is more travel and migration than is found in agricultural systems. In the information era, in the long term, it is possible that an enormous global community is no longer restricted by geography in that a global communication system makes the dominant information-related type of work possible anywhere.

Corresponding to each economic system, as Marx and Engels (1962) argued, those in power in the community (the elite) are likely to differ. Thus hunter-gatherer societies are led by those few older members of the tribe who survive and are respected as the repositories of the wisdom of the group. (Thus information leads to power?) In agrarian societies the land is the source of wealth so that the major landowners tend to dominate socially and politically. With industrialization comes the political and social triumph of capitalists – the owners of the factories that are the key to the wealth of the economy. It is argued by writers such as Bell (1973) that in the post-industrial era the new elite will be the 'technocrats' and managers who understand and can control the scientific and technical information which is now the real basis of wealth.

In each era human beings' relationship to their environment undergoes a radical shift. At first humans are parts of the ecological system – one more species competing for survival in a harsh landscape beyond their control. With the development of agriculture, however, over centuries humanity remakes the landscape and comes to control which species they are prepared to cohabit with. A process accentuated by industrialization where, in a still shorter timescale, industrial pollution can render whole areas virtually uninhabitable. It is to be hoped that in the post-industrial era, with a greater understanding of ecological variables, deliberate conservation of a multiplicity of habitats for all the species of the planet may prevail.

Each historical era can be seen as having its distinctive technology. Hunter-gatherer societies are characterized by a limited range of tools mainly made or even improvised by the users (spears, sticks to knock down high-growing fruit, etc.). In agricultural economies specialized craftsmen such as blacksmiths or carpenters may develop quite sophisticated human- or animal-powered tools. The distinctive feature of industrial economies is the development of other sources of power and the use of mass manufacturing techniques in factories. Water power was soon replaced by steam power in the early Industrial Revolution. Later on, of course, the internal combustion engine and electricity became increasingly important. The distinctive technology of the information economy is of course the digital electronic computer.

Whilst digital information technology can be seen as the defining characteristic of this latest era of economic development, earlier eras too had characteristic technologies of communication. Hunter-gatherer societies probably developed through a capacity to use speech; other means of communication, such as smoke signals and cave painting, were either economically or culturally significant too. Many agricultural societies developed writing and the use of mathematical technologies such as the abacus. In ancient Egypt and elsewhere, such communications were probably important in maximizing agricultural production and certainly were useful politically. In industrial economies printing was undoubtedly associated with the spread of scientific knowledge and technological innovation. Broadcasting has helped to spread new patterns of mass consumption in many economies. We have already discussed at length, and will develop further, the key role of computers and global networks in the current era.

Related to the issue of information technology is what IT is being used to convey: knowledge. If we assume that early societies were like the preliterate societies of today or yesterday, which have been studied by social anthropologists, then the most important type of knowledge can be assumed to be tribal custom – the inherited wisdom of the ancestors of the group. In more sophisticated agrarian societies the most important and certain traditional knowledge was often theological. In a few societies, traditions of scholarship were developed which often included practical and legal insights as well as theology. The Greeks and the Romans also developed methods of philosophical inquiry, which can be seen as the ancestors of the modern natural and social sciences. Round about the time of the Industrial Revolution philosophical thought took a more rationalist and empirical turn and the new physical sciences began to contribute greatly to the rapid development of technology. It may be argued that in the post-industrial era rational techniques of inquiry are being increasingly applied, not only to technological but also to social problems. Modern professions such as economists, systems analysts, operational research specialists, market researchers, etc. can be seen as developing essential expertise which must form the basis of informed social decision-making whether by managers in industry or by politicians. The power of these 'technocrats' – expert users of the massive databases increasingly made available by the new technology – can be seen to be inevitably increasing as we move further into the twenty-first century.

Box 2.7 presents an overview of the theory of the development of an information society which has been summarized thus far. It makes a formidable case for the major significance of the widespread adoption of modern information and communication technology as a major turning point in the history of human society. However, there are a number of critical objections to such a thesis, some of which were discussed earlier.

One major area of objection may be to the implication that such a scheme involves a rather nineteenth-century view of the inevitable progress of mankind as the result of technological and economic innovation. The author certainly would not accept that there is necessarily any moral, aesthetic or cultural superiority of the later stages in this process of change. Certainly from anthropological and historical descriptions some hunter-gatherer or agrarian societies may well be happier places than many industrial ones. It is clear, too, from the historical record that there is no inevitability to the transition from one type of society and economy to the next. Also there are many theories about the causes of such changes, none of which can be unequivocally regarded as established. However, it is worth suggesting that there is some sort of 'fit' between different types of society, economy and technology, as described in this account.

Another obvious area of controversy centres around the final post-industrial or information stage of economy and society. Have we (or perhaps the United States and Japan) already entered it – or is it the likely next stage of development? Are some of the descriptions of the likely impact of IT on society over-optimistic and utopian? In particular does such a society represent a real break in the economic and social realities of capitalist industrial economies? These are large questions which cannot be finally resolved in a book of this kind, but we will return to some of them in our final chapter. In any event, there is no denying the immense importance of IT in contemporary society, whatever its exact role in terms of causation.

Box 2.7 Societies, production and information (an optimistic view of history)

	Hunter-gatherer	Agrarian	Industrial	Information
Dominant sector of economy	Primary (extractive)	Primary (extractive)	Secondary (manufacturing)	Tertiary (services) or quaternary (information)
Main economic activities	Gathering Hunting Fishing	Farming Domestic Service Craft skills	Factory mass production	Research Education Design Finance Marketing
Standard of living	Marginal	Subsistence	Increasing	High
Location	Shifting	Home-centred	Factory	Optional
Population size and distribution	Tiny nomadic	Small settled and rural	Large urban and mobile	Enormous global community
Elite	Community elders	Landowners	Capitalists	Technocrats and managers
Ecology	Part of system	Transforms landscape	Industrial pollution	Conservation
Technology	Own tools	Crafts developed	Steam manufacture	Digital computers
Information technology	Speech, smoke signals, cave painting	Writing Abacus	Printing Broadcasting	Computers Global networks
Knowledge	Tribal custom	Tradition Theology Scholarship	Rationalism Physical sciences	Professionalism Social sciences

Defining and measuring the information economy

Earlier in the chapter we touched upon the difficulty of defining what an 'information economy' was. It is worth considering briefly how it can be defined and measured and apply this to some contemporary states.

An early treatment (1986) of this is a report by the Organization for Economic Cooperation and Development (OECD). This looked at the numbers of 'information occupations', which were very widely defined to include

Information machine workers:	bookbinders
Process control and supervisory workers:	sales supervisors
Communication workers:	stage directors
Scientific and technical workers:	metallurgists

All of these occupations do deal with information in some sense (but not necessarily with modern digital information technology), and using such definitions the report showed that the number of information workers had been increasing rapidly in developed countries since the Second World War, as Figure 2.3 illustrates. On this basis the USA certainly now has a majority of information workers in its employed population. But somewhat paradoxically such figures show a massive growth in 'information workers' (mainly those in semi-skilled clerical operations) *before* computers were widely employed in American industry.

Miles (1990) employs an alternative and perhaps more convincing approach to the definition of the information economy by focusing on the use of micro-electronic silicon 'chips'. For him the 'core' of the information economy is represented by producers of such chips, whilst the 'heart' consists of information technology producers and providers such as those involved in telecommunications and computer manufacturing, computer services (software) and communication services (VANS – value added network services). The rest of industry, he suggests, could be assessed for the degree to which it makes intensive use of IT by measuring the extent to which it purchases. In principle this seems a more convincing method of measuring the spread of the use of IT throughout modern industry, but unfortunately the author knows of no definitive figures available on this basis. In the long run, any such attempt is bound to be a rather rough and ready exercise since, for instance, as chips become more powerful the employment of one chip may represent a different degree of involvement with the technology. Equally, using many computers to word-process invoices represents less dependence on the technology than using one computer to control a whole set of production processes.

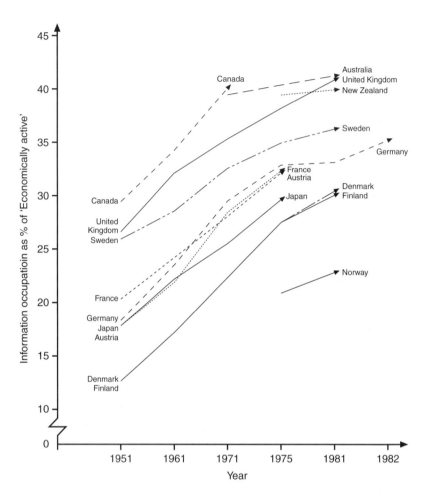

Figure 2.3 Estimated international growth in information employment
Source: OECD (1986)

IT and employment

One of the key variables in this discussion has been the extent to which people are employed in occupations affected by IT. But what is the impact on total employment of the use of computers?

Here we are considering three related topics. First, what an a priori economic analysis would lead us to expect the impact of innovations involving microprocessor technology to be. Second, we relate IT to the known causes of unemployment. Third, we consider some relevant empirical evidence. Here we are considering primarily the impact of IT on the quantity of employment; at a later stage (Chapter 6) we shall consider the impact of IT on the quality of employment available.

An economic analysis might appropriately begin at the micro (firm) level with a conventional but useful distinction between process and product innovation. In the former the innovation is used as a part of the production process to produce an unchanged product; in the latter a new or improved product (or service) involving the technology is developed. These would appear to be likely to have different employment implications.

As far as process innovation is concerned we would appear to have a conventional case of capital investment, in which *if* it is assumed that the price and quantity of the good to be sold and the materials employed is unchanged *then* the only rational justification for the investment involved must be a lowering of labour costs, probably involving job losses. This is the gloomy assumption upon which predictions of substantial job losses from IT are based.

Note, however, that there are alternatives for firms involved in process innovation – e.g. if more goods can be sold (even at reduced prices) the same (or even increased) total labour costs may be justified as the labour cost *per unit* of good sold is thereby reduced.

The product innovation case, conversely, would appear to have positive implications for the predicted demand for labour since a new product must surely produce a new demand for labour by the entrepreneur concerned, whilst an improved product would only be marketed if it produced greater profits and would be therefore likely to lead to an increased demand for labour.

At the macro (whole economy) level, unfortunately, it cannot be assumed that these findings can be automatically applied, since, for instance, process innovation by efficient firms may lead to the collapse of less efficient rivals (and the loss of their workers' jobs) whilst increased demand for the a new product (e.g. video cassette recorders) may lead to a loss of demand for rival older products (e.g. outings to the cinema).

Of the three major types of unemployment usually recognized by economists (frictional, structural and demand deficiency) the last two seem most likely to be of importance here. However, frictional unemployment may be slightly reduced by the availability of improved techniques of data retrieval and communication which can be used on behalf of, or by, the unemployed so as to match job vacancies and applicants.

Structural unemployment may result from either type of innovation as the new processes require (or appear to require) different types of labour from those made redundant. For example, older male welders are lost and young female data processing staff are demanded, or the products are produced in areas like south-east England or Japan where relatively high levels of employment are already found, whilst areas such as Tyneside (dominated by traditional declining product-producing industries) register high and increasing labour surpluses.

However, it is worth emphasizing, the major importance of the overall level of demand, in that, as we have seen, in circumstances when overall demand is buoyant, process innovation is likely to lead to an expansion of production and a richer society; product innovation, similarly, should mean that new products will be consumed in addition to the old rather than substituted for them.

Many of the gloomier predictions of the impact of IT have been based on a neglect of the economic realities of investment considerations. Technological possibilities are frequently mistaken for economic inevitabilities, as Graves (1986, 49) points out. Graves himself gives a long and gloomy list of doomed occupations, ranging from teachers in higher education, through postmen and check-out girls to transport workers. This sort of pessimism led Jenkins and Sherman (1979) to predict a loss of 23 per cent in the labour force between 1978 and 2003. It is amusing to look at some of the older works in the field and note the extent to which predictions have failed. Post Office mails business continues to mushroom (on word-processed junk mail), despite some decades of prediction that electronic mail was about to replace it. Cash-less purchasing, which according to Finn (1984) was to have paid for its installation costs by 1988, was only introduced into local Sainsbury's in 1990, and so on. Whilst something like the job loss predicted by Jenkins and Sherman occurred in the UK between 1978 and 1983, it is clear that it was overwhelmingly the result of a loss of overall demand in the economy, not of technological innovation (Brady and Liff, 1983).

Earlier in the chapter we saw some statistics (frequently quoted in connection with 'post-industrial' or 'information' society controversies) which show a considerable relative increase in the 'information-linked' and service industries apparently at the expense of manufacturing, but it is worth pointing out that much of the growth of these sectors has predated the application of microprocessor technology to them, whilst the decline of manufacturing (and agriculture in the developed world) is clearly linked to very heavy capital investment.

In the jumble of somewhat conflicting assertion it is refreshing to find some clear, if limited, empirical evidence in the shape of the regular PSI surveys of British manufacturing industry (Northcott and Walling, 1988). At first sight they appear to show a wide-scale adoption of microprocessor technology accompanied by very little reduction in employment (estimated at a total loss of 121,000 in the whole of British manufacturing industry between 1981 and 1985). However, the authors do caution us that only an estimated 12.5 per cent of manufacturing processes have yet been even partially 'automated', and that the larger job losses are associated with the more intensive users. Other findings are somewhat unexpected – for instance, on a regional basis there is no perceptible southern bias, and the expected contrast between product and process users fails to materialize.

In addition to the authors' cautions on their data we might add that only 10 per cent of the workforce are employed in manufacturing, and that job losses are direct ones within the plants concerned whilst a greater job loss may have occurred amongst rival plants which have not automated. More generally we might add that British manufacturing industry appears to have 'raised' productivity in recent years, not by investing in microtechnology but by eliminating 'uneconomic' plants and using labour more intensively (Massey and Meegan, quoted in Finn, 1984, 28). Japanese, American and newly industrialized country entrepreneurs may have, wisely, followed a different strategy, with serious potential consequences for British employment figures in the UK's exceptionally open economy.

Recommended reading

Darnton, G. and Giacoletto, S. (1992) Information in the Enterprise: It's More than Technology, Burlington, Mass., Digital Press (now available from the first author ISBN 1-902755-01-4). Develops the analysis of information economics in this chapter.

Moschella, David (1997) *Waves of Power: Dynamics of Global Technology Leadership 1964–2010*, New York, American Management Association. Excellent analysis of development of the IT industry.

Porter, Michael (1990) *The Competitive Advantage of Nations*, New York, Free Press. A classic.

Zerdick, Axel *et al.* (2000) *E-conomics: Strategies for the Digital Marketplace*, Berlin, Springer, for the European Communication Council. Excellent introduction to the changes the Internet is bringing about in the world economy.

3   Government, globalization and information technology

Topics

- Government and the economy
- The role of government in relation to IT
- National and regional approaches to IT
- Globalization, information technology and government

Here we consider the issue of how far government does, and should, affect the use and development of information technology. The role of giant international firms in IT, such as IBM, Microsoft and Toshiba, will be considered, as well as the dependency of other major international players (from Coca-Cola to NATO) on IT and global networks. Finally, we consider how far the use of information technology by multinational enterprises can be regulated by national governments.

Government and the economy

Government interventions that affect the information technology industry are only a special case of a whole host of interventions by governments in economic matters. The economic policies and attitudes of governments affect the economy as a whole, which in turn constitutes the environment for the IT industry. We begin, therefore, with a general discussion of the role of governments in influencing the economy by way of background to a much more detailed discussion of their impact on IT.

To what extent can the government affect economic success? There are three main schools of thought, with different implications both for the economy in general and action towards the IT industry: socialist/nationalist interventionism, free market/monetarist and Keynesian/mixed economy.

Socialist/nationalist interventionism

Most governments, historically, have not hesitated to intervene in the economy – especially to safeguard industries regarded as strategically vital (like IT). Beside this, socialist or communist governments may regard capitalist industries as exploitative and unfair, and some, or total, central planning of the economy as necessary and desirable. On both grounds (nationalism and socialism), the protection of 'infant industries' has been frequent.

Free market/monetarist

Adam Smith, the eighteenth-century Scottish economist, argued, in contrast, that the 'invisible hand' of the free market was the most efficient decision-making mechanism on economic affairs. The best government policy was one of *laissez-faire* (leaving market competition to decide). The government should maintain law and order and intervene only to break up monopolies and safeguard sound money. Britain's best-known recent Prime Minister, Margaret Thatcher, was much influenced by Milton Friedman, a modern American disciple of Adam Smith, who has argued for a minimum of government expenditure (and taxes) and control of the economy only through restricting the money supply.

Keynesian/mixed economy

Most economists and many 'moderate' politicians of all parties remain influenced by the English economist John Maynard Keynes who argued that economies were not in a natural balance, but that governments had to influence the level of demand by spending money in recessions and raising taxes in booms. He supported welfare expenditure partly because it helped government to balance the economy in this way. In post-war Britain, and in most economically developed democracies, governments have, in principle at least, remained committed to the goal of full employment and most have attempted to plan the economy to some extent. They have also tolerated or encouraged nationalized industries, boasted of their increased expenditure on welfare, education, housing and the like, and intervened to bolster the economies of depressed areas. Labour, Socialist and Democratic governments have spent taxpayers' money to support private industry, while Edward Heath, a British Conservative Prime Minister, nationalized Rolls-Royce to prevent the firm's closure.

Government policies towards IT should be understood in the context of these differences in attitude towards economic policy.

The role of government in relation to IT

Research and development

Perhaps the most obvious way in which government can be seen to have an influence on IT is through its influence on the research and development (R&D) cycle. Figure 3.1 simplifies this.

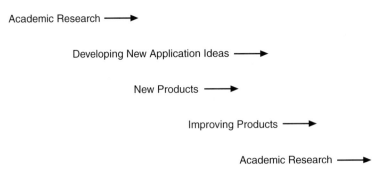

Figure 3.1 R&D cycle

The question of the role of universities and polytechnics, ministries of economics, trade, education and defence, specialist research bodies and firms in all this is a complex one, but in an industry changing as rapidly as information technology it is clearly a crucial one. There are the questions not only of the size of government support for the process but also the nature of the support and the stage of the process in which the government sees it as appropriate to intervene.

One constraint on most governments today is that the WTO (World Trade Organization) international trading rules theoretically prevent government subsidies to individual firms to develop particular products. This is to ensure there is a 'level playing field' between firms competing on an international basis. However, this does not prevent support for research institutes to benefit industries as a whole or 'pure' basic research in universities which can be converted into specific products by firms at a later stage. Defence and space research can also be commissioned by governments, which often has spin-off benefits for the firms concerned.

Several defence-related projects have led to fundamental developments in computing technology. In the United Kingdom the major pioneer of mechanical computing, Charles Babbage, was first encouraged, then discouraged, by the award and by the ending of substantial grant aid which was primarily directed towards the compilation of navigational tables for the Royal Navy. Similarly, the first leap forward in electrical computing was instigated at Bletchley in Buckinghamshire as part of a successful government-financed project to break the Second World War German codes.

In the USA, the pioneering ENVIAC computer was a government-financed project used in the development of the early H-bombs. Subsequently the industry's research and development has been massively financed and moulded by the federal government's defence and space projects. In particular the need to pack computing power into relatively small US satellites following the USSR's Sputnik triumph helped forward the development of micro-computing. The development of the Internet, via US Defense Department funding, has already been considered. Recent examples include the massive IT expenditure which will form the core of the National Missile Defense system.

In the other major world computing power, Japan, the Fifth Generation Project is only the latest major example of explicit government and industry planning which places the development of IT industries as the focus of a strategy for maintaining the international competitiveness of the whole economy.

British R&D on IT

Broadly speaking, viewed in comparative international terms, the general record of British (government) expenditure on R&D does not seem far out of step with other advanced economies. The problem, from the point of view of the need to develop commercial IT products, is that too much of this is allocated to applied defence-related projects and too little to both IT and academic research and its development towards civilian industrial uses. Additionally, the British industry's notorious reluctance to invest seems very evident in this area.

In the not-too-distant past, the 'Alvey' programme, made a promising start in addressing these problems by encouraging joint academic/industry R&D programmes with grant aid. This appears to have been very successful initially, but to have lost momentum with a change in government policy which has stressed that such initiatives should normally be financed through the EU programmes (which normally require a partner or partners in another EU country), and that government aid should be restricted to the early stages of the cycle. This is perhaps unfortunate, given Britain's record of successful scientific and technological innovations, which are not then properly developed and exploited by industry. However, such a move was intelligible in terms of the Thatcher/Major governments' pro-market philosophy.

Whatever the reason, even the early stages of the cycle seem to have been starved of funds – in 1987–8 only 35 per cent of 'alpha'-rated computer science proposals to the ESRC were approved. (The Committee of Vice-Chancellors, in their evidence to the select committee, suggesting that this was partly the result of the success of the Alvey initiative in generating new research proposals in the area.)

More recently the government's policy has been to focus its grant-giving activities for research through its 'Foresight' programme, which involves business representatives working alongside academics in spotting which research is most relevant to industrial and social needs and likely to be successful. Whether this is a sensible substitute for a more generous attitude to fundamental research in universities and the development of mechanisms for encouraging long-term investment in technology by industry and financial institutions is, again, somewhat arguable.

European IT R&D programmes

The first major European programme for research and development in IT was ESPRIT and is typical of the sort of activity financed by the EU. This programme provided EU grants for research programmes of a 'pre-competitive' nature in IT, which must be based on a collaboration between industry and higher education across national boundaries. ESPRIT continued for three phases (the last, 1991–4) and has been described as 'the most successful and prestigious of European technology programmes' (Economist Intelligence Unit, 1991). Over six hundred projects were funded, usually on a 50 per cent basis, involving 1,500 organizations. However, the Dekker review of 1993 recommended a more user-oriented approach in future.

IT-related programmes in the Fourth Framework Programme (which covered 1994–8) included 843 million ECU for telematics, 630 million ECU for communication technologies and 1,932 million ECU for information technologies – approximately £660 million a year (about one-third of the total R&D budget).

In the current Fifth Framework programme (1999–2002) the division between computing, telecommunications and applications was considered undesirable, given the growing convergence of technologies. A single Information Society Technology programme, with a total budget of 3.6 billion Euro, has replaced them. Areas of research and development covered by the plan include security and privacy; education and training; access for the elderly, the sick and the disabled; electronic commerce; electronic government; health on-line and intelligent transport. These are all elements of the parallel eEurope Action Plan discussed later in this chapter.

Structure of IT industries

Another obvious area in which the government may intervene is in the structure of the computer and telecommunications industries themselves. Here considerations of political 'ideology' are still more evident than in the R&D area. Nationalist governments may be concerned to promote a strong indigenous IT industry because it is thought to add to national prestige to be involved in such a modern industry, to serve as a resource for other sectors of industry and aid economic development, and for use in national defence (avoiding reliance on foreign, potentially hostile firms). The promotion of national 'flagbearer' firms was a common strategy in the early period of computing development. Conversely, authoritarian governments like the former Soviet Union may regard information technology as potentially politically destabilizing. China, for example, is still (in 2001) seeking to censor the websites available to its citizens. More free market oriented regimes will be anxious to promote free competition amongst independent entrepreneurs in this, as in other, areas.

British governments and industrial structure

The Thatcher government was preoccupied with the denationalization of British Telecom, and the establishment of competition for it and the creation of further privately financed broadcasting (satellite) channels. At the same time it showed no great concern at the takeover of ICL – the UK's major indigenous major computer manufacturer – by a Japanese 'multinational' in 1990.

This record contrasts with that of earlier governments, which seemed much more preoccupied with the development of an independent British manufacturing capacity – so that (old) Labour supported development of INMOS as a (private enterprise) chip-maker (also sold off to a multinational), and of ICL, as free enterprise 'flag-bearer' companies.

It would appear that the Thatcher administration felt that we had lost the international race in this respect. The leading UK IT manufacturer, STC/ICL, had only 4 per cent of IBM's turnover. The large negative balance of trade in IT hardware was not seen as a major problem provided good use was being made of the imported technology.

EU competition policy

All large mergers within the EU are now subject to Community-wide regulation. In assessing whether to take action the Commission will have to consider not only the avoidance of internal monopolies but also the maintenance of European industrial players capable of competing with the giant US and Japanese 'multinationals'.

In 1994 the Commission refused to allow Deutsche Telekom and two large German media companies to merge, which would have reinforced DT's almost total control of the German cable network. However, it allowed a proposed joint venture between BT and the US firm MCI on the grounds that it facilitated innovatory services in a competitive world market.

A single market in computers?

The European Union's primary objective is to create a large single competitive 'home market' for European manufacturers which will enable them to compete effectively on the world stage. In terms of IT this means that, for instance, standard 'Eurocomputers' will be sold and marketed to one Euromarket from one European point of manufacture! How realistic an objective is this?

Some progress towards this has already been made. Tariff barriers have already been removed between all EU countries on computers, as on all else. The 1992 'single market' measures have meant a substantial reduction in delays at national borders and in paperwork involved in crossing boundaries, but VAT rates are still not standardized, hence some administrative barriers remain.

Within the Euro single currency zone (most of Europe – but not including the UK) transaction costs associated with changing currencies have been phased out from 2002. Certification problems (see our discussion of standards below) have diminished as a result of the 1992 single market agreement, and a European Court decision which held that goods certified as safe in one EU country can be sold in any another.

However, there remain considerable problems in achieving Euro-standard computers. One major area is that of standards. All sorts of standards affect computers, not just operating systems, but also file formats, protocols for transmitting data which *may* be standardized under OSI (see pp. 114–15) and also such things as paper size (e.g. A4 is a European standard largely unknown in the USA), electricity supply voltages, the number of lines, etc., on domestic televisions which might be used as monitors. All of these need to be standardized if a standard product is to be possible.

Consumers in any European country – let us call it 'Transylvania' – may still prefer to buy 'made in Transylvania' products. This is still the norm outside the UK in Europe – though 'Euro-preference' may evolve! Perhaps, in time, the EU will insist that goods be marked only 'Made in Europe' not 'Made in France' or 'Made in Britain'. Equally, governments may still wish to favour domestic producers. The EU has directed (July 1992) that all government contracts over 200,000 ECU (£144,000) should be open to competitive tender, including those for computing services and some telecommunications contracts. But governments will probably still be able to manipulate specifications to suit domestic manufacturers and find reasons to prefer their bids.

National needs, tastes and preferences are still likely to vary. The most obvious example of this is language differences. Accents on French or German texts fade into insignificance when we consider the case of Greeks with a completely different alphabet. But markets are also likely to vary according to the needs of national educational systems and the existence or otherwise of large 'hobby markets', business preference for faxes rather than e-mail, and so on.

The United States and IT competition

In the United States the federal government has often taken a strong line on safeguarding consumers against monopoly exploitation. Two notable examples are the decision to break up the Bell Telephone company and the more recent decision to prosecute Microsoft for the abuse of monopoly power, with a real threat to break up the company into separate components. This is covered in more detail in Case Study 3.1.

Case Study 3.1 **Microsoft and the courts**

USA versus Microsoft

30 May 1989	Federal Trade Commission starts anti-trust investigation of allegations of anti-competitive pricing policies and secret features of operating system to frustrate development of competing application products.
20 August 1993	Justice Department takes over the case.
14 February 1995	US District Judge rejects settlement between Justice Dept and Microsoft as too weak.
20 May 1995	Acquisition of Intuit dropped following Justice Department opposition.
21 August 1995	Another District Judge approves previous settlement following successful Appeal Court action.
20 October 1997	Justice Department sues Microsoft for violating previous settlement by requiring computer makers to install Internet Explorer web browser if they want to license Windows 95.
7 November 1997	Texas launches first of 20 State probes into Microsoft.
11 December 1997	Judge Jackson issues an injunction restraining Microsoft from requiring computer makers to install Internet Explorer.
23 June 1998	Federal Appeals Court rules in favour of Microsoft on this.
19 October 1998	Trial of two further anti-trust lawsuits against Microsoft begins in Jackson's Washington District Court.
5 November 1999	Preliminary ruling by Jackson finds Microsoft has used its monopoly power to harm consumers and other businesses.
7 June 2000	Judge Jackson accepts US government proposal to divide Microsoft into operating systems and applications companies.
28 June 2001	Federal Appeals Court reverses order to break up Microsoft and sends case back to new judge, but found merit in anti-trust allegations.
6 September 2001	Justice Department in new Republican administration abandons attempt to break up company.

2 November 2001	Mediator appointed by new judge announces settlement between Microsoft and Justice Department – but some States are unwilling to accept its terms. The terms include an independent technical team to monitor compliance; new versions of Windows to be made available to rival developers; provisions against the automatic loading of Windows by PCs at switch on; and the end of discounts to OEMs in exchange for their exclusively installing Microsoft wares.
11 November 2001	The European Commission is reported to be considering fining Microsoft £1.7 billion for deliberately making its software incompatible with that of its competitors.
20 November 2001	Microsoft reported to be considering a deal to supply hardware, software and support to the 14,000 poorest schools in the USA to compensate consumers for the monopoly profits they have made.

Sources: www.washingtonpost.com and www.guardian.co.uk

Use of IT by industry

It may be desirable for an economy to have major IT hardware and software producers, given that the industry has, as we have seen, represented the leading edge of industrial development in the past half century. However, not every country can, or should, achieve this, since production, to be competitive, must be on a massive (global) scale. Free-market economists would generally argue that the law of comparative advantage means that countries should concentrate on those areas of production to which they are best suited. Hence New Zealand might concentrate on rearing free-range sheep, and the UK on producing communication content (e.g. English dictionaries and interactive English lessons) rather than hardware.

What is essential to a successful economy is that every industry should deploy IT to maximum effect. All economies will require distribution and consultancy services, an IT-literate workforce, and a telecommunications infrastructure. Multinational companies may, perhaps, be relied upon to adopt new IT, but small and medium enterprises (SMEs) are often thought to require government encouragement to adopt such innovations.

In Britain, as far back as 1988–9 in their replies to the Select Committee on Industry, the use of IT by industry was seen as crucial by government spokesmen. But the view taken by the administration of the need to respect market forces has inhibited the adoption of many of the measures which might be considered to encourage usage. Thus direct subsidies have apparently hardly been considered, whilst the idea of tax incentives was rejected partly on the basis of Treasury advice that much of the expenditure thus indirectly subsidized would be made in any case. The Department of Trade and Industry has thus resorted mainly to the use of publicity campaigns, some aid to research and development (as previously mentioned), and a limited scheme to subsidize information technology consultants for small and medium-sized firms (House of Commons Industry Committeee, 1988–9).

In practice, investment in IT by British industry has suffered from the same malaise which has affected all such capital investment in recent years, if not decades. Thus although successive PEP surveys have shown the majority of British manufacturers adopting some IT, this has been on a piecemeal basis, mainly in relation to process innovation rather than product innovation, and at far below the levels of Japanese and American competitors (Northcott and Walling, 1988).

Public procurement and government use

A major influence that governments can have on the IT market is through their status as the major purchasers and users of IT equipment. For instance, UK government IT spending is estimated at well over £4 billion a year.

In spending such large sums, governments may influence suppliers for good or evil. One notable influence governments may have is in developing good practice standards. Thus Britain's CCTA (Central Computer and Telecommunications Agency) commissioned the development and adopted SSADM (the Structured Systems Analysis and Design Method); PRINCE (PRojects IN Controlled Environments), the government's project control methodology for IT projects; and CRAMM, the CCTA Risk Analysis and Management Methodology. Not only are government agencies required to use these procedures, but major suppliers of information services and developers of products for the public services are usually required to adopt them as well.

Similarly in the United States, government, in addition to the Internet developments discussed later, has developed, through the National Institute of Standards and Technology, a number of commercially adopted Federal Information Processing Standards and promoted a single programming language: ADA. Although ADA has not been as widely adopted in the US as SSADM and PRINCE have in the UK. So far the EU has failed to adopt common system development standards, even within its own machinery, and thus has been unable to promote them throughout European industry.

The degree to which the UK can influence industry through its procurement arrangements is limited by membership of the EU. As has been already remarked, EU Directives now require that all large projects be put out to tender via the EU official journal.

There have been some attempts to promote rational public sector purchasing. One early attempt was through GOSIP: the UK government OSI (Open Systems Interconnection) Profile – a procurement specification covering OSI-based data communications. This was also adopted by a number of other EU countries. However it seems likely that this has largely been abandoned in favour of commercial de facto standards such as IP/TCP (Springett, 1994).

We shall return to the topic of democratic government's use of IT in our final chapter.

Training of skilled personnel

In relation to the successful application of IT in industry generally, as well as in the development of the IT industry itself, it is clear that training and education plays a vital role. With a knowledge-based industry, a high level of individual skills, attitudes and knowledge is clearly economically vital. It is surely no coincidence that the most successful, IT-led economies – the United States, Japan and Germany – are also those with the highest levels of higher education and industrial training. Government policies towards education and industrial training are therefore clearly of vital relevance to IT.

Whilst some good work has been done in British schools, with some imaginative backing from the BBC, there can be little doubt that they are handicapped by policies which resulted in the purchase of IT equipment becoming the subject of Parent–Teacher Association raffles rather than being automatically provided as a key learning resource. Information technology is now a core element of the National Curriculum prescribed by central government, and some specific funds have been allocated – particularly since the 1997 government pledge to ensure that all schools will be connected to the Internet.

Whilst the UK government has verbally favoured the expansion of IT courses, in practice one might argue that there are few practical incentives to students to choose such courses. Employers continue to favour 'Oxbridge' Arts graduates in recruiting to management training schemes. Government fails to provide any special financial incentives for technology and engineering students. Higher sums are paid to university-level institutions to provide laboratory-based courses, but these do not necessarily cover the much higher costs.

The former Manpower Services Commission did successfully insist, amongst other things, on all Youth Training Schemes including an IT element, and the Department of Trade and Industry successfully fostered local Information Technology Centres, although the overall expenditure by industry on training in general and IT in particular remains well below that of Britain's overseas competitors. There are some signs that local Learning and Skills Councils and industry generally are becoming more aware of training needs. But such bodies operated until recently in a climate of government hostility to quangos (quasi autonomous non-governmental organizations) and 'feather-bedding' industry, which has all but eliminated the Industrial Training Board levies and reduced government expenditure on training.

A recent government initiative, which has been extensively utilized by colleges and private IT training agencies, to offer IT training to adult learners has been a system of individual learning accounts. Every adult has had a sum credited to them by the DES which can be used towards the purchase of any approved course in a number of areas including IT. Unfortunately, however, no proper system of quality control was exercised over the approval of courses in the private sector and the scheme has now been suspended in the wake of revelations that a minority of training providers were effectively defrauding their students and the taxpayer.

The EU has subsidized a range of IT training programmes throughout Europe, including NOW (New Opportunities for Women) and (massively) Youth Training.

Telecommunications and broadcasting

In contrast to the relatively lightly regulated computing industry (including the Internet) both telephone and broadcasting industries have been heavily controlled by governments for a combination of technical, economic, and political reasons.

One major reason for this is that both areas were initially, and to some degree still are, 'natural monopolies'. Telephones, until recently, required landlines, the installation of which requires the use of public land (e.g. under or alongside roads) or private land (when powers of compulsory purchase may be necessary to complete a network). It made no sense to duplicate local networks (from exchanges to offices and houses) since this would require enormous additional disruption and be unlikely ever to justify a vast additional investment. This means that whoever owned the local network would have a local monopoly. In Britain and most of Europe, abuse of the monopoly was prevented by a government-owned PTO providing the service on a non-profit basis. In the USA, as we have seen, the Bell Telephone companies were licensed to operate regional monopoly services, but under strict federal price controls.

A similar technical requirement applied to broadcasting is that a shortage of broadcasting wavelengths (particularly in the long and medium wavebands) meant that there had to be international agreements implemented by national governments on their allocation. There was also the consideration that it was difficult or impossible originally to charge listeners (and later viewers) for broadcasting services. Thus broadcasting could only be financed through advertising, which was thought, in Europe at any rate, to require government regulation – or be provided on a non-profit basis, usually by government-controlled bodies.

Additional political considerations applied particularly to broadcasting. The power of the media was rapidly seen to be enormous. Hitler and other dictators in the 1930s used radio as a major means to power. In the Second World War the airwaves were full of rival propaganda broadcasts. More recently in Rwanda, and in the former Yugoslavia, populist broadcasting incited 'ethnic cleansing' on a massive scale. In contemporary Italy Senor Berlusconi has successfully supported his bid for political power through control of a chain of TV stations.

In many countries national governments insist on controlling broadcasting through state broadcasting that reflects the government party's line. In the United Kingdom an alternative solution was an attempt to 'neutralize' the power of the new media by setting up an impartial public service broadcaster: the BBC. (Even the BBC failed to stay neutral during the General Strike and the Second World War.) In Holland a legally regulated system of politically balanced broadcasting stations has operated.

Only in the USA did an historical commitment to free speech and capitalism result in a relatively uncontrolled, advertising-financed, more competitive broadcasting system. But even here the Federal Communications Commission allocated wavelengths and set some standards on content. This has been heavily supplemented by the power of advertisers, in practice, to censor any 'offensive' content. In the UK and elsewhere quangos such as the Broadcasting Complaints Commission have been set up to enforce complaints about indecency and unfairness.

It can be argued that recent technical developments have greatly weakened the economic and technical case for high levels of regulation. The introduction of mobile telephones has enabled rival broadcast, rather than wired, telephone networks to be created much more cheaply than in the past. (However these do require the allocation of broadcast wavelengths and the construction of either transmission masts on the ground or the launching of satellites in geo-stationary orbit in the airspace of one or more states.) The use of digital transmission systems has enabled many more messages to be sent down wired systems simultaneously and the creation of many more broadcasting frequencies. The possibility also now exists to transmit along power cables, television cables and even gas pipes, thus abolishing even the local exchange-to-house monopolies. Above all, the availability of hundreds of channels of broadcast material, on both terrestrial and satellite digital channels, let alone virtual broadcasts on the

Internet, weakens the likelihood of effective regulation and the case for controlling conventional (analogue) terrestrial broadcasts.

The political climate in most countries has moved in a free market direction favouring deregulation and competition. Thus much of the EU effort so far has been concentrated on telecommunications because it is obviously vital in linking Europe together, because telecommunications is seen as crucial technologically, and because national telecommunications markets have been dominated by cosy arrangements between monopoly national PTOs (public telecommunications operators) and a few 'national' manufacturers (some of these being subsidiaries of multinationals). The Council of Ministers has now agreed and has largely implemented a policy of the full liberalization of all communications services, including public voice telephony.

ISDN (Integrated Services Digital Network) is being strongly encouraged (with BT being a European pioneer), mainly with technological progress in mind. This involves converting the telecommunications network to a binary transmission system, opening up additional channels for moving image transmissions, for example, and conforming to international standards which would enable suppliers from all over the world to compete on equal terms.

An EU directive of June 1990 introduced a policy of ONP (open network provision). The objective here is more obviously economic and political. Essentially the idea is that the main network provider in each country must open up access to the network to competitors on equal terms to those upon which it offers access to its own parts or subsidiaries. In most countries PTOs have previously insisted that all (first) telephone sets are provided by them. In some, PBXs, mobile phone, radio pagers, modems and telex machines have had to be supplied by them, whilst in others telex or mobile phones are not available. Britain has been rare in having a competitive provider of telephone services (Mercury) and a separate regulatory body (Oftel – Office of Telecommunications). The EU has favoured a more competitive regime throughout Europe and has brought about the creation of Oftel-like bodies in each country.

This was politically quite subtle since the former Thatcher UK government, for instance, whilst unenthusiastic about EU regulation, was keen on fostering competition, especially abroad in line with its own domestic measures.

The Commission has also announced that PTOs are to be investigated for price-fixing international calls through the CCITT. The proposal is to harmonize internal and external charges and to ensure that calls cost the same in opposite directions.

The EU 1989 Broadcasting directive has already included regulation of such subjects as advertising, protecting children and guaranteeing a role to independent producers. A separate audio-visual policy supplements this in relation to the development of HDTV (high-definition television).

Encouraging superhighway development

Governments are increasingly recognizing the economic centrality of the existence of a superhighway in the age of the information economy.

In the United States, former Vice-President Gore, whilst still a senator, sponsored the High Performance Computing and Communications Act of 1991 which provided \$2.9m over five years to provide high volume data highways linking the NREN (see Chapter 2); this has been followed by the High Performance Computing and High Speed Networking Act of 1993 which aimed to spread the NREN to all health care facilities and schools. The former Republican leader of the House of Representatives Newt Gingrich was also an enthusiastic superhighway protagonist. NREN operates at a gigabyte per sec (i.e. 1 billion bytes = 300 large novels). In 1998 a further 'Next Generation Internet Research Act' was agreed which authorizes the development of a yet faster (a thousand times the previous Internet speeds), more reliable, and secure net to link one hundred universities. Facilities for tele-surgery and other medical services were particularly stressed by the White House in their press release.

The EU is also sponsoring the development of European networks, including the European Nervous System to link EU governments. For instance, in February 1995 the new European passport/visa control system came on-line linking countries from Spain to Germany.

The British government's approach has been mainly to encourage private enterprise to develop networks competitively in response to market forces – although it has financed JANET and subsequently SUPER-JANET. The main thrust of policy has been to encourage competition to British Telecom in the shape of rival networks such as Mercury, and especially by licensing cable companies on a local basis. To encourage the latter, BT was for years specifically prohibited from broadcasting along its wires, although the cable companies are allowed to offer telephone services on their cables. An estimated 70 per cent of the UK should be cabled by 2004 at no cost to the Treasury/PSBR (public sector borrowing requirement).

Regulation

A further important area of government intervention which affects not only the IT industry but the whole of industry are the rules which have been adopted to regulate the use of information technology. These include rules to preserve the privacy of individuals (data protection), to prevent the abuse of computers and the Internet, and to protect people's intellectual property. These will be dealt with in more detail in the next chapter.

National and regional approaches to IT

It is often assumed that existing technology is the independent result of scientific and engineering know-how, and the world beating its way to the door of the inventor of a better mousetrap. (The role of a free market economic system being explicitly acknowledged by the more sophisticated.) However, in relation to information technology in particular, it is clear that the development of the technology itself, and the pattern of its employment, has been fundamentally affected by government activity.

The current nature of the world's use of IT has, therefore, been shaped by the decisions of national policy-makers. In this chapter we consider some of the different ways in which policy-makers have approached this task.

Government and IT in the UK

In the UK, parliament, mass parties, big 'cause' pressure groups and the like have been largely irrelevant to the making of policy on IT. Most of the public (and MPs) have not appeared to understand or care about IT issues as such – although in recent years there is an increasing recognition of the importance of IT to economic and industrial success.

However, the last Conservative (Major) government did announce an information society initiative in the wake of EU initiatives. In early 1996, following considerable developments at the international (G7 – Group of Seven leading industrial nations – and EU) level, the government did announce its own 'information society initiative' which put additional emphasis on its efforts to encourage the use of IT, especially by small and medium enterprises (SMEs) and in education. This was followed by the announcement that it had set up a Cabinet committee to coordinate strategy on IT and a consultative Green Paper in November – *Government Direct* – which discussed how the government planned to apply IT to the delivery of better service to industry and citizens.

The New Labour government of Tony Blair followed up these developments with a modernization strategy for government centring around the increased use of IT in government initiatives to spend more on bringing the Internet to schools, and some further initiatives to encourage industrial use of IT. In a White Paper, *Opportunity for All in a World of Change* published by DfEE and DTI, the government proposed five University Innovation Centres to help SMEs to apply IT, an Action Plan to improve IT skills, the building of a 'world class' technical education system, spending £30m to facilitate broadband access for people and businesses, and measures to promote digital TV to give Internet access for people without PCs (see www.dti.gov.uk/opportunityforall).

So far civil servants and ministers in the Department of Trade and Industry (DTI), the Ministry of Defence (MoD), the Treasury and the

Department for Education and Skills (DES – previously DfEE), plus the Prime Minister if interested, have made policy influenced by the 'interest' pressure groups they consult. These include the Confederation of British Industries (CBI), universities, manufacturers' associations, British Telecom, and the Trades Union Congress (TUC). The European Commission also, of course, plays a role since IT is increasingly central to the economic objectives of the Community as considered below. The pattern of policy-making can thus be roughly described as a 'corporatist' one in which co-opted members of affected groups share in decision-making in return for delivering cooperation with, and legitimation to, the resulting policies.

It would appear, therefore, that success in influencing the government on these issues would seem to depend on an understanding of the subtleties of the Whitehall (rather than Westminster) lobbying system, and not on a grasp of formal party and legislative politics. This is not to deny the importance of political 'ideology'. Attitudes to state intervention and the market, European collaboration and nationalism will affect the assumptions as to what is possible by the behind-the-scenes policy-makers.

A (1989) parliamentary Select Committee report was not too encouraging: 'The overall impression we have gained from all the evidence is that the government has no strategy for Information Technology and fails to coordinate the various aspects of the subject in which it is invariably involved' (Select Committee Report §111). As the description of the policy process offered above might lead one to conclude, piecemeal behind-the-scenes decision-making led, in the past, to uncoordinated policy-making. Since September 1999 a more proactive approach to policy on IT may be appearing. Policy is coordinated from the Prime Minister's office by an 'e-envoy' who is a member of the staff of the Cabinet Office. The Secretary of State for Trade is responsible for the government's e-agenda, with two junior ministers specifically responsible for e-commerce and e-government. The UK Online Action Plan gives 94 detailed recommendations in 25 priority areas and annual reports are now published on progress towards these. Monthly reports are also made to the Prime Minister.

The e-envoy's core objectives are:

- to make the UK the best environment in the world for e-commerce by 2002
- to ensure that everyone who wants it has access to the Internet by 2005
- to make all government services available electronically by 2005.

However, the small sums actually allocated for expanding broadband access, and a continued reliance on encouraging competition in the private sector as a means of achieving ambitious targets, makes the likelihood of achieving of such targets debatable at least.

In summary, then, it is argued here that an understanding of the UK IT industry, and the crucial role of government policy towards it, requires a knowledge of the general industrial context of government policy towards the economy, education and training and the European Community. We have also argued that, in the United Kingdom, unlike the situation in say Singapore, government policy towards IT has been poorly coordinated. Given the international context in which the IT industry, in particular, operates it seems difficult to envisage a viable future for the industry except as part of a unified and dynamic European industry.

Europe and IT

European policy-makers have stated that they see IT as vital to the future of European industry. Telecommunications was explicitly highlighted as an area for European decision in the Maastricht Treaty of 1992 (Article 129 on Trans-European Networks); in 1993 the Commission proposed spending 150 billion ECU over ten years on telecommunications, and the 1995 Commission appointed a Commissioner with sole responsibility for IT/Telecommunications (Martin Bangemann). Bangemann urged the EU to 'put its faith in the market mechanism as the motive power to move us into the Information Age'. In collaboration with the G7 group of major industrial countries eleven pilot projects were agreed in February 1995 to support the birth of the 'global information society'.

Europe's first Action Plan on the information society (1994) was based on four main elements:

- First, the adoption of a statutory and legal framework for liberalizing the infrastructure – increasing competition, interconnection and inter-operability in telecommunications; intellectual property rights, electronic and legal protection, media control and international relations.
- Second, the Commission was to act as a catalyst for initiatives by the private sector in fields of trans-European networks, services and applications including teleworking, research networks for universities and others, telematics services for SMEs, road and air traffic management, trans-European governmental networks and urban information super-highways.
- Third, social and cultural aspects – use of IT to promote cooperation based on linguistic and cultural diversity.
- Fourth, the promotion of the concept of the information society.

The plan was updated in a 'Rolling Action Plan' in 1996 which preserved the same general strategy, but emphasized five new key objectives:

- Improving the business environment, particularly through ensuring that the necessary conditions are available for *electronic commerce* – copyright, data protection, digital signatures, etc.

- Investing in *life-long learning* as well as in appropriate schools.
- Increased investment in research on the development of innovative information and communication technologies.
- *Putting people first* – job creation and increased opportunities for citizens.
- Modernizing *global rules* which affect e-commerce etc. WTO (World Trade Organization) negotiations were seen as central to this.

The current statement of strategy for the EU builds upon these earlier efforts but places much greater emphasis on the Internet. Adopted in June 2000, the eEurope Action Plan emphasizes the three main objectives of a cheaper, faster, secure Internet; investing in people and skills; and stimulating the use of the Internet.

These objectives are to be achieved through setting up an appropriate legal environment, supporting new infrastructure and services across Europe (mainly through private sector funding) and applying an open method of coordination by monitoring progress towards defined bench-marks annually.

Much effort has gone into the legislative framework for an information society. In November 2000, the index of relevant legislation on the EU website ran into 17 pages! Some fairly large sums have been expended on research and development, but the reliance on private capital to develop a European telecommunications infrastructure is a questionable element in this strategy.

Given the size of the domestic American and Japanese markets, the existing strength of their IT industries, and the support they receive from their strong national governments, European manufacturers (particularly non-German manufacturers) are unlikely to be able to compete without acting in a concerted manner in a single market place.

Given the barriers to creating a single European market we have observed, and the lack of political will to overcome them in some quarters, the prospects for success must be limited – although some consolation may be derived from the likely long-term increase in the size of the market (even if incompletely integrated) as a result of the disintegration of the Eastern bloc.

USA

As we have already seen to some extent the USA's approach to the development of the IT industry is a curious mixture. Nominally its government is the chief world apostle of the free enterprise market approach to economic development. Certainly in many respects the freedom enterprises have to set up (and close down) where they will, and the presence of a large affluent home consumer market has facilitated the growth of dot.com millionaires out of businesses started in Silicon Valley garages.

The dot.com boom and bust discussed in Chapter 2 highlights the availability of investment finance for speculative ventures in the USA. It is noticeable that in the UK much of the risk capital for these ventures also came from across the Atlantic.

The government's aggressive attempts to curb monopoly in the telephone system and to regulate monopolistic businesses such as IBM and Microsoft also seems to reflect a commitment to the 'free enterprise way'.

However, we have also seen that many of the most important developments in US and world computing (including the initial development of mainframe computers and of the Internet) were in fact closely linked to massive defence spending by the federal government.

Japan

In contrast Japan, although nominally also a free-market economy, has in practice worked through a system of close collaboration between government and groups of banks, associated major companies and their smaller suppliers. A very successful post-war group decision to move from the manufacture of imitative cheap copies of Western products to the creation of innovative high-quality consumer electronic goods shows the potential for such a system.

What is perhaps surprising is the comparative failure to date of the Japanese to capitalize on their success in the consumer electronics field (videocassette recorders, games consoles) to make similar breakthroughs in the computing and Internet areas. This is despite a determined effort in the shape of the Fifth Generation Project to become innovators in the advanced areas of super-computer and artificial intelligence research and development.

Moschella (1997, 200–2) suggests some reasons for the problems Japan has faced. These include, of course, general financial and economic problems, some of which relate to political corruption. Another problem is that it is difficult to coordinate the group of economic players centring around MITI (the Ministry of International Trade and Industry), who are mainly successful export-oriented producers of automobiles and electronic goods, with those related to the Ministry of Posts and Telecommunications. Although Japan has a high standard of living and a highly educated population, home computing developed more slowly than in the USA or the UK, partly because of language problems and partly because rival producers used incompatible versions of MS-DOS, which reduced competition. Telecommunications remain largely in the hands of a monopolistic state system.

Thus, factors relating to government economic and industrial policy seem to have somewhat undermined a considerable early success story.

NICs

An interesting group of countries, in terms of the impact of the IT industry, are the newly industrialized countries (NICs), mainly to be found around the rim of the Pacific Basin. Hong Kong, parts of mainland China, South Korea, Taiwan, Singapore and, perhaps, Malaysia have successfully pursued a strategy of involvement with information technology industries which has raised them, in some cases, from underdeveloped countries offering little but cheap 'sweat shops' with unskilled assembly facilities to increasingly affluent and sophisticated economies – symbolized by the construction of the tallest building in the world in Kuala Lumpur, Malaysia.

Whilst most of these economies have prospered by a deliberate strategy of involvement in global trading and an intensive effort in educating and skilling the population, perhaps the most interesting example of a deliberate development effort focusing on information age industries is that of Singapore (see Case Study 3.2).

Less-developed countries

In contrast to the NICs there are still, of course, a large number of poorer countries still relatively untouched by the 'information age'. Arguably the gap in information resources between industrial and non-industrial nations is increasing their competitive disadvantage and hence the 'development gap'. This may be accentuated by information poverty reducing the quality of policy decisions by both government and businesses. IT applied to developed world manufacturing may reduce the demand for energy and raw materials supplied by the 'South' and reduce the advantage given to its economies by cheap labour (Sirimanne, 1996).

Amongst the problems poorer countries face, arguably the major factor in many cases is the lack of an educated population – this probably being more difficult to overcome than the obvious infrastructure problems of the lack of a reliable electricity and telecommunications infrastructure and of the capital resources required to compete effectively in an age of technology. It is noteworthy that India, which despite many problems of poverty, has some excellent higher education facilities and is becoming one of the major software producing and data-processing centres of the world.

Using high-speed data connections routine back-office functions can be carried out in low-wage economies remote from the USA and Europe. Sirimanne (1996) reports that Chinese operators have re-keyed the name and phone number of every American twice for a US CD-ROM product. BBC reports have indicated that some UK firms, in exporting their call centres to India, have trained local staff to speak with British accents and supplied them with appropriate weather and sporting information to enable them to chat informally with clients as if they are in the same country.

Case Study 3.2 **Singapore: from intelligent island to global infocomm capital?**

Singapore is a crowded small island off the coast of Malaysia with a population of four million. From a relatively low baseline in colonial times, its economy is now on a par with that of many European countries (GDP per head $26,300 in 1998).

Singapore's economic strategy has been to develop an open trading economy with high-quality infrastructure which serves as a base for over five thousand multinational corporations to trade with South-East Asia and the Pacific rim. Over half the population is employed in finance, commerce and services.

A key element in this strategy has been the development of Singapore as the 'Intelligent Island', with a highly educated English-speaking workforce that is computer literate and linked by good telecommunications (including free narrow-band service). By the end of 2000 it was claimed that 60 per cent of Singapore homes were connected to the Internet.

The government's Information and Communication Technology 21 campaign is a five-year plan 'to develop Singapore into a vibrant and dynamic global infocomm capital with a thriving and prosperous economy and a pervasive and infocomm-savy e-society'. A key part of this strategy is the provision of broadband network access to every home and business on the island, using a combination of state and private capital. By the end of 2000, 274,000 users of the Singapore ONE network were claimed. ONE offers more than 200 applications and services to users. In addition, high-capacity links to the rest of the world are in hand – for instance an 8.4 billion terabytes/sec fibre-optic link to India was due to open in 2001.

The government has not only focused schools on 'technopreneuralism', it encourages the submission of tax returns on-line with a lucky draw (top prize over US$10,000), uses an electronic road pricing system and is developing a smart card system to pay for public transport.

A controversial element in government policies is a somewhat authoritarian stance that discourages political opposition and attempts moral censorship through control of the local ISP. This may be somewhat at odds with its economic and technological ambitions.

Source: Financial Times (2001), Coutsoukis (1999)

Globalization, information technology and government

Globalization is the thesis that the increasing global interdependence of states, individuals and social and economic organizations is reducing the autonomy of individual states (Tansey, 2000, 45). We examine it here because it seems to be partly attributable to the effects of the spread of global information technology networks and also to have profound implications for the future development and use of the technology.

The background to globalization is a combination of powerful economic, social, political and technological factors.

One of the most controversial of these is dominance in international trade of multinational enterprises (MNEs) considered in the previous chapter. According to Flaherty (1996, 11) MNEs account for 80 per cent of traded technology and 75 per cent of the world trade in commodities (such as cotton, sugar, steel, etc.). Although there are over 37,000 MNEs, a mere 300 of them are responsible for 80 per cent of the world's foreign production.

We have already discussed at some length the vital role of global communications networks, clearly these are increasing the degree of social, economic and political interdependence between different societies throughout the world.

A more controversial factor is the current dominance in the global economy of capitalist ('free market') rules for international trade. The International Monetary Fund and World Bank determine the rules for international currency exchanges and are a source of capital for states whose economies are in difficulty – but often only subject to such states agreeing to curb state expenditure and raise taxes. The former General Agreement on Tariffs and Trade (GATT) has been succeeded by the WTO (World Trade Organization), which enforces tougher free trade agreements, including international treaties on intellectual property rights. The 'hard' major currencies of dollar, euro and yen are desired and accepted by the inhabitants of smaller, less prosperous economies which must often do business on terms dictated by the central banks controlling these currencies.

A major political factor in determining the shape of the current world political system is US military and diplomatic power, along with the collapse of the Soviet Union and the desire of China to adopt the economic if not the political system of the 'West'. The United States is the strongest political influence on every continent and uses this influence to support 'freedom' in the sense of capitalism as well as liberal democracy.

Another technological factor is the relative ease of travel and migration through air and motorway transport. With greater knowledge of conditions in other parts of the world through broadcasting, printing and the Internet, there may well also be more of a psychological incentive to move from poorer, less stable societies to richer, more settled ones – hence the probably unprecedented levels of mass migration and certainly international leisure travel.

Thus many factors facilitate a series of challenges to the self-sufficiency (autonomy) of modern states; these are summarized in Box 3.1.

A graphic illustration of the threat to (smaller) state autonomy posed by multinational enterprises (MNEs) is to compare their financial resources, as does Table 3.1. It can be seen that many MNEs are comparable in economic resources to middle-sized, let alone small, states.

Global company strategies and IT

Clearly global communications and information technology has shaped the rise of multinational enterprises and the strategies they adopt.

One much noted feature of globalization is the domination of many consumer markets by brands marketed on a global basis. Goods such as Playstations, Coca-Cola drinks, McDonald's hamburgers and Gucchi handbags are bought by consumers of similar income, sex and age profiles the world over. In many cases manufacturers previously marketed similar or identical goods under different names but are now unifying them. For example 'Marathon' chocolate bars in the UK became 'Snickers' as in the United States, and Oil of Ulay cosmetic products were renamed Oil of Olay. (There is no such thing as either olay or ulay!) As the media become global, advertising messages must be intelligible across the world. Thus a

---

Box 3.1 Challenges to the nation-state

Internal instability
- threat from mini-nationalisms, ethnicity

External instability
- need for regional/global security

Economic dependence
- on global economic and financial organizations

Social integration
- development of world standards for human rights, professional behaviour

Technical integration
- dependence on world communication networks and leading-edge technical developments increases vulnerability

Ecological interdependence
- threats of pollution, global warming etc. insoluble within state boundaries

Source: Tansey (2000, 46)

Table 3.1 Multinationals and countries compared

Rank	Company/state	Company sales/GNP (billion dollars)	Rank	Company/state	Company sales/GNP (billion dollars)
1	USA	7,100	28	General Motors	169
2	Japan	6,964	40	Royal Dutch Shell	110
3	Germany	2,252	41=	Poland/Myanmar	108
4	UK	1,095	45	Portugal	97
14	Russia	332	46	Wal-Mart Stores	94
23	Indonesia	190	54	AT&T (US)	79
24	Mitsubishi	190	57	Philippines	72
27	Turkey	169	58	IBM	72

Source: *The Observer*, Finance Section, 9 March 1998, p. 9

product placement in a Hollywood film or TV series, an Internet website, or a sponsorship message on a T-shirt in an international sporting event, all need to be intelligible throughout the global marketplace.

On the production side, multinationals are increasingly developing a strategy of global sourcing of materials and components with a networked global coordination of operations. Thus a car manufacturer such as Ford will produce perhaps five basic engines in three plants (one in North America, one in Europe, one in Asia). Valves may be bought for all plants from China, paint from Venezuela and Italy – depending on the cheapest reliable place of production and transport costs. Levels of production and consequent purchasing are controlled by the level of global demand for each product. This is only possible by the creation of central databases accessible across a world network (perhaps in the form of a company intranet).

Despite massive centrally coordinated purchasing, design and production, actual products can be flexibly adapted to local markets given sophisticated software design tools, intensive market research and computer-aided manufacturing (CAM) techniques. Thus cars or jeans can be adapted to the known physical characteristics of smaller Japanese or larger Texan customers!

Large automated plants offer advantages of scale in production without sacrificing reliability and economy. Smaller local manufacturers thus find it difficult to compete.

By operating on a global level, rewards to technical and commercial innovation are maximized; massive research and development teams can be employed, thus giving additional competitive advantage to multinational firms.

As we shall discuss at greater length in the next chapter, increasing technical standardization on a global level enables firms to manufacture components for other firms a continent away and reduces any advantage to local firms manufacturing to distinctive local specifications. Such distinctive local specifications might include the use of imperial not metric measures, distinctive plugs for electrical appliances, and so on.

Most major multinational firms are now quoted on one, or all three, major stock markets (New York, London, Tokyo) which between them operate on a 24-hour basis. These are linked in a global trading network that enables investors in any developed capitalist country to be a part-owner of almost any 'multinational' company. This is facilitated by US Mutual Funds, UK Unit Trusts and investment companies that enable even small investors to develop multinational portfolios. Thus firms legally based in one country, but operating globally, are increasingly owned by multinational shareholders. In practice, though, it is worth remarking that most multinational enterprises are predominantly still staffed at executive level and owned from one country – usually the USA, but sometimes Japan, Germany or the UK.

For and against globalization

For business students with an interest in information technology, globalization may seem like an obviously good thing. It appears to promote efficiency and economy in production, and gives individual consumers more choice of products and services from a global marketplace 'at the touch of a button'. A global exchange of ideas between citizens of different countries is made possible. It can be argued that globalization promotes economic development by encouraging the importation of modern business practices into less-developed countries.

However, it is clear that to many groups globalization is a phenomenon to demonstrate and protest against. Recent meetings of world leaders to consider financial and economic issues have been greeted by massive demonstrations against globalization representing an amalgam of protest groups from extreme anarchists, through green activists through to peaceful and highly respectable Church people.

Their objections include that globalization gives power to multinational firms effectively responsible to no one; that it is effectively Americanization since the major multinational firms are US-owned and institutions such as the World Bank are controlled by the US government; that it destroys local culture and independence; and that market forces result in extreme ecological damage, including global warming. We shall return to some of these issues in our final chapter.

Recommended reading

Financial Times (1999) *Mastering Global Business*, London, Financial Times. Good practical business perspective on globalization from a practical business perspective.

Moschella, David (1997) *Waves of Power: Dynamics of Global Technology Leadership 1964–2010*, New York, American Management Association. Includes some useful material on the impact of government as well as its US perspective on change in the IT industry.

Tansey, Stephen D. (2000) *Politics: the Basics*, London, Routledge, Ch. 2 and references. General political background to globalization and the power of the nation-state.

4 Regulating computing

Topics

- Computers and privacy
- IT standards
- Intellectual property and IT
- Organizational information management rules
- Governing the Internet
- Legal regulation and computer abuse

This chapter is concerned with the need for rules about the use of computers and who should enforce them. This involves a consideration of the need to protect individuals against the abuse of IT by governments, multinationals and other firms and individuals. We discuss the need to protect intellectual property (including copyright, patents, trade marks, design right, etc.) in a global information economy and the (opposing?) case for freedom of discussion and innovation. This leads to an analysis of how organizations should manage their data, software and other intellectual property. Finally, we consider the role of government regulation and self-regulation, especially on the Internet.

Computers and privacy

After 15 years of White Papers and government reports, the UK government passed the first Data Protection Act in 1984 for two main reasons: first, to protect the privacy of the individual against the increasing use and capabilities of computerized information systems; second, to allow the UK to comply with the Council of Europe Data Protection Convention. The Convention allows participating countries to refuse personal information to be transferred to countries that do not have adequate data protection laws ('data havens'). This could have placed the UK at a disadvantage in the international IT market.

In 1998 a new Data Protection Act (DPA) was passed which came into effect in stages from 1999. This was a response to the 1995 European

Community directive on data protection, which required a strengthening of the earlier legislation in response to both technological change and increasing disquiet by consumers. All 15 European Union countries now have very similar laws. The USA and Canada will be discussed briefly at the end of this section. In most countries, data protection law continues to be influenced both by consumer worries and by the need for acceptable status in the eyes of the international trading community.

Computers are commonly seen as a threat to privacy for a variety of reasons, which were conveniently discussed in a UK government 1975 White Paper. This listed five features of computers posing a special threat to personal privacy and linked them to corresponding possible abuses. First, they facilitate the maintenance of extensive records systems and the retention of data. Such records tend to grow 'out of control', and organizations collect more data than is necessary for the original task. Second, computers make data easily and quickly available from many different points, which makes possible unauthorized access to information, its theft or alteration. Third, data can be transferred from one information system to another, making possible the compilation of centralized dossiers on individuals and the resale of private information. Data can be combined to give new information using powerful relational databases which make the merging of records cost-effective. Finally data is in machine-readable form which means that few people may know of the data or the uses to which it is put.

It is worth giving a general outline of the UK Data Protection Act 1998 as an illustration of the sort of legislation now generally found throughout the European Union and elsewhere. (In this section 'formerly' means under the previous Data Protection Act 1984.)

The scope of the Act is to regulate the processing of personal data by any person or organization. 'Personal data' is that which relates to a living individual who can be identified from the data, and other data likely to come into the processor's ('data controller's') possession. It includes expressions of opinion about individuals and indications of intentions by the data controller towards them. 'Processing' means obtaining, recording or holding the information or data and carrying out the organization, adaptation, alteration, retrieval, consultation, use, disclosure, alignment, combination, blocking, erasure, or destruction of the data.

The DPA does not cover information relating to organizations – only data held about individuals.

The Act defines five main groups: 'data controllers' (formerly 'users') – all UK organizations or individuals who determine the purposes and manner in which any personal data are processed; 'computer processors' (formerly 'bureau') – any person or organization processing data on behalf of a data controller (commercially or otherwise); 'data subjects' – individuals about whom the personal data is held; 'recipients' – the persons to whom personal data is disclosed; 'third parties' – anyone other than the first three categories above.

The Office of the Information Commissioner (formerly Data Protection Registrar) maintains the Data Protection Register and enforces the law and codes of practice. The Commissioner may issue an enforcement notice requiring rule-breakers to comply with the DPA, or, in extreme cases, issue deregistration notices making it illegal for offenders to hold or use personal data. The Commissioner was at first designated as Data Protection Commissioner, but renamed Information Commissioner on 30 January 2001 on acquiring responsibility for freedom of information matters as well as for data protection.

Data controllers must notify to (formerly register with) the office a description of the personal data to be processed and the categories of data subject to which they relate; the purposes for which the data is processed; recipients to whom they disclose the data; any countries outside the European Economic area they may transfer it to; and a declaration as to any 'assessable processing' they plan to undertake.

Data users must adhere to the rules listed in Box 4.1. (These eight principles are similar but not identical to the eight principles listed in the previous Act – they are largely taken from the EU directive.)

Data subjects have three main rights under the principles:

- to obtain access to personal information;
- to receive compensation through the courts;
- the rectification (through the courts if necessary) of inaccurate data.

Box 4.1 **Data protection rules**

Personal data shall:

1 be collected and processed fairly and lawfully in accordance with schedules 2 and 3 of the Act (see p. 109)
2 only be held for one or more specified, lawful, purposes and not be further processed in any manner incompatible with that purpose or those purposes
3 be adequate and relevant and not excessive in relation to the purpose for which they are processed
4 be accurate and, where necessary, kept up to date
5 be held no longer than is necessary for the stated purpose
6 be processed in accordance with the rights of data subjects under the Act (e.g. information must be supplied to data subjects on request, not be likely to cause damage or distress)
7 have appropriate technical and organizational measures taken against unauthorized or unlawful processing of personal data and against accidental loss or destruction
8 not be transferred outside the European Economic area unless adequate level of data protection exists in the area concerned

The DPA lays down a general framework of law, supplemented by guidelines from the Information Commissioner and regulations to be made by the Home Office. Inevitably there will be uncertainties about the applications to individual cases. These will become clearer as the DPA is implemented.

Some important detailed exemptions to note include that the DPA does not apply to a home computer user holding only personal, family, household or recreational data. One does not have to register the following personal data:

- data held for the detection and prevention of current crime;
- data used for statistical or research purposes (e.g. census);
- data for national security;
- publicly available information (e.g. electoral roll).

It is a condition of all these exemptions that they are not disclosed without consent, or used for any other purpose.

However, the Act does apply to individuals and organizations using IT for a business or profession, including public and government bodies (e.g. limited companies, DHSS, trade unions, commercial clubs). If more than one individual or organization controls the content and use of a collection of data, both must notify the Commissioner.

UK developments

Some key issues raised in recent DP Registrar's and Information Commissioners Reports are touched upon here.

Proposals for national identity cards/numbers have become more frequent in recent years. The danger of National Insurance numbers (NINO) (or new style driving licences with photographs, or some other document) becoming a 'de facto' national identity number/card was observed by the Registrar. Use of NINOs is spreading, although the Registrar persuaded ministers not to use it for the Student Loan Scheme. The danger is that numerous disparate records can be accumulated to produce a comprehensive picture of data subjects without their knowledge ('data matching').

The confidentiality of personal financial data is another key area of concern. The practice amongst banks and other financial institutions of swapping credit data, and (especially) making agreement to do so a condition of holding an account, was queried – especially 'white' data on accounts which are not in breach of credit agreements or limits. Other financial databases which generated anxieties were the insurance industries' Comprehensive Loss Underwriting Exchange (CLUE) and Impaired Lives Register; the Consumer Credit Trade Association's Gone Away Information Network (GAIN) and the Council for Mortgage Lenders Anti-Fraud Scheme.

Case Study 4.1 **Revising the Data Protection Act in the United Kingdom (95/46/EC)**

It has already been emphasized how important international flows of information have become and the centrality of IT to EU industrial strategy. It is not surprising therefore that the EU should have sought to adopt a minimum standard of protection for consumers in the area of data protection. Several hundred million consumers are now covered by this important directive, which is therefore worth some detailed discussion.

The EU wished to harmonize data protection legislation in the member countries as part of its programme to create the 'single market'. A draft directive on data protection was issued in 1991; this proved controversial and so a revised directive was issued in October 1992 following debate in the European Parliament. Following protracted negotiations in the Council of Ministers and opposition by the UK government and others, a directive was finally issued in October 1995 with implementation by member states due to take place by 1999. Many features of the directive were already to be found in the UK 1984 Act.

From a British point of view it is worth emphasizing some features not in the UK DPA 1984 which have now been included in the 1998 legislation. Manual data is now included: 'if the data processed are contained or are intended to be contained in a filing system structured according to specific criteria relating to individuals, so as to permit easy access to the personal data in question' (s.15). A fundamental principle is that personal data may only be processed with the consent of the data subject. Data users have a duty to inform data subjects the first time that their personal data is communicated, except where the information is already public or the communication is required by law. A major emphasis is on data protection as part of the right to privacy – which was not previously explicitly recognized in UK law. An independent EC data investigation authority has been established with wider powers of investigation, access and intervention than the former UK Registrar (who could only investigate under a warrant issued on reasonable suspicion of an offence). The directive clarifies and simplifies procedures for notifying the supervisory authority and provisions for codes of conduct (trade associations to be involved). Non-profit organizations are now included in the scope of the legislation. A reference to 'free movement of data' in the full title of the directive emphasizes that the measure is part of a package of policies intended to promote a single European market in many different goods and services. There is a rule that no data may go to countries with no or inadequate DP law (with more exceptions than in the original draft as these include the private sector in the USA!). Subjects may refuse to exercise access rights at the behest of a third party (see UK developments below). Some exemptions have been introduced for journalists and artists. Extended compensation to individuals for unfair processing has been introduced. File controllers must take appropriate technical and organizational measures to protect personal data. Consideration must be given to any relevant EC recommendations – this applies whether or not they are registered.

Reactions to the directive varied according to the group concerned. There was considerable controversy over the inclusion of manual data (the UK government was opposed, as was the Confederation of British Industry). This has been included in the new Act but with a long transition period. Civil rights proponents have welcomed the reference in article 1(1) to the object of the directive being to safeguard a right to privacy. 'Consent' provisions were criticized at the draft stage as unworkable, but the UK Registrar argued that consent can usually be obtained on collection. Registration provisions were criticized by industry as creating bureaucracy – this has been reduced (compared with draft and previous UK practice) by exempting some classes of data from the need to register – but not from the need to abide by general principles of consent, subject access, fair and lawful processing, etc. The UK Registrar was particularly unhappy about allowing the unfair collection of data if an explanation is afterwards provided to the individual concerned, but was pleased by the prospect of some strengthening of her powers to collect information.

The development of a sophisticated market in personal data has also led to increased concern in recent years. Earlier comments by the Registrar were reinforced by an investigation agency offering to supply to MPs, for a fee, details of people's telephone calls, bank accounts, mortgage repayments and arrears on utility bills. The Home Office now accepts that safeguards on this are inadequate and legislation is necessary. Banks have tightened their security somewhat – they were criticized for using one internal password for calls about customer accounts.

The Police National Computer formerly contained code markings indicating HIV status of subjects – these are being removed at the Registrar's behest. Technological developments to the Internet and document image processing (DIP) were also considered. (The Internet because of the sheer volume of data available; DIP because of the uneditable nature of the material held.)

In the 2001 Annual Report the Commissioner was much exercised by the issue of employer monitoring of employee e-mails and access to the Internet. She saw this as undoubtedly covered by the 1998 Act. 'Any monitoring must therefore address the specific risks that an employer faces, it must be a proportionate response to those risks, it must be conducted with no more intrusion than necessary and employers must be open with their employees about its existence.'

The European and international dimension of the Commissioner's work also loomed large in the 2001 Report, given that there are no national barriers on the Internet. This is clearly likely to increase in future years given the international response to terrorist threats.

Examples of the impact of changing technology on the Commissioner's work include the formulation of a code for the use of CCTV cameras and a consideration of how far it is legitimate for law enforcement authorities to use data on people's locations derived from their use of mobile phones.

A useful summary of some of the problems in the implementation of the 1984 UK Act is to be found in a 1993 report of Comptroller and Auditor General (an independent officer of parliament who reports to the House of Commons Select Committee on public accounts). He argued that, after ten years of operation, enforcement by the Registrar was limited by the small budget and staff available (100 staff including only 13 part-time regional investigators and a £3.4m budget). About a third (approximately 100,000) of data users were not registered – one in three small companies did not realize they should register. Two-thirds of the small companies and more than half of the large ones did not understand their obligation to abide by the data protection principles. Public awareness of the Registrar is limited to about a third of the population, even though four out of five regard protecting rights to personal privacy as important.

The Registrar was seen as making little effort to ensure that more firms register, but as putting more effort into pursuing those who do not re-register (a disincentive to register in the first place!). Registration documents are usually only cursorily checked (using OCR technology to ensure correct quantity of ticks). The Registrar lacked power to investigate the facts of applications. It was concluded that people who complain did receive quite good service, with two-thirds cleared up in six months and 90 per cent within a year. (This was much better than, for example, the Solicitors Complaints Bureau.)

Few compliance notices are issued and compliance to them is not systematically monitored. Only twelve formal notices requiring compliance to DP principles were in force and only three prosecutions have been made for failure to comply. 'Formal undertakings' to abide by the

Act have often been used instead since 1992 (200 in first 18 months). The only systematic effort at monitoring compliance has been an investigation of the direct marketing industry – over a third of companies checked advertising direct mailing lists for rental, and almost half of those obtaining personal information from off-the-page advertisements were found to be in contravention of registration requirements or DP principles. The Register is no longer available in public libraries – but extracts are sent out free, on request, and by 1999 the whole register was available on the World Wide Web.

In conclusion, the Comptroller recommended that there should be better publicity and more stringent registration and compliance procedures, better monitoring and more efforts to contact unregistered users.

How little progress has been made on some of these issues can be gathered by looking at two recent (2000) research reports by a market research firm on behalf of the Commissioner. Only a third of firms were clear who was responsible for enforcing the Data Protection Act, whilst half of the general public were unclear about their rights of access to information held upon them by organizations. This was despite a television public information campaign.

IT standards

An important area of rule-making in relation to IT – if at first sight somewhat technical – is the adoption of standard interpretations of technical specifications. This is particularly important in the area of communications since if two devices are to be used in conjunction (perhaps several thousand miles apart joined by wires or radio waves) they must not only be physically compatible (e.g. be capable of attachment to the same circuit)

Exercise 4.1 **Data protection**

1 List as many organizations as you can think of that hold information about you on computer.
2 How complete a biography could be written of you using this information?
3 Check on the website of the Information Commissioner (or your national equivalent). What relevant files are kept by some of the organizations you have identified?
4 Consider making a request for the information held upon you. (NB There may be a charge for this.)

The Information Commissioner is at:
http://www.dataprotection.gov.uk

but also interpret relatively arbitrary signals in the same way (e.g. the first ten digits may be interpreted as the address from which the signal has come).

Even a stand-alone computer workstation, however, is customarily assembled from parts made by a variety of manufacturers who must agree on the meaning of technical specifications given them by the assembler, whilst bought-in software must assume an operating system and technical performance by the hardware which needs to be described in a standard-ized way.

It is worth distinguishing clearly between different levels of standardiza-tion in ascending order of the degree of state interference in the process of setting them (see Box 4.2).

De facto *standards*

Standards relate to different aspects of device and process design and performance. For example, some standards are merely *informative*, so that PCs are customarily described by a series of standard performance and design indicators – for example, a measurement of ROM capacity (say 128 MB); a measurement of hard disk size (say 100 GB); a measurement of the speed of the central processor unit (say 750 MHz), etc. For more tech-nical purchasers a series of defined *bench marks* measuring performance in carrying out carefully defined standard tasks are also available. These reduce the cost for buyers in making comparisons and enable sellers to publicize the value they offer. Other standards are concerned with *variety reduction* – for example, ROM is almost always measured in multiples of 32 MB. Other standards relate to *quality* – for instance reliability, durability

---

Box 4.2 **Levels of standardization**

'De facto' standards are specifications for a form of product of service volun-tarily accepted as mutually beneficial by producers and users.

'De jure' standards are specifications that have some form of legal recogni-tion, often through national or international Standards Institutes who generally nominally represent the public interest but are often somewhat producer-dominated.

Regulations are legally enforced specifications usually in the interests of public health or safety, the environment or consumer protection.

Certification is an institutional arrangement to ensure that specific products conform to a standard – e.g. BEAB (British Electricity Approvals Board) approved.

and safety minima. As has been emphasized, *compatibility* is particularly important in information technology – for example, with Windows, Unix or Excel.

Davis (1987) suggests that when IT standards evolve 'naturally' through the workings of the competitive process they are often characterized by:

- *Narrow windows* of opportunity during which later and better products can supplant early market leaders. In many cases better alternatives exist to the standard product but too many people are locked into it for change to take place. Good examples are the former dominance of DOS and the present dominance of Windows operating systems which maintain their position because so many applications packages assume their prior installation.
- *Blind giants.* Government agencies may have power to influence standards by buying on a massive scale but lack a vision of the needs of subsequent users or the potential of the technology.
- *Angry orphans.* Early users of losing alternative products are locked into outmoded designs and are faced with heavy conversion costs.

De jure *standards*

The European Union explicitly, and many other governments implicitly, has adopted a policy of legislating using accepted standards. Most standards in IT (including telecommunications) are defined by a complex international network of bodies culminating in the International Standards Organization (ISO) and the International Telephone and Telegraphic Consultative Committee (CCITT). On a European level the main European equivalents are CEPT, CEN, CENLEC and ETSI (see Glossary). These bodies are dominated by representatives of manufacturers and PTOs.

The politics of standards

From a European point of view the main problem with *de facto* standards is that they usually benefit the firms dominating the market at the time at which they evolve. These will tend to be major US firms such as Microsoft or IBM, or possibly consortia of Japanese firms which have a demonstrated capacity to cooperate for these purposes.

If an overseas manufacturer, or consortium, creates a standard it is naturally at a competitive advantage. European governments do not wish to have to specify in purchasing goods and services that they conform to standards pioneered by a foreign competitor rather than their national manufacturers. But national standards break up the single European market, hence the EU enthusiasm for OSI (Open Systems Interconnection). Even the official standards-setting process is dominated by large manufacturers (often US/Japanese) and may neglect consumer interests. OSI is designed to ensure that telecommunications and computing equipment from different manufacturers can be used together. In Europe, the European Workshop on Open Systems (EWOS), composed of representatives from seven standards organizations, fosters and coordinates the programme. New European machinery has been set up which delegates the details of standard-setting required under 1992 directives (designed to create a single European Market) to the appropriate standards bodies. New bodies created include a European Standardization Board and Council to coordinate activities. All new IT and Telecommunications technical standards are now European rather than national.

Intellectual property and IT

Intellectual property law is a difficult and hotly contested area, partly because of the practical problems of asserting 'rights' in such an insubstantial area and partly because of its crucial practical economic importance. Hence giant international corporations frequently sue each other for millions of dollars in intellectual property cases and IT firms like Microsoft employ literally hundreds of lawyers. In recent years multinational corporations have been assessed by financial markets largely in terms of the brands and patents they control and their capacity to innovate intellectually – to research, develop and market new products. This may be an area that appears rather difficult and remote to students, but they should appreciate that it is at the centre of modern business activities – especially those of the key information-based industries.

The importance of 'intellectual property' in an era of information industries can, therefore, hardly be overstated. We have seen that industries based on information and technological innovations designed to optimize their use have become the leading edge of economic development in the late twentieth century and are likely to remain so in the twenty-first. It can therefore be argued that protecting investments in producing information is basic to the world economy. If, in a capitalist economy, those who invest heavily in producing information cannot achieve a financial return, they will cease to make such investments; in which case, the engine which is driving contemporary world economic growth will grind to a halt.

The problem with information, including technological innovations, is that it is so insubstantial. It cannot easily be locked in a safe or protected by guard dogs if it is also to be exploited. To be used effectively it must normally be spread around numerous workers or consumers who can carry it away in their heads, on easily transportable floppy disks, or transmit it across the net. The owner of information may not even know that it has been 'stolen' since, unlike diamonds or gold, it can be in two places at once. It is usually easily duplicated in a form indistinguishable from the original. (This is especially so with digitally stored information.) This means there is a major problem for information businesses: how to profit from information without losing control over it. To this end almost all governments have enacted laws giving the producers of information rights over their product. The authors, who benefit from royalties on this book, are naturally pleased that this is so!

But there is a balancing act to be done as far as governments are concerned if the public interest is to be served. Consider the case of a pharmaceutical company that makes a medical discovery and produces a new drug which cures a virulent disease. The manufacturing cost of such a drug may be a few pence, but the benefit to patients, at the extreme, may be many additional years of life. If the company retains a monopoly of the production of the drug it is in a position to reap enormous profits representing the difference between the production cost and the benefits to consumers. This may be justified by pointing to large investment in research and development necessary to make such discoveries. However, some potential patients may well not be able to afford the high prices charged, thus not only creating unnecessary misery to the individuals concerned but heavy losses to the community in which they live. The community loses the contribution that the untreated patients might have made and may have to care for them in a weakened condition, or for their dependants. Again, if the company retains exclusive rights to exploit the new discovery it may block researchers in universities, or other companies, from building upon the original discovery.

More generally it may be argued that the life-blood of both democracy and scientific enquiry is the free exchange of ideas. Can any ideas really be seen as the exclusive production of one individual – let alone a corporation? Only in rigorous testing and debate will ideas be evolved and assessed, and property rights may well impede this. For instance, if a company has a financial interest in a drug or a genetically engineered plant or animal, and testing reveals undesirable side-effects on patients or the environment, will it not be tempted to suppress inconvenient evidence?

In a rapidly evolving area such as information technology it may be especially important that rival researchers and developers can freely borrow and criticize ideas from each other if swift progress is to be made. As Sir Isaac Newton observed, most scientific and technological progress is a case of others 'standing on the shoulders of giants'. Hence, as we shall see in more detail later, many users of the net – which originated in an academic context – feel that the free exchange of information is a primary value and that intellectual property law is an inhibiting capitalist irrelevance.

Before we are in a position to evaluate these arguments it is perhaps desirable to have a clearer idea of the nature of intellectual property rights, how they apply in an information technology context, and what use businesses make of these rights.

Varieties of intellectual property

Generally speaking, because of the importance of freedom of discussion and the existence in many democracies of constitutional guarantees of freedom of speech (e.g. the First Amendment to the US Constitution), there is no general property right in ideas as such. Everyone is free not only to have their 'own' ideas but to adopt other people's at will. Indeed it is arguable that almost all the ideas we have are taken from someone else, hence it would be impracticable to charge for them as a general rule. Only in a limited number of situations does the law protect property in information. These are outlined in Box 4.3 and discussed in more detail in the following section. It is worth cautioning readers that this discussion is primarily in terms of English law and that some considerable differences are to be found internationally, both in the nature of the law and the extent to which it is enforced in practice. In an age of global communication flows, such variation in national laws is, to say the least, awkward for the many businesses concerned.

Patents

One of the best-known forms of intellectual property is the patent. Patenting is a legal procedure to enable the inventor of a useful physical device to benefit from it for a limited period by registering with national (or, in Europe, international) authorities. The Patent Office establishes who has produced the innovation first and gives them a monopoly over the licensing of the use of the invention for a normal period of 20 years (subject to payment of fees by the patent holder to the Office). Since this is a limitation on other people's freedom to trade it is only granted in exceptional cases where the invention is demonstrably a novel advance in the area in question which advances the state of art – not merely a logical next step in the development of a technology. Such a monopoly is potentially a very valuable property since if an invention is produced and sold by the million even a tiny royalty can lead to enormous revenues. Alternatively, if a commodity becomes essential to some types of business or consumers they can, in effect, be held to ransom by the patentee.

In terms of information technology, patents will clearly normally apply

---

Box 4.3 **Varieties of intellectual property**

- Patents
- Copyright
- Design right (registered design)
- Trade marks and service marks
- Commercial confidentiality

to revolutionary new hardware devices, but not to software. In the United Kingdom the 1977 Patent Act specifically excludes programs alone from its scope – although they may be included if they are an integral part of a physical device. In the USA, however, the law has broadened the definition of an invention to include 'virtual devices' in software form. There is also controversy over the meaning of 'invention' as opposed to 'discoveries' of existing natural laws or phenomena. Generally speaking scientific discoveries have traditionally been made freely available to the whole scientific community without charge, but there is an increasing trend to attempt to patent new discoveries by scientists. A particularly controversial example of this is the discovery of genetic information – including human DNA patterns. Again USA practice has been more open to patenting innovation than the European position.

Registration creates a valuable database of technological and scientific discoveries which businesses neglect at their peril. The European Commission estimates that European industries are wasting £20 billion per year reinventing patents (Patent Office, 1994a, 3). In such cases not only is the research and development expenditure wasted but the 'reinventor' may have to pay royalties and possibly damages to the prior patentee. It is no excuse for the violator of a patent to show that they invented their device separately or even before the patentee. This reinforces the need for businesses to ensure that they protect their own inventions and do not violate the rights of others.

A further complication to patent law has been touched upon – registration is mainly on a national basis. This means that to protect an innovation internationally the patent has to be registered overseas as well as at home. This can lead to quite a large legal bill which, however, would pale into insignificance against the possible losses if a competitor were to register the patent in large markets such as the USA, Japan or Europe.

Copyright

Copyright is in many ways a much simpler matter than patent rights (particularly in the UK, most of Europe, and in other countries which are signatories to an international treaty on the subject known as the Berne Convention). In such countries copyright is automatic (there is no need to register with an authority to obtain its protection), does not require payment of fees, and now (since a 1997 EU Directive) lasts up to 70 years from the death of the 'author' of the 'work' concerned. In the USA there is a procedure for registering copyright with the Library of Congress and protection, since 1978, lasts for 75 years from registration.

As the terminology suggests, copyright developed as a protection for literary, artistic, dramatic and musical works, giving authors and artists protection from unauthorized copying of their original productions. In one way it has been interpreted very broadly to include any substantial text

Box 4.4 **Comparison of patent and copyright**

Patent	*Copyright*
Covers inventions objects, processes of being used and made	Covers 'literary, artistic, musical and dramatic works (including software)
Must be 'novel' – new inventive step	Must be 'original' (not copied)
Must advance state of art	Only requires some skill, labour or judgement
Complex registration	Automatic in UK (no copyright required)
'Independent creation' not a defence	'Independent creation' a defence
Underlying ideas protected, object need not exist	Only expression of idea protected (i.e. specific words images, etc.)
Protection for 20 years	Protection for lifetime plus 70 years

(including digitally recorded text) of any kind which is in some sense original and requires some kind of skill, labour or judgement. Thus software programs, railway timetables and terrible daubs or jingles are all covered by the legislation. (As far as software in the UK is concerned this was first explicitly stated in legislation in the 1985 Copyright (Computer Software) Amendment Act and confirmed in the Copyright, Design and Patent Act 1988.) In another way, however, the protection offered by copyright is very limited because it extends only to the words written or lines drawn, not the ideas which these express. Thus if you were to paraphrase every line in this book and publish the result as *Commerce, Computers and Social Affairs* the author would probably have no recourse in copyright law. Hence the inventor of the first electronic spreadsheet (SuperCalc) could claim copyright for every line of code with which it was written, but was powerless to prevent other programmers writing other spreadsheets which operated in a similar, but not identical, way and could be used for the same purpose.

Design right (registered design)

A further category of intellectual property, akin to copyright, is design right which protects the appearance of three-dimensional objects. Automatic protection is for a maximum of 15 years for original non-commonplace designs. In the European Union increased protection (up to 25 years) can be obtained by actually registering a design with a Patent Office. From an information technology point of view it is worth pointing out that specially enhanced provisions are made for the protection of the design of computer 'chips' in European law as a result of a European directive (Patent Office, 1993, 8).

Trade marks and service marks

A more generally useful type of protection for businesses is that accorded to trade marks (technically known as 'service marks' when applied to services rather than goods). In common (e.g. English and US) law there is a protection for traders against rivals 'passing off' goods and services as theirs. Hence if a business can show that it has traded as 'Brown's Shrewsbury Beer' for years, and that it has a reputation for a high-quality product and a rival starts selling cans of an inferior brew with a similar label, but actually made in Washington by Smiths, then this is an offence – effectively a fraud on beer drinkers.

The problem may be to establish that you have an established reputation or, in less clear cases, that there is no intention to deceive – where, for instance, two software engineers called Jones settle in Tallahassee within a year or so and both trade as Jones Tallahassee Software in good faith. To avoid such problems, businesses may register trade marks with Patent Offices and thus establish a preferential claim on that mark in a particular line of business. This protection will apply immediately from registration, even if no trading has yet taken place. For instance, it was reported (*Guardian*, 2 July 1988, 5) that Herr Engelhardt of Bavaria had registered 'Lady Di' as a trade mark with the German Patent Office the day after her death and was even threatening to sue Princess Diana's brother for damaging the commercial potential of Diana's name by 'turning Althorp into a theme park'.

Clearly trade marks such as IBM, Microsoft and Intel are capital assets of considerable worth whose value has been built up by extensive advertising and the maintenance of known standards of performance.

Commercial confidentiality and contracts

In many cases information held by businesses is of considerable value but cannot easily be protected by a patent and would be insufficiently protected by copyright. Examples might include the recipe for Coca-Cola, a list of existing or potential clients of a system consultancy, or the business strategy of a telecommunications firm. The form in which such information is expressed is not important, so copyright is irrelevant; and the nature of the information is not so revolutionary as to merit a patent. Businesses may be forced, or prefer, to keep such information in confidential files (paper or digital), and whilst some reliance can be placed on locks and passwords, inevitably some employees of the firm must be entrusted with the information. The law of theft applies to documents and disks but not to the actual data that they hold.

Common law does place a duty on employees to keep such trade secrets confidential and employees can be disciplined for unauthorized disclosures, or they and former employees sued in the civil courts for damages arising out of a breach of confidence. Breach of confidence in relation to computers was considered in *Format Communications Manufacturing Ltd* vs. *ITT (UK) Ltd* (1983 FSR 473). Employees' paid activities result in copyright/patent rights to employer, so that the result of an employee's normal work as a programmer would automatically belong to the business not the employee. However, difficult issues may arise if employees have ideas outside of their normal range of work which they develop partially or wholly in their own time, or if employees leave and develop their work with a subsequent employer. Further restrictions can sometimes be placed on employees as part of their agreed contract of employment; for instance, they may be restricted from taking up new employment in the same industry within a fixed distance of their present job, or have to agree that any patents or copyright material relating to the employer's line of business produced by them during or resulting from a period in employment is assigned to the employer. There is a danger, however, that such clauses may be ruled by a court to be illegal as a 'conspiracy in restraint of trade'. It may well also be the case that the employees concerned have few financial resources to make good the enormous damage their leaking of information has caused (in legal parlance they are 'men of straw').

Software as intellectual property

As we have seen, software code is covered by copyright, but the adequacy of this to protect the rights of the authors of the code (or their employers) is debatable. Physical copying outside of contracted permission is, of

---

Exercise 4.2 **Intellectual property (answers on p. 134)**

What legal protection could exist for:

- *Great Expectations* by Charles Dickens
- *The Satanic Verses* by Salman Rushdie
- The idea of a vegan cook book series
- 'Good Veg' description of a vegan cook book series
- A railway timetable
- Drawings for a new mountain bike
- Song title: 'The Power of Love'
- Fully operational time machine
- A silicon chip for a computer-controlled industrial robot
- A spreadsheet program
- A revolutionary new computer operating system

course, illegal – but what of more subtle reuse of coding efforts? Any translation of code without permission (e.g. into source, object or another language) is an illegal 'adaptation'. The analogy with, say, this book being translated into Polish is clear. The original writer retains copyright and a translator must seek permission to use the original work and pay royalties to the originator as agreed. The translator, however, then has copyright over the new adaptation of the text.

Non-literal copying is, as we have seen, more problematic (there is no UK case law but some very expensive cases have been fought in the USA involving, Apple, Microsoft, Lotus and others). To return to our original example, the 'idea' of spreadsheet columns, rows, formulae, macros cannot be copyright, but the 'expression of the idea' could be: perhaps the screen layout, the wording of menus and command syntax.

Tests include:

- How differently could the idea be expressed?
- Did the creator of program A see program B (to which it is similar) before writing it? (See the US case of *Whelan* vs. *Jaslow* (1987).)
- Is the 'borrowing' a 'substantial part' of the work?

In order to maximize legal protection through copyright it is necessary for code developers to be able to establish that they were first in developing software. They need to document the development process carefully so that this can be used as evidence of 'priority' in court. They may leave 'footprints' in code in the shape of comments, or even by starting a series of lines with their initials. Once marketed, contracts should make clear that copyright remains with the developers (if that is the intention), and printed copyright statements/marking (©) can be made on the packaging. The familiar copyright mark '©' only has special effect in the USA, where it does ensure protection for foreigners.

A software registry such as that run by the National Computer Centre in Manchester for the UK allows the deposit of code to establish independent date verification and acts as a stand-by resource in case a supplier ceases to trade. A similar effect may be achieved by sending material in a sealed envelope to a legal practitioner by registered post.

Customers can be restricted in their use and copying of software by contracts which restrict use to one user, x-users, users on one named site, licences, etc. But the formerly common practice of 'shrink-wrap' contracts in which the statement of terms of the licence is not seen until after the product is unwrapped has little validity. In common law contracts must be agreed before the exchange of goods and the 'consideration' (i.e. the payment in cash or kind).

Organizational information management rules

The theme of this chapter is the need for rules to control the use of information and its associated technology. Clearly, if the managers of organizations accept the proposition that information is the major asset of the modern organization then they should have a strategy for employing that asset to best advantage. A part of that strategy should be a framework of rules to ensure that all employees are aware of the import-ance of information, to safeguard that information and help to ensure it is used to best advantage. A mere set of rules cannot, in itself, ensure that the best and most imaginative use of information is achieved. In the next chapter we shall consider how a dynamic vision of how an organization can develop its information resources might be agreed and implemented, but an essential prerequisite of this is that data, software, and intellectual resources should be properly held, safeguarded, catalogued and con-trolled. The objectives of rules to control information in organizations (see Box 4.5) are therefore likely to be quite complex and to overlap – they may even conflict. There will be a tension between establishing rules which are short and simple enough to be effective and enforceable and the complexity of the task in hand.

We have already discussed at length the need for compliance by organ-izations with legal requirements such as copyright and patent law, data protection, and contractual requirements. Beside the moral responsibil-ities everyone owes to obey the law, give others the just reward for their labours, and to protect the privacy of customers, fellow employees and others, the expense and embarrassment to the organization, and the disas-trous potential professional impact of discovery if found in breach of such laws, should be considered.

At first sight the expense of compliance with data protection and other rules may seem an unfortunate economic overhead. In practice many of the requirements for compliance are necessities for the effective use of the technology. For example, the requirement that data held should be the minimum necessary and kept up to date is clearly desirable for effi-cient operations. If information is not secure, then it can be accessed by competitors and used by them or altered by customers or employees for their own benefit, thus incurring considerable losses. A register of

---

Box 4.5 **Objectives of organizational information rules**

- Compliance with legal requirements
- Efficient use of software resources
- Achieving 'competitive advantage'
- Establishing and exploiting intellectual property rights
- Security

software may be necessary to ensure compliance with contractual obligations under copyright laws, but it is also desirable that all users within an organization should have the same up-to-date version of software which can be supported by the relevant department and allow users to exchange files without difficulty.

Achieving 'competitive advantage' means simply making better use of data, software, etc. than the competition, a theme we shall return to in the next chapter. Rules in themselves cannot, of course, make this certain, but a regime which ensures that someone is responsible for overseeing and supporting individuals' use of information within the organization can at least encourage best practice within the organization to spread from one individual or department to another.

Establishing and exploiting intellectual property rights is an area which can make a crucial contribution to the profitability of a company, or economic viability of a voluntary or public sector organization. Individuals in organizations may develop software that solves a problem met with frequently elsewhere, but frequently no one recognizes that such an application could be commercially marketed. Consultants can be paid to develop an expensive system for a department but then allowed to walk off with a software system developed at the organization's expense and sell it to its competitors!

An important point with virtually all intellectual property is that rights have not only to be established (for example through patenting) but also constantly defended and asserted. If a competitor uses its patented idea a firm must ensure that any such use is recognized and royalties paid. This means the marketplace must be monitored and legal action taken or threatened as required.

Security – safeguarding valuable data on clients, industrial processes, strategic and tactical plans (e.g. marketing campaigns) from external threat, accidental damage, dishonest or negligent employees – is a vital area which if neglected can have disastrous results. This is dealt with at more length later in the chapter (see pp. 129–31).

There are many problems in enforcing any set of rules of this sort, however sensible the rules may be.

One particular set of problems stems from the growth of 'end-user computing' in which hundred or thousands of independent machines function in the same organization. (The Woolwich Building Society had over three thousand PCs some years ago.) This makes it difficult to monitor the use of software, the data upon the machines, and the security standards applied. Some departments within the organization may be purchasing independently and amateurishly.

Other problems stem from a lack of knowledge and commitment by busy end-users and managers anxious to solve day-to-day problems and lacking a broad perspective on the overall information strategy of the organization (assuming one exists).

Implementing effective information management rules

The effective implementation of information management rules within an organization therefore requires the definition of clear policy to which top management must be seen to be committed. To win such a commitment information managers will probably need to stress the positive business advantages of such rules, as well as the role of such rules as a protection against threats such as viruses.

Responsibility for implementation must be clear – including departmental managers' responsibilities when acquiring software as well as those of auditors and computing staff.

It is important to educate all staff on the importance of the policy and areas such as copyright law, the commercial need for documentation, etc. Help and training needs to be available.

A clear disciplinary code and procedures in relation to the illegal use or import of software and the unauthorized release of information of all sorts must not only be set out but publicized and taken seriously.

One important tool which needs developing in this area is a software register – a database of acquisitions, authorized users, location of documentation, contracts, back-up copies, maintenance help and training available, etc. Whilst such information is useful for compliance purposes it is also invaluable in preventing the continual reinvention of the wheel by users and the coexistence of incompatible versions of the same software or the purchase of redundant new software.

A 'software auditor' is required to conduct regular checks. 'SPAudit' and similar commercial products will scan hard disks for up to 650 software packages. Many commercial network products also ensure 'version control'. If all programs can be kept on server machines, this simplifies rational control. Networking of machines also makes possible the automatic backing up of data – something which unprofessional users are often poor at doing. Virtually every year at the authors' university at least one student has a major crisis centring on the loss of a project or dissertation draft on a hard disk which has failed and not been backed up on to a floppy.

There is a need for a positive regime. The end-user department or 'help-desk' which is responsible for enforcing rules should be seen as a useful ally – not just as 'Big Brother'. The manager of the software register should have a mission to spread good practice rather than merely eliminate breaches of discipline.

On a still more positive note there is a need to encourage and document 'in-house' developments: to review imaginatively and manage the exploitation of software. End-user managers and systems departments have important complementary roles in this.

Governing the Internet

Since 1992 the Internet Society (ISOC), which is globally representative, has been responsible for coordinating international networks. Reporting to this are the Internet Architecture Board (IAB), Internet Research Task Force (IRTF), the Internet Engineering Task Force (IETF) and the Internet Assigned Numbers Authority (IANA). The IAB etc. have basically always proceeded by open informed debate and consensus, publicizing draft standards over the net through requests for comments (RFCs) before issuing standards documents (STDs). The IP/TCP standards are the main devices whereby inter-operability of the net is maintained.

A good example of the decentralized decision-making characteristic of the net is the addressing system which broadly speaking takes a form like *Username@computername.institutionname.networkname.domainname.* Domain name (or zone) is usually com/edu/gov/mil/org or net in the USA, representing the sort of organization the computer belongs to; overseas the last part of the address is usually a national identifier. Allocation of detailed addresses is decentralized to the network manager at each level.

There are, however, some government-imposed rules. The core of Internet (NSFNET, NASA Science Internet, etc., which is being integrated into the National Research and Education Network (NREN)) is financed by the US government and subject to the rule that the network is for non-commercial use.

'Netiquette' prohibits excessive game playing (where it uses up too much capacity), advertising, intentional damage to others' files, public obscenities, etc. This may be policed by local network administrators withdrawing an account, or even by 'flaming' in which hundreds of offended users flood your account with protesting or rude messages. Conner-Sax and Krol (1999) suggest two ethical principles prevail: individualism and protecting the network. Everyone should be allowed to do their own thing: providing this does not prevent others from doing theirs.

Legal regulation and computer abuse

The normal laws of the land *do* apply on the net – including those on libel, copyright, data protection, obscenity and computer abuse.

Some complications flow from the international nature of the net – copyright provisions differ from country to country and jurisdiction in the case of acts across borders may be unclear.

The likelihood of detection of 'net crime' is also very low, generally speaking, because of the enormous number of files and the lack of expertise and attention on the part of police authorities. However, it is worth pointing out that messages are generally traceable to their originating address. Because of the 'packet' transmission technology employed, all messages must carry both a destination address and an originating address. This allows the tracing back of a message to its originator, except where the message is re-sent by an intermediary who refuses to disclose its origin. In a Swedish legal case the Church of Scientology successfully insisted on tracing a message sent through such an 'anonymous re-mailing' FTP service, threatening the intermediary with confiscation of their equipment (*Time International*, March 1995).

Tracing the origin of a transmission may be of little use, however, since 'hackers' can operate unauthorized accounts on installations with slack security – maybe even via a modem and a stolen mobile phone. Alternatively Internet cafés and the like may not check the identity of users.

Computer crime

Computer crime is often thought of as the activity of spotty teenage 'hackers' pitting themselves against the security experts of Microsoft, the virus-checker writers, or the banks, for the sheer joy of winning an intellectual contest – or in the hope of international fame (or notoriety). Such incidents do occur, and in the case of virus writers can have enormous and expensive international implications. However, most computer crime is of a technically unsophisticated nature. Two of the most commercially significant types of crime are the simple confidence trickster operation and the insider theft. In addition we shall consider the use of the net for criminal sexual activities and for terrorism – activities which have certainly tended to give the net a bad newspaper image and helped to fuel demands for government action to control or 'clean up' the net.

'Hacking' – gaining unauthorized access to protected files without necessarily altering them – even has its defenders as a useful hobby activity. 'Ethical' hackers merely seek to test out the security of software or organizations, and then to reveal the problem before it can be used by those with criminal intent. A few experienced hackers of this sort are said to have gone on to set up security consultancies and been paid by firms to do what they formerly did for free. Such activity however is criminal, in the UK at least (see below), and may have negative consequences in that unintended damage may be caused. The temptation, once access has been achieved, to show off by revealing information or leaving messages in the files may well be difficult to resist.

More difficult to defend is the creation of viruses or worms which seems to be still largely a 'show off' rather than a deliberately dishonest or greedy activity. Here programs of more or less destructive effect are smuggled – usually as attachments to e-mails – on to other people's computers where they may do anything from (say) merely displaying a silly message on St Valentine's Day to multiplying non-stop until they occupy all the memory space on the host computer. (The latter is known as a 'worm'.) The motivation would appear to be usually to show that the perpetrator is cleverer than the professional virus protection writers who attempt to guard against such devices. The perpetrator may not anticipate the millions of pounds worth of communications bandwidth and time they could potentially be consuming, or the disastrous consequences of invading the memory of a hospital, atomic power station, or airline computer.

Confidence tricksters find the web a congenial environment for their work, since it is easy to appear to be what you are not. One man or woman can pose as a multinational giant by means of a slick web page or a misleading address. Thousands of potential 'marks' can be approached at minimal cost. The simplest 'con' may often be the best – offer a bargain, accept the money and then disappear. A slightly more sophisticated, and by now fairly well-known approach, often used by Nigerian computer thieves, is to ask to use the respondents bank account to evade currency controls and offer a commission on the large sums it is proposed to move into your account. Somehow, in the end, it is your money that moves into *their* account! Having been involved in a transaction which is illegal (at least in Nigeria), the mark may well feel in a poor position to involve the police.

Although computer crime is usually associated with the web, it is thought that many offences are actually committed by employees on internal networks or machines. In some cases it may be that no technicalities are involved – an authorized user merely misuses information available to them. In other cases, slack security means that passwords can be easily misappropriated and the criminal cannot easily be traced. For instance, a black policeman's ID was stolen in a police station and racist messages then sent out in his name in order to discredit him. The more technical stories may well be apocryphal, such as that of the bank computer programmer who allegedly creamed off every fraction of a penny or cent created when interest calculations were performed into a secret account of his/her own and became a multimillionaire! The extent of this sort of insider 'white collar' crime is widely thought to be much greater than that reported because firms do not wish to admit to the poor security which these crimes often reveal.

A more often reported and controversial type of 'cybercrime' is the use of the net for illegal sexual purposes. It should be noted that the definition of what is criminal in this respect varies greatly from one jurisdiction to another. For instance, in Sweden and Holland the display and viewing of images of sexual intercourse may not be regarded as a crime, whereas in Saudi Arabia and Singapore it certainly is. It might be argued that imaginary sexual experiences on the web are an outlet for activities and feelings which, if expressed in behaviour in the real world, would do their objects considerable harm. Conversely the possession of large quantities of pornography is said to be a characteristic of sexual offenders such as rapists and 'peeping toms'. It is also clear that the pornography industry exploits poor men and, especially, women – often from the less-developed countries. Worse still it may involve the exploitation of children and/or the injury, mutilation or even death of non-consenting victims.

A possibly still more dangerous feature of the use of the web for sexual purposes is that its interactive nature enables naïve people to be entrapped through chat rooms or dating agencies into relationships which may not be all they seem. The classic danger is that of teenagers being entrapped by paedophiles, who initially may pose as children themselves.

'Soft' pornography is certainly a major feature of web traffic – apparently the *Playboy* website is the most visited of all. Some studies have claimed pornography constitutes the largest sector – or even the majority – of web traffic. All this certainly reduces social and political support for the web and makes it easier for governments who wish to attempt to censor it or restrict access.

Allegations about terrorist use of the web also serve to render it suspicious in the eyes of many, particularly perhaps those who have not made much use of it. It is certainly true that advice on bomb-making and many provocative political statements are to be found on the web. E-mail can be used to set up assignations or even discuss bomb plots. Few would suggest, however, that this is a major category of web traffic, but some would argue this justifies government surveillance in order to catch out a dangerous, if tiny, minority. It is clear, however, that the increased use of digital networks, using standardized technologies, to manage vital economic infrastructures such as telecommunications, electrical power systems, transport, banking, gas and oil storage, water supply and emergency services does present a vulnerable target for terrorist sabotage (Clement, 2001, 2), and in the wake of the attack on the World Trade Center raises important security issues.

Security measures for individuals, families and organizations

What effective precautions can be taken to prevent the misuse of information on computers? This question must be seen in social context since the answer varies according to who is being protected from what. Are we considering an individual's personal computer; a family, perhaps with several computers, some attached to the net; or a commercial organization with both internal networks and external connections to the rest of the world?

It is also worth distinguishing between the technical fixes for security problems and the development of a security-conscious approach. Technical fixes can always, in the long run, be overcome by a cleverer programmer than the one who wrote the defensive device. A security-conscious approach is essential for even the most sophisticated devices to be effective. Perfect security will always be impossibly expensive and excessively inconvenient – the objective would normally be to have good enough security to make someone else a much easier target, while still being able to work effectively.

For individuals with their own computer it is necessary to decide how important it is to protect the data on the computer and what level of inconvenience you are prepared to suffer. If you have valuable data then it can be protected from external threat by not connecting to the Internet, keeping your computer in a locked room, using a password to prevent flatmates or burglars logging on, and chaining the PC to a large piece of furniture. It is possible, of course, to go one step further and keep no data permanently on the hard disk or lock a removable hard disk in the safe. Clearly at some stage you may be accused of paranoia and taken off to a therapeutic environment, or decide to use a ballpoint pen and paper instead, given the inconvenience!

Whatever your level of security, wherever the computer is situated, and whatever it is used for, one important issue must not be neglected: backing up data in case your security fails, or in case of technical disaster. For individuals this may just be a case of copying new, or amended, files on to floppy disk. Ideally a copy should be stored in a different location – for instance, at work for home computers, perhaps with a firm specializing in disaster recovery for organizations. For larger operations, automatic back-up procedures will be applied using more sophisticated technology.

A link to the web involves additional security procedures. At the very least a virus-checker should be installed. For organizations, more elaborate precautions in the shape of a 'firewall' barrier between web-linked operations and internal operations may be appropriate.

For families the question of protecting the welfare of children from contact with inappropriate material and people must clearly be considered. A first line of defence must surely be an explanation of what the computer should, and should not, be used for and why. Clear ground rules that, for instance, there should be no contact with people met through chat rooms without parental consent should be adopted. The dangers of downloading material of dubious provenance must also be made clear. If there are limitations on the sort of material to be viewed then, again, the nature of the ban and its rationale need to be made explicit.

A second line of defence is for parents to take an interest in what children are using computers for and possibly to insist that any PCs with web access are situated in family living rooms, not bedrooms.

The third possible line of defence is the installation of software that limits access to some parts of the web. Various approaches to this exist. Children can be limited to defined 'suitable' sources. Alternatively, software exists to scan and censor sites which use designated words thought to be harmful. Another approach is to have web pages voluntarily classified by the publishers and accept only those declared to be suitable for children. The obvious problems here are that many useful sources of information may be unnecessarily cut off and that harmful material may still manage to evade the somewhat mechanical methods of censorship employed.

Insisting on using computers in family rooms, making clear that disks may be accessed by parents from time to time, or employing software censors all suffer from the obvious problem that older children in particular may feel they are not being sufficiently trusted. Children may also see parental controls as a challenge to circumvent and a reason to acquire greater computer knowledge than the parents who seek to exercise authority in this way. (For a more detailed discussion see Waltermann and Machill, 2000.)

Issues of trust may also be of some importance in achieving security in an organizational context. Heavy-handed regulations banning private e-mails or surfing of the web are widely ignored and may generate resentment from employees who, as parents, feel they are being treated like children. Attempts to limit employees' full access to the web may mean that the organization fails to benefit from non-obvious information that could be very useful. Banning private e-mails may reduce opportunities for employees to form informal links, which can greatly reinforce morale – or send them off for longer face-to-face gossip sessions which impede productivity still further.

As argued above, the most important step is to generate an understanding of the importance and rationale of security issues and for clear rules to be known and consistently enforced. Password systems must not only exist where appropriate, but passwords must be hidden and regularly changed.

With the increasing importance of e-commerce, the safeguarding of customers' confidential information and respect for data protection principles can be key issues in commercial success. Customers will not buy online if they believe they thereby compromise the security of their credit card numbers or reveal their bank balances to all and sundry.

An important mechanism for ensuring the privacy of data in transmission across an open system, such as the net, is the use of encryption. This is the use of a coding system that prevents anyone intercepting the message from understanding it without a knowledge of the 'key'. In principle this is no different from the techniques used by spies for centuries, but with computers much more elaborate techniques can be applied which are virtually impossible to break without a supercomputer and a lengthy processing operation – possibly not even then. Clearly this is a useful tool which can help to protect commercial or state secrets.

Government action to control the net?

As we have seen, the ordinary laws of the land do apply on the net, even if they are somewhat difficult to monitor and enforce because of the volume of traffic and some official ignorance. This may raise the question of whether special government measures are required to control the Internet. In many ways the author would argue for a presumption against special legislation of this sort. Failure to enforce one set of laws hardly justifies putting more laws on the statute book. Why should it be illegal to do on the net what is legal on the telephone, in the press, or in conversation on the street? General democratic principles favour freedom of expression and the Internet is a global exercise in this.

It is true that the Internet can be used to promote and organize terrorism, subversion, pornography and drug dealing. It can also be used to promote ethics, religion, fine art and the family. All these things can be done, also, on the telephone, by letter or in newspapers.

An important point is what precedents are considered in relation to the Internet. If the example of the post is taken, then there seems no reason why e-mail should not be treated in the same way as 'snail-mail'. In general, in a democracy, post is uncensored and the Post Office is not responsible for its contents (legally it is a 'common carrier'). Similarly, although newspaper editors are legally responsible for what they publish, they are only to be sued after publication, not censored in advance. Nor would the operator of the train or other vehicle which carries news reports to their destination be guilty of libel (say) if they did not know the contents of what they delivered. However, if the precedent of videos, cinema, television and broadcasting is considered, these newer, more visual media, often with an element of monopoly in their delivery systems, have been subjected to more prior censorship and licensing, even in 'democracies'. Thus there is an argument about who is responsible for the content of a web page – the person who composed it and maintained it, or the Internet Service Provider (ISP) on whose server it is kept – and some pressure for ISPs, or even the government, to censor Internet content.

The first UK Data Protection Act was an example of special regulations being made for computers. But the later European Directive, and the UK Act based upon it, quite rightly saw data protection as part of a broader principle of the protection of the privacy of individuals. In the second version of the legislation paper files are subjected to regulation similar to computer files.

The UK Computer Misuse Act 1990, passed to deter 'hacking', does creates three criminal offences specific to the use of computers:

1 The *unauthorized access offence*: causing a computer to perform any function with intent to secure unauthorized access to any program or data held on the computer. The penalty for this offence is a fine or maximum of 6 months in prison.

2 The *unauthorized modification offence*: intentionally, and without authority, altering computer-held data, with the intention of impairing the operation of the computer, hinder access, or impair the reliability of a program or data.

3 The *unauthorized access offence with intent to commit a more serious crime* (e.g. fraud). The penalty for this offence is a heavy fine or up to five years in prison.

One might argue that six months in prison is a rather tough penalty for peeking at someone else's files. The 'access with intent' offence was either already covered by legislation concerning the substantive crimes the access was connected with, or should be part of a more general offence covering all actions which reveal an intent to commit a crime. The remaining offence is arguably covered by the offence of criminal damage to property.

Another interesting area of legal regulation relates to encryption. In the USA it was, for a long time, illegal to export advanced encryption programs on the grounds that this put state security in peril. The CIA and FBI then tried to limit the capacity of domestic encryption facilities to that which they could break, despite a lack of legal authority to intercept encrypted e-mails. The United Kingdom has gone one step further in the Regulation of Investigatory Procedures Act (2000) by requiring ISPs to install equipment which enables MI5 (counter-intelligence) to monitor e-mail traffic and empowering ministers to issue warrants to actually read e-mails. Users of encryption can actually be imprisoned for failing to deliver their decryption keys to MI5, even if they have actually lost or forgotten them.

In a BBC Radio 4 interview on 28 September 2001, after the World Trade Center disaster, the former Home Secretary, Jack Straw, criticized former opponents of the RIP Act on the grounds that they had given comfort to terrorists. Similarly it was alleged that terrorists were using advanced encryption techniques which hid messages in pornographic images (www.usatoday.com/life/cypber/tech/2001-0205-binladen.html). Another article claimed that Phil Zimmerman, the inventor of the PGP (Pretty Good Privacy) encryption system 'was crying every day ... overwhelmed with guilt' (www.washingtonpost.com/wp-dyn/articles/A1234-2001Sep20.html). There seems to be no evidence, at the time of writing, for any of these allegations. On 25 September 2001 an FBI briefing revealed that hundreds of e-mails by the terrorists were sent 30 to 45 days before the attack and traced by the Bureau afterwards. However, plain text messages, not even a simple code, were employed (Campbell, 2001). Similarly, Phil Zimmerman continues to defend PGP as a means by which opponents of dictatorial regimes can have free discussions on the net (Interview, BBC Radio 4, 28 September 2001).

It seems that encryption draws attention to traffic which otherwise is unlikely to be detected amongst the vast quantity of ordinary messages. The National Security Administration in the United States has apparently taken delivery of an on-line storage system (Sombrero VI) which can store a million gigabytes of data, but this is already being regarded as too small for the job of archiving 90 days of Internet traffic (Campbell, 2001, 3).

Answers to questions on intellectual property

What protection could exist for?	Answer
Great Expectations by Charles Dickens	Copyright expired – author dead 70+ years. (Intro, illustrations; typography, possibly)
The Satanic Verses by Salman Rushdie	Full(!) copyright protection
The idea of a vegan cook book series	None
'Good Veg' description of a vegan cook book series	Could be trademark
A railway timetable	Copyright
Drawings for a new mountain bike	Copyright (possibly design right)
Song title: 'The Power of Love'	None – too short
Fully operational time machine	Patent – if operational
A silicon chip for a computer-controlled industrial robot	Design right
A spreadsheet program	Copyright
A revolutionary new computer operating system	Copyright – but idea can be expressed in other code. Patent if it has hardware features

Recommended reading

Rowland, Diane and Macdonald, Elizabeth (2000) *Information Technology Law* (2nd edn), London, Cavendish Publishing. Comprehensive recent text on UK and EU law includes data protection, intellectual property law, contract and legal issues relating to e-commerce and e-crime.

Part II

The workplace and IT

5   IT and organizations

Topics

- Organizations and IT: background
- Competitive advantage and IT
- Information strategy
- Managing IT projects
- The future of IT and organizations

Computers have grown in importance within modern organizations from an obscure back-room tool to a dominating feature of the whole organization. In this chapter we consider the ways in which information technology is managed; the central role its use now plays in enabling organizations to compete in the marketplace (or perform a socially useful role in the case of non-profit organizations); and how the planning of IT has become central to the strategy of the whole organization, often leading to its total reorganization. The consequences of this are explored in an analysis of the political forces unleashed within organizations by such changes, and of the likely transformation in the nature of organizations and the role of managers as a consequence of IT.

Organizations and IT: background

Processing modes and IT organization

We saw in Chapter 1 that originally computing was a specialized and technical operation carried out by experts on large and expensive machines in isolated air-conditioned environments. Naturally, when such machines were first employed by commercial and other organizations they were deployed in specialized and largely separate 'data processing' (DP) departments. If a query was made by managers which involved a non-routine analysis of the data, the expectation was that DP would take several days – if not weeks – to produce an answer. Such a department might well employ large numbers of staff. Many of these staff would be involved in routine clerical coding operations reading data off paper and punching it onto cards or tape with equipment similar to typewriters.

Some organizations retain substantial operations of this type. The technology has naturally changed somewhat though, with much data now being machine-readable and remote terminals for non-DP staff to obtain on-line access to the system, both to punch in current data and read off an analysis of yesterday's data, being commonplace.

With organizations such as banks, insurance companies, the Department of Social Security, and the like, such operations may have become vital to the core functions of the organization; they still largely exist, however, in a separate organizational ghetto from the mainstream professionals who meet the public, design and market new products and make the strategic decisions for the organization.

As computing became more a part of routine business operations conducted on familiar equipment, and utilizing standard techniques whose many capabilities were increasingly appreciated by ordinary managers, the role of IT departments has changed so that in many organizations the main role of the 'systems' department has been to develop new systems which are increasingly operated on a day-to-day basis by the main departments with an interactive relationship with the live data on either a section of the organizational mainframe or even a departmental 'mini' system.

Technical planning, maintenance and control of the system (including acquisition of new equipment) remained a systems responsibility. Early on most new systems were written in-house by the systems department personnel in a standard 'third-generation' language such as COBOL. Such 'systems' departments tended to be largely staffed by computer specialists, but an important role was played by business or systems analysts who interpreted business needs to more technically oriented personnel. These departments could be divided into project teams or separate systems analysis and programming divisions.

The rise of the personal computer, and the availability of a myriad of commercially available 'fourth-generation' applications software, has seen the emergence of a new type of IT department – the Information Technology Centre (ITC). In many cases user departments are buying in and/or developing applications for themselves. Increasingly, some technical specialists are more familiar with the latest PC-based developments in their area than are the IT personnel of the company. The role of IT personnel in such a department is predominantly advice to, and training and coordination of, end-users. Maintenance of micros may be an ITC responsibility, or this may be contracted out to the suppliers or a specialist firm. Ensuring that networked machines retain compatibility despite numerous different systems operating upon them will also be important.

Increasingly firms may in fact be relying on outside contractors to develop and provide IT services so that a fourth type of IT department might be included here: the out-sourced IT department. Such a department may be on or off the premises and may be what was previously a part of the company but is now an independent firm or profit centre. Such an organization will be in a contractual relationship with the host company providing defined services at a fixed cost. (This will be embodied in a formal service agreement.) Such departments are often specialist suppliers of integrated IT systems, perhaps based on their own brand of software or hardware.

It is worth remarking that in many organizations all four styles of computing are working side by side, often with variously named IT departments also coexisting. The names used here are indicative of current commercial practice, but there is no standardization of either nomenclature or of function for IT departments.

Changes in the power and status of IT departments

Thus new relationships are developing between managers and IT specialists. Originally the IT specialists designed, implemented and operated a separate IT function on behalf of end-users (often on a batch system). The DP department was largely autonomous, making its own decisions, but was not particularly influential. Now, predominantly in larger organizations, users are operating systems on an on-line basis, but systems have been developed by the professionals and are still controlled and modified by them. Increasingly IT departments come under pressure to deliver systems which are regarded as crucial to the organization's major objectives. Greater influence, but less autonomy results.

Increasingly now systems are being developed by the users and are 'owned' and controlled by them. IT professionals are operating as advisers and coordinators, rather than as controllers. In many cases, as we have seen, formal service agreements exist between IT departments and users defining the user as the customer and making the IT department financially dependent on success in fulfilling the agreement for survival. An important and relatively new area of expertise for IT professionals is in the formulation, monitoring and control of effective service agreements, either as a member of an integrated user department or as a member of a slimmed down systems department which concentrates on strategic coordination planning and purchasing rather than the direct provision of IT services.

The role of IT professionals

As IT becomes increasingly central to the success and, indeed, survival of organizations (see pp. 142–9), and central to the operations of virtually every organization, what are the implications for the status of IT personnel? At first sight IT professionals might well be cock-a-hoop – if IT is so important shouldn't IT professionals takeover the world? Certainly there is some evidence that IT functional heads are becoming directors/vice-presidents of companies/corporations as IT expenditure expands and IT becomes more central to each company's competitive strategy.

However, the opposite implication for IT professionals might be derived from all this – that 'IT is becoming too important to be left to IT experts' (Kaye, 1990, 93). There is much evidence that most organizations have instituted extensive procedures to keep the process of IT development both under financial control and responsive to the competitive position and needs of the business. The IT professionals have to justify what they want to do in business terms whereas in the early years of computing they were often given a budget and left to exceed it in peace!

Another consequence of the development of IT through all departments is the spread of IT skills and knowledge to professionals and managers throughout the organization: 'We are all information technologists now.' In some cases 'users' may feel that they have greater knowledge of the applicability of IT to their area than the nominal IT specialists. Such claims cannot always be reasonably dismissed. IT specialists must increasingly justify their positions – particularly when IT departments cannot deliver new systems built by traditional systems development methods in third-generation languages as rapidly as users can adapt sophisticated fourth-generation applications packages or buy in and adapt specialist products from third-party developers.

Stages of data processing growth

Gibson and Nolan, two American researchers, put forward a perhaps more sophisticated description of how information technology and business management interact. Their original four-stage model of data processing growth (see Figure 5.1), and Nolan's more elaborate and later six-stage model (Figure 5.2), illustrate different but linked and important points. The original four-stage model suggests how the use of IT spread throughout organizations in the early years and the efforts organizations

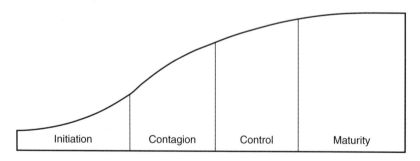

Figure 5.1 Gibson and Nolan's four-stage model
Source: after Gibson and Nolan (1974)

Growth processes

	Stage I Initiation	Stage II Contagion	Stage III Control	Stage IV Integration	Stage V Data administration	Stage VI Maturity
Applications portfolio	Functional cost reduction applications	Proliferation	Upgrade documentation and restructuring of existing applications	Retrofitting existing applications using database technology	Organization Integration of applications	Application integration 'mirroring' information flows
DP organization	Specialization for technological learning	User-oriented programmers	Middle management	Establish computer utility and user account teams	Data administration	Data resource management
DP planning and control	Lax	More lax	Formalized planning and control	Tailored planning and control systems	Shared data and common systems	Data resource strategic planning
User awareness	'Hands off'	Superficially enthusiastic	Arbitrarily held accountable	Accountability learning	Effectively accountable	Acceptance of joint user and data processing accountability

Transition point

Level of DP expenditures

Figure 5.2 Nolan's six-stage model of IT growth

Source: Nolan (1979)

had to make to adapt to, and control, this. They distinguished four stages – initiation, contagion, control and maturity – accompanied by an 'S' curve representing expenditure levels within the organization.

Earl (1989) and McFarlane and McKenny (1992) argue that this four-stage model can be applied to all technological innovation and, in particular, successive waves of information technology innovation. Thus, first the application of mainframes to data processing, then the use of personal computers, and thereafter office automation and telecommunications are all subject to such organizational learning curves.

Nolan's (1979) more elaborate six-stage model (Figure 5.2) can perhaps best be seen as two superimposed 'S' curves – one for batch processing the second for on-line/database technology. This is supported by Nolan's own stress on the 'transition point', which he describes as being a transition from 'computing' to 'managing data'.

The four-stage model can be seen as a clearer theoretical model which seems more generally useful, whilst the six-stage model is a useful 'descriptive' variant giving a rich picture of development of data processing in 1970s USA (possibly the 1980s in the UK) but less useful in the long run.

What we can learn from these two models?

Clearly IT has to be adapted to the stage of development which an organization has reached. A process of 'organizational learning' is at work – e.g. slack control may be desirable in the earlier stages of the development of a technology but this will require stiffening with time. Factors which are affecting the optimum management of technology will include not only internal organizational development but the way in which technology is developing outside the organization and the development of managerial know-how.

Competitive advantage and IT

So far we have been considering the management of IT in organizations from the point of view of the IT function. It is, however, more important to consider the broader purposes for which IT is employed by organizations and the role of IT in achieving these. We therefore briefly turn to a consideration of the needs of organizations, followed by the role of IT in serving these.

In Britain, and in most countries in the early twenty-first century, most organizations must be set in the context of a market economy. To survive, most organizations must demonstrate that they can serve customers' needs better than others. Ultimately the price of failure to compete with other organizations is stagnation and bankruptcy. If customers can obtain similar goods and services at a better price, to a better specification or more conveniently elsewhere, then the organization's supplies of cash will dry up and it will ultimately cease to exist. In a market economy success is relative and we will therefore consider first in general terms how organizations can achieve an advantage over other similar organizations and then how IT can assist with this objective.

Achieving competitive advantage

Four alternative strategies for achieving competitive advantage suggest themselves: doing it better, marketing it better, doing it differently and making yourself indispensable.

Doing it better

First, the customer may be brought to think that your firm is doing the same thing better in some way than others – either the product or service is better than others, or it is as good as others and produced more cheaply, or perhaps it is delivered more conveniently to the consumer.

The obvious way to do this is to deliver a better, cheaper or more convenient product. A higher specification product (e.g. a more durable one) can be produced to higher quality standards (e.g. fewer defective goods sold), with better production methods or cheaper sources of supply than competitors can find. The same product or service can be delivered to the door of consumers on demand rather than forcing them to wait for or collect the product. Thus more sales and/or greater profits can be achieved.

Marketing it better

On a cynical note it must be pointed out that an alternative is to convince your customers that they are getting some or all of these advantages without necessarily delivering them. A large sales or marketing effort may, to a degree, be a substitute for superiority in the actual product. In the long term, though, it is probable that consumers in most markets cannot be fooled indefinitely. But, in any case, it must be said that many excellent products have failed to sell because the consumers did not know about them. In many cases effective brand management of a good product or service can effectively create a demand for, say, Coca-Cola which is different from the demand for soft drinks. Producers can create a sort of monopoly by establishing a difference between their version of the product and other versions.

Doing it differently

An alternative strategy to achieve competitive advantage is to innovate, as we touched upon under the heading of intellectual property (see pp. 115–25). If your product really is different in kind to the competition then a substantial competitive advantage may well result. Your new product will certainly be protected from competition by a time-lag before your competitors can invest in the necessary plant or skilled personnel to produce the new product. You will probably generate a marketing advantage through being first in the field – including free publicity in the media and perhaps identification of the product with your brand name. As discussed earlier, additional protection may be available under patent law, design right and copyright.

Making yourself indispensable

A more subtle strategy is to attempt to engineer a situation in which your service or product is taken for granted. The customer does not stop to make comparisons but automatically re-orders your product or service. An example might be book or record clubs automatically delivering the current choice of the month. At one stage IBM were happy to accept the myth that 'no one ever got fired for buying IBM'. Corporate clients' employees were trained in IBM technology, their managers were offered upgrades on existing equipment on 'favourable' terms, and the effort required to move out of an assumption that the next generation of equipment would also come from 'the Big Blue' was considerable.

Achieving competitive advantage with IT

Authors such as Naisbitt and Aburdene (1985), Kaye (1990) and Earl (1989) have documented how IT is becoming increasingly central to many modern organizations' strategies.

IT has come to play an important role in virtually all large successful organizations in relation to computerized accounting systems, word processing, filing information in databases, modelling the future of the business through spreadsheets, maintaining stock control, and so on (see pp. 4–10). But most of this would only indicate that IT was an important service function like personnel or accounts. Even so, it is worth pointing out that in order to compete on equal terms with other firms – performing with equal efficiency and economy – IT has become an essential tool of modern management.

What is happening in a number of organizations is more fundamental still, however, in that either what the organization does is fundamentally dependent on information technology and/or its capacity to compete with other organizations in the field is fundamentally affected by the use made of IT.

Many organizations actually sell products incorporating the new technology, so that it is crucial to such organizations that they keep abreast with the latest developments in that technology or risk losing out to the competition. For example, pop recordings have been sold in many formats from vinyl 78s, through various tape formats to multi-

Case Study 5.1 IT and competitive advantage: Ford

Ford: IT in automobile manufacturing

The most obvious use of IT in car manufacturing is the employment of robots on production lines. In fact, although this happens, it is relatively rare. Use is mainly confined to areas such as paint spraying where great precision is required and health and safety considerations preclude the use of human beings who are, generally speaking, still cheaper to train than specialist robots are to manufacture.

As the pioneers of the concept of production line manufacture, Ford have been notable in the employment of IT – not only to control production lines but also to link the input and output of these lines to suppliers and customers. Their 'just-in-time' (JIT) manufacturing system gained them considerable economic advantage when first employed by lowering production costs through reduced holdings and wastage of stocks, thus reducing the working capital they needed to employ.

By setting up a wide area network linking manufacturing plants, dealers and suppliers communicating through standardized electronic forms – a system known as electronic document interchange (EDI) – Ford enabled its plants to produce only the models that have been ordered by dealers for their customers using stocks of parts delivered the day or night before assembly. To function efficiently such an arrangement requires not only agreement on technical standards for inter-communication but a high degree of commitment and trust between the commercial partners. Every stage in the production process is rendered a vital one, and a failure to deliver one category of part could bring a plant to a halt.

We have discussed earlier Ford's global production strategy (Chapter 3), but another feature of this system which is worth remarking upon is the use of computer-aided design (CAD) tools. This enables a few basic products to be customized to suit a large number of markets, whilst computer-aided manufacturing (CAM) systems enable a single production line to produce a wide variety of variations on a single product on one production line.

Case Study 5.2 IT and competitive advantage: American Airlines

American Airlines: SABRE booking system

American Airlines (AA) pioneered the use of automated booking systems for airlines connecting a central database by WAN to travel agents in the USA and in Europe. By providing both flight information and reservations, not only for AA but also for many other airlines, about half of all US travel agents were persuaded to install the system.

Before anti-trust actions prevented it, Sabre displayed AA flights preferentially, thus achieving competitive advantage for its parent company.

Thereafter SABRE remained a source of revenue for AA since other airlines pay booking fees to the company and each booking also provides a cash float to the company.

More recently, the SABRE operation has become a separate company specializing both in the sale of booking systems for other industries and in enabling maximum advantage to be taken of the extensive information gathered in by such systems. Such systems yield valuable information on the needs of customers which can then be used to adjust flight times and pricing policies. Airlines now offer a variety of fares, depending on departure time of the flight and even on how many passengers have already booked. This enables planes to fly at passenger levels much nearer capacity and thus more profitably.

The President of American Airlines has suggested that the information asset represented by the SABRE operation is as valuable to the group as several multimillion pound jumbo aircraft.

Source: Harvard Business Review (1991, 10–17)

media CD-ROMs; recording companies must judge which new formats represent the next wave of innovation in the market and invest accordingly.

Earl (1989) gives a number of rather subtle examples of cases where suppliers of goods and services have tied their clients and customers into their own systems, thus creating a considerable advantage to themselves. A good example is ICI's expert system for agricultural representatives. This consists of a system installed on a laptop that diagnoses crop problems and then suggests remedies. The remedies include non-chemical solutions and products of other companies, thus increasing its usefulness and credibility. But in the hands of an ICI sales representative such a system will be a powerful sales tool.

Kaye (1990) suggests four key ways in which IT may be employed in

Case Study 5.3 IT and competitive advantage: J. Sainsbury plc

Sainsbury's were amongst the first UK grocery chains to introduce modern information technology in the shape of bar codes on each package sold. The width of each line on a bar code can be read by a laser reader attached to a computerized till as a number which yields a code for each product.

The obvious advantage of the system is quicker work by till operators, reducing labour costs and/or customer waiting times. In addition more labour is saved by no longer having to use in-store labour to attach price labels to each product. Price flexibility is maintained by the till translating a product code into a price, rather than printing a price on the good at the factory or packing station. Although this system yielded an advantage to early innovators in the field it is now so standard that it has to be adopted to merely keep up with the competition.

However, if data from the tills is combined with data on deliveries and wastage, an accurate picture of sales and stock levels in each store can be made available over a company-wide network to central managers. This can be used both to analyse and improve sales performance and strategies and also to organize a daily delivery system. Such a system enables Sainsbury's to minimize stock levels in shops and regional warehouses (thus cutting the amount of working capital invested) and reduce shortages in stores (thus maximizing sales). An EDI network linking HQ, warehouses and suppliers facilitates this.

A second round of retail IT innovation also found Sainsbury's amongst the early adopters of a new technology. This was the introduction of electronic swipe loyalty cards to allow the accumulation of a small discount towards money-off vouchers to be spent on another visit to the store. Sainsbury's biggest rival, Tesco, have taken this one stage further by rewarding bigger customers with more valuable discount offers. Although the purpose of such cards seems obvious – to encourage regular spending in the same chain of shops – it has the major bonus of creating a massive database of transactions by each individual. Such information can be used to analyse shopping behaviour and, potentially, to identify individuals who, say, prefer organic foods or who frequently buy pet food. Specific groups of consumers can then be targeted for special offers and other attempts to build up an individual customer relationship. To date, however, Sainsbury's do not appear to have made much use of this facility.

A third wave of innovation in retailing is the introduction of web-based shopping with deliveries serviced from the national network of shops. So far Tesco have been more successful in achieving a high volume of web-based sales. But it is interesting to see that Sainsbury's have made information derived from their loyalty card scheme available to their on-line customers as the basis for their first shop. This cuts down the clerical labour involved for the customer.

Sources: Flowers (1988, 203–6), and trade literature

Case Study 5.4 IT and competitive advantage: the Open University

Since 1970 the UK Open University has not only used IT in the preparation and broadcasting of its broadcast television and radio programmes but also for:

- a huge desktop publishing operation of course units based on academic staff use of Macintosh computers;
- administration of large numbers of student applications, student records ($c.$ 100,000 examination scripts and nearly one million assignments per year) and fee administration;
- distribution of course units and other material to students;
- use of computer-marked assignments employing optical mark recognition techniques.

Today there is also extensive use of home PCs for e-mail access to tutors, student access by WAN from local study centres to university minis and mainframes, telephone conferencing, bulletin board self-help groups, and so on.

The university is a publicly funded non-profit institution that has proved extremely cost-effective and has consistently performed highly in academic quality reviews of both teaching and research activities. It is now the largest university in the United Kingdom. It competes successfully outside the UK on a self-funding basis with many private, as well as public, higher education providers.

Source: Eisenstadt and Vincent (2000)

Exercise 5.1 **Competitive advantage**

To which of the categories of competitive advantage, introduced earlier (p. 143), does each case belong?

strategies to achieve competitive advantage (see Box 5.1). Changing corporate frontiers and cutting out the middleman means a transformation in relations with customers, the possible elimination of branches or agents, the introduction of direct telesales operations, and so on. Thus an insurance company which has always operated through brokers and self-employed sales teams organized through local offices might decide to work, in future, through a direct sales staff working from headquarters or from their own homes. Holiday travel tour organizers may similarly decide to cut out travel agents and sell direct to customers via TV and other media.

Moving to a global market strategy involves a transformation in the international business structure of multinational companies. Thus, as we saw above, Ford have adopted a global strategy for producing, selling, and resourcing a wide variety of models based on a small number of engines and body shells.

A product and service strategy of developing new 'information-rich' products may well involve the creation or expansion of research departments to find new products and services, the design and development of new manufacturing plants on greenfield sites, or an evolution away from manufacturing a product to providing customer solutions.

The adoption of production and servicing strategies which involve adopting new IT-dependent methods for producing goods and services include CAD/CAM and JIT as already described. This involves new relationships with suppliers and the need for new integrated information systems. One further example of this is the creation of giant call centres handling all customer service enquiries for an organization at a central point. With the aid of a sophisticated database and expert systems a 'one-stop shop' is created to prevent customers being shuffled around from one department to another when they telephone with an enquiry.

Box 5.1 **Corporate strategies to use IT for competitive advantage**

- *Corporate frontiers* – cutting out the middleman
- *Market strategy* – moving to a global strategy
- *Product and service strategy* – developing new 'information-rich' products
- *Production and servicing strategy* – adopting new IT-dependent strategies

Information strategy

What is a strategy?

'The art of war especially the part concerned with the conduct of campaigns, choice of operations to be attempted and getting forces into favourable positions for attempting them' (*Pocket Oxford Dictionary*). (As opposed to 'tactics' – fighting immediate battles to achieve a fixed objective.)

A business strategy, then, is a relatively long-term planning document (or set of ideas in someone's head) which focuses on the broad objectives of the business and how they are to be achieved. It considers such matters as:

- Which new markets are we going to attack?
- What new products need to be developed?
- How are we going to obtain the people and capital we require?
- Where should we be operating?

In particular it is concerned with deploying resources effectively to meet long-term objectives.

Information strategies versus IT strategies

As we have seen, information is a major resource for all businesses and therefore must be a part of the strategic planning process.

It is sensible to divide this into two parts – the information strategy and the information technology strategy – to emphasize that the technical strategy should serve the business needs of the organization and that the whole management of the company needs to be involved in defining their business needs before the technical question of how these are to be supplied can be sensibly addressed.

Preparing an information strategy

A very clear vision of what information needs to be available to the organization's corporate policy-makers at every level should be the starting point for the formulation of a strategy to ensure that this is made available. Only by consulting those decision-makers at every level can this be done effectively. Both 'bottom-up' and 'top-down' approaches can and should be applied.

As an example of a 'bottom-up' approach, in the Berkshire Constabulary, for instance, 26 workshops, with ten people from different areas of the organization in each, were held recently as part of the process of generating such a strategy. Unusually, in this instance, two police constables were seconded for a full year to lead the process of producing a strategy through a broad consultative process. Many of those consulted remarked that they had never before been asked what resources they required to do their jobs! The result does seem to have been an unusually solid commitment to the resulting strategy on the part of the organization.

Kaye (1990) recommends a 'top-down' approach, bringing top policymakers together in an 'open information visioning' process in which they are invited to consider what information is available to someone, somewhere, within the organization and the strategic uses which could be made of this information if it were available to the central policy-makers. The IT function can then design and cost a system to make the key information thus identified available. Another example of such a top-down strategy is business process re-engineering (BPR), discussed in detail later in this chapter.

Key issues in information strategies

Earlier in the chapter we introduced the topic of how the optimum use of information resources is likely to be crucial to the competitiveness of organizations in the future. We saw the importance of identifying the key IT projects for the firm that will reap competitive advantage. Thus a major part of the strategy must be to give priority to those projects which will have a major impact on the quality and nature of the goods and services provided by the organization and the efficiency with which these are produced and marketed. In other words, we are interested in identifying *key applications* of the technology.

However, another major consideration is becoming increasingly prominent in recent management thinking on information strategies. This is the development of a high-quality *information infrastructure* which enables the development (and abandonment) of new applications rapidly and flexibly, plus the pooling of strategic and tactical information throughout the organization.

Key issues for IT strategies

Of course there is also an important role for more technical IT strategic planning, as well as that directed to securing competitive advantage on which we have concentrated.

As we saw in looking at competitive advantage, market leaders like Sainsbury's and Ford are crucially dependent on IT to obtain greater efficiency than their less-automated competitors. This is usually obtained by *system integration*. One of the major objectives of many information technology plans is thus to achieve greater links between existing systems so that a more effective cooperation between departments can be achieved.

For instance, fundamental decisions have to be made about the extent to which a centralized and networked system is to be sought, and how this is to be achieved. Thus issues of possible downsizing (moving from mainframe to client–server architectures) and, of course, the whole question of end-user computing must be addressed.

In the past many companies have either become unacceptably dependent on one mainframe manufacturer (often IBM), or failed to achieve integration between different departments or sites because of equipment and software incompatibilities. Increasingly, large organizations are likely to turn towards an intranet-based solution to this dilemma.

In addition, of course, policies must be formulated to ensure high-quality systems development (perhaps the adoption of specific methodologies like SSADM and PRINCE for in-house development of large systems), the protection of the firm's intellectual property, conformance to legal requirements on health and safety, and data protection through software audits and quality reviews.

Business process re-engineering: old ideas in new clothes?

Thus, if the whole nature of the business is being changed by IT, so will its entire structure. For instance Rank Xerox has restructured its operations by hiving off its local sales and servicing operations into independent businesses run by ex-employees but linked to headquarters by an electronic information system.

A recent movement which emphasizes the potential of IT in transforming the nature of businesses is business process re-engineering or redesign (Hammer and Champy, 1995).

Case studies are quoted (e.g. Earl, 1994) in which dramatic improvements in the efficiency of businesses have been achieved with this approach. For instance, Xerox claim inventory savings of $500m; Texas Instruments a saving of 70 per cent in the time taken to develop customized semi-conductors; National Vulcan Engineering a policy issue time reduction from six months to 24 hours, with staff savings of 90 per cent.

This is a multifaceted movement, which Earl conveniently summarizes as having six main features (see Figure 5.3). The first three are a 'new triangle' of features, including the possibility of a rapid 'top-down' (executive led) transformation in the efficiency of businesses based on an analysis of the fundamental business processes using the potential of IT. Most of the quoted case studies focus upon the use of central databases shared by all parts of the business, often through a global WAN. Texas found that the process of producing a new chip involved transit through 15 buildings, over 15,000 miles on eight planes and 15 trucks, requiring 40 customs signatures tracked through 18 databases. Treating all establishments as 'a virtual factory' processing orders through a single reservation system enabled the quoted savings to be made.

The older 'triangle' of features are also seen to be vital, however, comprising a redesign of jobs and changes in the business's culture and the employment of systematic techniques for analysing the processes employed.

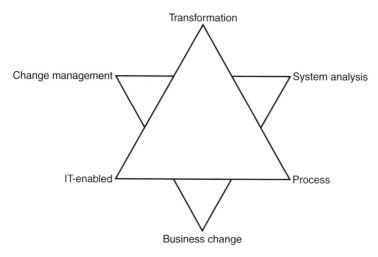

Figure 5.3 Business process re-engineering or redesign
Source: Earl (1994)

The organizational implications

Necessity of an integrated strategic planning process

Kaye (1990) has argued for this involving three interrelated parts:

- overall business strategy;
- information technology strategy;
- organizational planning.

The need for such an approach is, of course, an integral part of BPR.

End-user computing

We have considered this in more detail elsewhere, but it is relevant to stress here that such developments may well raise complex questions about relationships between the different IT departments, and how to coordinate related system developments in different user departments adequately.

Implementing information strategies

As we shall see in more detail later, recent research has suggested that, in practice, IT strategies, are frequently unimplemented. How can the likelihood of implementation be increased?

Undoubtedly part of the reason is the failure to link IT strategies to business needs and to realize the organizational implications. If the strategy is seen by top management to be central to business success, then it is more likely to succeed. Business-like system development using established methodologies such as SSADM, may also be a factor. At least three other (related) requirements may also be suggested:

- to 'sell' the strategy;
- to fit IT to the business's culture (or vice versa);
- to plan for the manpower requirements of the policy.

Selling the strategy

An extremely expensive and complex IT strategy should not be implemented if top management are not committed to it. The best way to obtain commitment is to involve the directors in its formulation, so that it becomes 'theirs'. If the strategy is not seen as their idea initially it must be sold to them with a realistic view of the costs involved (including allowance for inflation, unexpected project delays, training, etc.). Many IT managers have tried 'salami' tactics – getting commitment to stage 1 in the hopes of embroiling the organization in later stages of a broader undisclosed overall plan. The snag is that such tactics may well deal a fatal blow to the manager's credibility as the further implications of the first commitment are revealed.

Furthermore, an integrated strategy is unlikely to be implemented in a coordinated way unless: (a) it is seen as a corporate (not just an IT department) policy, and (b) those responsible for implementation – user departments as well as IT personnel – actually understand where their projects fit into the strategy. Hence an extensive effort in publicizing the objectives and benefits of the strategy must be undertaken. Ideally a series of meetings at which the managing director publicly endorses the strategy should be held. A possible supplement or substitute for this, used in a number of successful schemes, has been the use of a video explaining the strategy, with the aid of prototype screens etc., which is shown to everyone in the organization in departmental meetings.

Fitting IT to the business's culture

Another major problem may be to fit the IT strategy to the existing organizational culture or, if this is not possible, to undertake the difficult task of changing the organization's culture to fit the new strategy.

Organizational culture is difficult to define and rather intangible; but it is of key importance. Basically it is people's understanding of how the organization works – 'how we do things here'.

If an organization, for instance, has discouraged middle management, in practice, from exercising initiative – emphasizing instead virtues of loyalty and reliability – then an IT strategy which relies upon end-user computing and expecting these same people to 'change their spots' is likely to fail unless new expectations are made clear and rewards offered to those who respond.

Very important and relevant here are ideas such as Zuboff's distinction between informating and automating approaches, which we shall explore in the context of job design in the next chapter.

Changing culture is a complex matter involving internal propaganda (as above), changes in structure and rewards, and – perhaps above all – changing people.

Planning manpower requirements

'Changing people' may mean many things. It may involve the provision of formal training in the new technology for existing staff. New staff may have to be appointed. Staff should be redeployed in a rational fashion within the new structure. At the extreme, existing staff may be asked to reapply for newly defined jobs. If necessary, again, early retirement and (preferably) voluntary redundancy arrangements may have to be defined. More will be written on the industrial relations aspects of this later (see pp. 191–4).

In summary, what is being advocated here is an 'organizational development' approach to the implementation of IT – what is often required is not just individual staff being trained, but a transformation of the whole organization.

Managing IT projects

Systems analysis

In Chapter 1 we outlined the nature of systems analysis; here we emphasize the way in which systems analysis is a process which needs to be managed within an organizational context. Methodologies like SSADM have been developed in recent years in an attempt to overcome the general unstructured nature of systems development. There are other reasons for using structured methodologies. A common reason cited as to why projects fail is the lack of user involvement in the development process. The user is the expert in the system and needs to be consulted at every stage. Structured methodologies foster this involvement. Often the development has been from the technology driving the solution. Structured methodologies analyse the problem and devise a solution independent of any technological solution. In addition to defining certain techniques for analysis and design, they put the emphasis on solving the business issues of the system before addressing the technical issues. They are used to address the early stages of system development.

Another way of defining user requirements is to carry out prototyping. This approach is 'user-driven' where users with particular expertise work with the systems analyst to develop a working system. The prototyping approach makes great use of computer-based tools. It often reduces the need for lengthy investigation, and therefore user requirements, and needs can be defined very quickly. Using the computer-based tools enables systems analysts and users to develop a number of different scenarios easily. Prototyping is increasingly being specified as part of the system life cycle, allowing for a system to be developed gradually using an iterative process.

With a perceived lack of user involvement in system development, and increasingly lengthy waits to implement new systems, organizations have looked to find new ways of getting new systems working sooner. There was often a backlog of computer applications, with consequent user frustration. One approach was to buy an off-the-shelf application package. This would be implemented quicker than a bespoke piece of software but it had the disadvantage of not always fulfilling all the requirements. An alternative approach was end-user computing. This was further encouraged by the advent of microcomputers where users had easy access to computing power and the development of new programming languages, which did not need in-depth, skilled and specialist knowledge. End-user computing would encourage the focus on the business and the problem rather than on the technology and the solution.

After the detailed investigation has taken place and a way forward has been agreed, the system can be designed. This addresses the issues of the hardware requirements, how data is to be physically stored, the information presentation and the user interfaces for input and output of data. Computer programs will need to be written and tested, both individually and collectively. The users of the system will have to be trained and test the system themselves before converting the data to the new file structures and changing over from the old to the new system. After the new system has been running for some time, it will need to be evaluated to see whether the objectives have been met and the benefits realized. Needs will change and the system will be amended and enhanced until a fundamental need for change is required and the whole system life cycle starts again.

Techniques such as data flow diagrams, logical data structures and entity life histories are central to structured methodologies (such as structured systems analysis and design methodology (SSADM)). Methodologies like SSADM, developed by the Central Computer and Telecommunications Agency (CCTA), have been developed in recent years in an attempt to overcome the general unstructured nature of systems development. There are other reasons for using structured methodologies. Information systems projects have suffered in the past from being implemented late, over budget, of poor quality and not to customers' specifications. Added to that customers have often been very critical in terms of their involvement on the project. A common reason cited as to why projects fail is due to the lack of user involvement in the development process. The user is the expert in the system and needs to be consulted at every stage. Structured methodologies foster this involvement.

SSADM covers the life cycle from inception and initial feasibility through to the physical design of a solution to the particular problems and requirements highlighted. It encompasses a set of tools and techniques, three of which (data flow diagrams, logical data structures and entity life histories) were discussed in Chapter 1. These tools and techniques need to be applied to analyse and design the requirements of the customer. Its aim is to model the requirements and specify a system that solves the problems and meets all requirements. There are other facets of system development identified in the project procedures which are seen as supporting SSADM. These cover issues like risk, quality, estimating and overall management of the information systems project.

Initially the feasibility of the project is determined by looking at the requirements. It uses data flow diagrams and logical data structures to assess the current system and examine possible solutions to the problems and requirements highlighted. The feasibility options are then presented to the Project Board for selection. The options should contain both business and technical ideas, and costs and benefits of each, in outline to provide solutions.

Following the selection of the feasibility option the project team will need to investigate the current environment to understand the problems of the system and any new requirements to enhance its effectiveness. They will again use data flow diagrams and logical data structures to understand the processes and the data in the current environment. A number of business options will be defined. Each of the options will be different depending on its impact, functionality and costs and benefits. Again the options are presented to the Project Board for selection. Often in the past the development has been from the technology driving the solution. Structured methodologies analyse the problem and devise a solution independent of any technological solution. In addition to defining certain techniques for analysis and design, they put the emphasis on solving the business issues of the system before addressing the technical issues.

After analysing the requirements of the system the project team need to specify the required system and use relational data analysis to create the required data model. This model provides the basis for the physical database.

Where a prototyping approach has been applied to the development of requirements, these can be elaborated to produce a number of working versions of the system. There are two main approaches to prototyping: either 'evolutionary' or 'throw away'.

The 'evolutionary' approach takes the computer code generated at the prototyping stage and uses the code as a basis for developing the eventual working system. On the other hand, the 'throw-away' approach uses proto-typing simply as a means of developing a model of the system. More advanced and sophisticated tools are then used to develop a working system. Prototyping is increasingly being specified as part of the system life cycle, allowing for a system to be developed gradually using an iterative process.

After the requirements have been specified the project team need to investigate the technical options available. They develop a number of options again for selection by the Project Board.

In developing options for the Project Board the technical team should always seek to provide at least three options which offer a realistic set of alternatives. They might illustrate what one might describe as 'Rolls Royce', 'family saloon' and 'utility vehicle' solutions to the design problem. Such options will vary in cost and the quality of service and relia-bility they offer.

Use dialogues are then created and design is undertaken to convert the logical design into a physical design on a computer.

Project management

Any information systems (IS) development brings about change (for example, changes to the procedures, different roles and responsibilities). An IS project is the process of identifying a business need at the start and implementing a new procedure/product at the end. Any process capable of being managed with a start and end point (for example, the construc-tion of an office building, the development of a pharmaceutical drug) is a project. A project involves people and often it is the people who are the key to a successful project. If not enough care is taken over the people who have a stake in the project, it is more than likely to be perceived as having failed. The person who manages this process is the project manager.

The task of managing a project is complex. It involves a large number of interrelated activities, such as:

- planning and control
- communicating with stakeholders
- organizing people and procedures
- managing risk and quality
- managing people.

In its simplest form, project management involves two main issues:

- leadership
- administration.

On many projects, leadership is the dominant discipline. As we have said, people are often, if not always, the key to project success. Project managers must strive for success through managing people both within, and external to, the project team. Leadership is about dealing with interpersonal behaviours, gaining commitment to the project, motivating the project team to get the best out of the people on the project. The leader has to build and maintain team spirit, set up systems of communication for the project, foster creativity within the team and provide the inspiration and vision for the team to work towards delivering the project objectives. On other projects there is the need to spend a great deal of effort on administration – on planning, estimating, scheduling and controlling the project.

Probably the most important phase of any project is the initiation phase. Many research studies have indicated that the major key to success is the definition of clear and unambiguous project objectives, a vision and a strategy (Pinto and Slevin, 1988). The emphasis must be on the start-up process. The best way to start a project is to hold a launch workshop or something similar. The launch workshop will enable a project manager to set the project off by building commitment and team spirit between all people who have an interest in the outcome of the project. The initial task is for the project manager, along with the senior management of the organization, to make everybody aware of the project objectives. After that the team need to agree on the success criteria – how the project is to measured (e.g. time, cost, quality) – in order to ensure that all participants are heading in the same direction. Roles and responsibilities must be issued and delegated, if necessary, and a management control must be prepared. The outcome of the initial phase of the project is often the project initiation document (PID). This document incorporates all the issues addressed in the launch workshop but also needs to address the project risks. The project team must identify all known risks and describe the risks, assessing their impact and the likelihood of the risks occurring, and then categorizing (for example, into high, medium and low). The actions required to deal with risks are identified and these risks, categories and actions are documented in the risk register.

After the launch of the project, the team spend some time planning the project. Why do we need to plan? Development of an information system is a complex activity and, with the multitude of elements (hardware, software, etc.), it needs to be planned in advance to have any chance of succeeding. The team need to demonstrate a clear understanding of where the project is going to customers and users of the eventual system. The project manager needs to know where the project is in relation to the time and cost requirements (if any) in order that corrective measures can take place. Without a plan the project manager will not be able to make informed decisions.

Two key ways to start the planning process is to develop a work breakdown structure (WBS) and a product breakdown structure (PBS). Both are hierarchical structures. The WBS breaks the work down into smaller parts until an individual activity is identified. For example, a part of the systems analysis is to interview users. The project manager needs to identify all the users who will be subject to the process 'interview users'. For each interview there will be activities – take notes, document interview, etc. These will be the lowest level on the WBS. This will allow the project team to estimate as accurately as possible the effort required and the duration of the activity. Perhaps more important to the project and the customers is the PBS. It examines the products required to be produced (management for planning and control, quality and technical) and again breaks down into smaller meaningful products. They can be complete deliverable products (for example, feasibility study report, functional specification) or transitional products (weekly/monthly meeting minutes).

The important point to realize in project planning is that the project manager and team cannot hope to plan the whole project in detail at the outset of the project. A project may takes years to complete and implement. It is quite difficult to predict what is going to happen in two months' time, let alone two years. In the early stages of the project the team should concentrate on milestone planning, where the key phases are identified with target dates for completion. End of phases are normally signified by a major deliverable in the PBS. The project team can then plan the next phase of the project in detail.

Many activities in the project are dependent on others being completed first. For example, design of a new system will not begin until there has been a thorough investigation of the problems, requirements and the current system. Other activities will occur in parallel – several interviews can be carried out by different systems analysts at the same time. These activities, identified on the WBS, can be shown using a network diagram, which is a representation of the activities and dependencies. The important thing to show is the critical path – the activities which, if delayed, will cause the project to miss its completion deadline.

Before a network diagram can be prepared the duration of each activity on the WBS has to estimated. There are many estimating techniques (function point analysis, COCOMO) to help the estimator. However, the estimates can only be reasonably made for activities in the foreseeable future. Many projects are planned in detail at the outset and, as we have identified, it is difficult to forecast into the future. On other occasions estimates are made to satisfy a political situation (making a low bid in tendering for a project). IS projects are well known for having very optimistic estimations, with the result that they have invariably been implemented late and over budget. Above all, estimates need to be thoroughly researched to make them realistic. They need to take account of unforeseen situations, and contingencies must be added.

After a network diagram has been developed, the project manager can then schedule and resource the project by allocating team members to activities. The project manager can develop a Gantt, or bar chart, which illustrates the sequence of activities. They can be prepared for individuals on the team to show their workload in the future. Much of these planning techniques are now developed using computer tools (such as Microsoft Project and Project Manager's Workbench) that automate the process and produce the diagrams and charts automatically.

Projects IN Controlled Environments (PRINCE) is a project management methodology used by both the public and private sectors to aid the project management process. It has a defined structure in the planning process:

- project plan
- stage plans
- detailed plans
- individual work plans.

The project plan, showing the main activities, milestones and resources, is produced at the beginning of the project. A PRINCE project contains a number of different stages and the stage plan shows in detail the activities required for a particular stage. Detailed plans are produced if further sub-division is required. Individual work plans show each person's individual roles within the stage.

After dealing with the planning process, the project manager needs to monitor the progress of the project, ensuring that the project follows the plan and making decisions on what needs to be done to keep the project on track. The project manager needs to establish a way of gathering data about resource expenditure. The easiest way is to get the team to complete timesheets. The actual effort can then be compared with the plan to identify variances. Experience of the member or an underestimation of the effort required are examples of the reasons for the variance. Bar charts can be used to show the progress of the project. There are many different ways in which a project manager can deal with project delays. For example:

- add more staff
- require existing staff to do overtime
- reassign staff
- give extra training or supervision
- replan the project.

Whatever approach is taken the project manager must act decisively with due consideration of the facts and risks. The project manager must make all the team, customers and sponsors aware of the actions, the reasons behind them and their impact on the project. Progress needs to be reported regularly. These progress reports can be either verbal, by way of meetings (weekly, monthly), or written. PRINCE uses a number of formal control mechanisms (end-stage assessments, mid-stage assessments, high-light reporting) to monitor the project.

Control of the project management process is one issue. The project manager also needs to control the quality of the products. Different team members will have a different definition of quality (for example, reliability, responsiveness, user-friendliness). Poor quality will mean more corrections required and additional work. Inspections or walkthroughs are an important part of monitoring quality. These activities must be clearly identified in the WBS and the project plans.

Quality issues must be addressed throughout the project. The project manager will need to keep the issue of quality at the forefront of his/her mind. Another concern is the issue of changes to quality or the objectives of the project. Sometimes changes occur through the request from customers. Business needs may have changed, new personnel may suggest new approaches or there may be new legislation requirements. There must be a mechanism set up to enable these changes to be processed quickly and efficiently. All change requests must be costed and assessed regarding the impact on the project. The project manager must make the customer fully aware of the implications.

In addition to these technical skills of project management (i.e. planning and control) the project manager needs to have good communication and interpersonal skills. Projects are much more complex because there are many more people who have an interest in the outcome of the project, with companies taking a strategic organizational view when undertaking projects, not a narrow departmental view. The project manager must look to satisfying the needs of all these interested parties. There is the need to negotiate with customers at the very start of the project in setting the contract. The project team will need to be motivated throughout the project, and particularly towards the end when enthusiasm is likely to wane.

Leadership will play a big part in the success of the project manager and the project. Leadership involves, amongst many other attributes, inspiration. There have been many great leaders in the past – Churchill, Montgomery, Nelson, Wellington – who inspired their people to great success. Leaders identify themselves with their team and commit themselves to the goal. The project manager is able to motivate the team by delegation, recognition and responsibility. Leaders focus on three needs (Adair, 1991):

- task needs
- team needs
- individual needs.

The leader must give due consideration to all three issues as they are fundamental to the success of the project. The team needs to focus on the common task and objective. The project manager needs to keep the team together in striving to deliver the objectives. The individual team members must have their own needs satisfied. The project manager must adopt an appropriate style (e.g. autocratic, democratic) that allows individuals and teams to flourish. The project manager must also exhibit a number of traits (for example, honesty, inspiration, visionary) to win over the individuals in the team to allow them to perform to their best.

Performance appraisal is an important facet of leadership. By this way project managers can offer recognition for achievement, thereby motivating individuals to perform better. As well as project objectives the project manager must set individual objectives against which they will be measured. Negotiation will play an important part in this process. If there is a gap between performance expected and performance achieved, reasons will have to be examined and an agreement reached whereby that gap can be bridged.

Many organizations are now employing project teams to deliver their strategic objectives. One responsibility of the project manager is to recruit individuals and staff the project. An effective team is invaluable in delivering project objectives. It is important to form a team that will work well together. There have been many studies on what makes an effective team. What is important is having a balanced team, minimizing conflict and stress.

As the project nears completion, the project manager needs to plan the implementation. This will involve establishing training programmes, conversion of data, user acceptance testing and the method of changeover. The project closure is formally marked by a meeting at the end of the project. All interested parties should be involved, with the objective being to:

- ensure that all work has been completed (WBS and plans)
- check that all products have been delivered (PBS)
- ensure that all sign-off/acceptance letters (project closure notice) have been completed
- review any lessons to be learned from the project.

The project review is an important part of the project. Unfortunately this is often neglected as part of the project life cycle. The lessons are hidden deep within the experiences of the project and are not instantly available. Initially, the project team can learn about the project process (from initiation to closure) – the methods, tools, techniques (for example, planning, control, quality, risk) that were used. However, the longer-term objectives of the project (for example, the benefits and overall quality) cannot be assessed until some time after implementation (perhaps two or three years). Eventually, however, every project should be assessed to determine its value to the organization.

Computer projects and power in organizations

The process of deciding what IT projects will be implemented has, in most organizations, become a highly political one in that there are many proposals for system development but only a very limited number of systems personnel, an awareness that budgets tend to be exceeded in system development, and that the decisions are crucial to the success of the organization.

Competing types of proposal will often include:

- individual departments requiring urgent updating of existing systems
- proposals for new systems from individual departments (e.g. a new marketing database system)
- the IT department's own proposals for strategic technical improvements (e.g. to upgrade mainframe to accommodate increased overall demand)
- 'go to jail', legally required, new systems (e.g. perhaps a pollution monitoring system)
- systems required by planned new products and services
- strategic projects designed to create competitive advantage from the board.

It may be imagined that lively interdepartmental discussions can easily ensue, even if system development goes to plan. Where overruns and complications from one project start to affect another, still further problems may ensue.

The prioritization of all these projects will normally have to be resolved at board level, or just below it, either through a process of *ad hoc* bargaining or as part of the strategic planning process.

Robert Block, a very experienced IT consultant, concludes in his book (Block, 1983) that the main reason that IT projects fail (and many do!) is that the project manager has failed to appreciate the political factors affecting them.

Similarly, research on the implementation of IT strategies in firms (including that done by Alan Warr, 1991) shows that most are not implemented, the main reasons including:

- top management insufficiently committed to strategy
- political factors
- projects not implemented in a coordinated way.

The last point usually means that differing departmental interpretations of project briefs have not dovetailed.

As a result, many recent official, academic and practical publications are stressing the crucial importance of correctly identifying the forces favouring and inhibiting the adoption of proposed IT innovations, and negotiating sufficient support among the 'stakeholders' in an organization to ensure their success. For instance, Wilcocks and Mason (1987) speak of a 'political cultural contingencies approach' to system development in which these sorts of considerations are paramount.

Stakeholders in organizations

A major part of such approaches is the identification of all those who may be said to have an interest (or stake) in the organization concerned and who, therefore, are likely to be affected by the operation of a new information system. If they can be convinced that the innovation is in their interests their cooperation may be anticipated; if not, their opposition may well explain the eventual failure of the project.

Obviously different 'stakeholders' have different degrees of influence and interest in specific projects; this also has to be weighed – as has their commitment to the overall success of the organization (naïve system analysts sometimes assume everyone is most concerned about this).

The following comments describe the different types of stakeholders listed in Table 5.1.

You as an IT professional may be the '*promoter*' of an IT project – or there may well be a split between a high-status (director or vice-president) 'project sponsor' and a lower status 'project manager'. Normally, once committed, the promoters of the project will find their professional futures bound up in its success. Clearly the larger the number, and the more influential the people who can be identified with a project, the better its chances.

Trade unions will be considered in more detail later, but bear in mind that they should not be assumed to be hostile or united on such issues. Many British organizations include representatives of several trade unions who may take different attitudes, perhaps according to the status and skill

Table 5.1 Stakeholders in information technology projects

Internal stakeholders	*External stakeholders*
Promoter	Shareholders, banks, etc.
Board of directors	Customers
Employees	Trade union organizations
IT or data processing department	Suppliers
Client department(s)	Competitors
Other departments	Government agencies
Managers	Local community/environment

Source: Adapted from a figure in Boddy and Buchanan (1987, module 2, 30)

of their members, or, very likely, according to whether the union will gain or lose members (and its members' pay or job security) as a result of the changes.

Shareholders are unlikely to be directly involved in implementing IT projects, but on major projects their known or presumed attitudes may be influential. For instance, major IT systems may require extensive investment and may not immediately pay back. Will the shareholders (or in some cases other financial investors) be willing to produce more funds or to wait for the investment to pay off? Again, in some cases, there may be a division between types of shareholder/financial backer on these types of issue.

Suppliers may be relatively indifferent to the organization (e.g. electricity companies) or crucially dependent on it (e.g. many of the suppliers to giant retail organizations such as Marks & Spencer), and hence more or less willing to cooperate with it. At the same time, their cooperation may be essential for the implementation of a project (e.g. just-in-time manufacturing systems), although usually they will not be concerned about purely internal systems.

Competitors may have a vital influence on the viability of IT projects. For example, if they are already offering an IT-based service to customers the organization may have little alternative but to do the same (e.g. automated till machines – ATMs – outside banks).

Data processing: Existing IT departments (whatever they are called) will have pronounced views on IT projects (particularly if originating from outside themselves). For example, some traditional DP departments have attempted to ban the use of PCs, whilst a new IT centre may enthusiastically espouse a user initiative based on the same technology.

Government agencies can have a vital influence (see Chapters 3 and 4), including:

- physical plant may require local authority planning permission
- Health and Safety Executive regulations
- recent detailed regulatory requirements by bodies such as the Financial Services Authority or the Federal Trades Commission
- Information Commissioner
- industrial tribunals.

Other departments will clearly have different perspectives. Most obviously accounts/finance may take some convincing and can, on occasion, destroy a project's viability with short-sighted economies. However, a less obvious, but sometimes major, problem may be where two or more departments feel they 'own' the same (or, at least, overlapping) data. If a system is designed by IT specialists with one 'customer' department in mind, and it is then discovered that the projected system cuts across the needs of another 'user' department, chaos and conflict may break loose.

Customers are seldom consulted, although any system should ultimately be designed to meet their needs (otherwise they will go elsewhere). Marketing departments may effectively represent customer interests internally. Different customers may want different things and ideally a flexible system will take account of this. Again some organizations have a few powerful customers who must be consulted if a system is to work; others have a lot of customers whose cooperation will sometimes be required to make systems work – for example, mail order or e-commerce companies (see the earlier discussion of competitive advantage on pp. 142–9).

As the costs of IT systems increasingly go into millions, each company's *Board of Directors* increasingly involve themselves in IT systems. With an overall strategy or a major costly project, board commitment becomes essential; strangely, it is not always sought or obtained.

Managers may be affected in many different ways by IT systems. Few, if any, managers these days would admit to opposing information technology, but many may be anxious about its impact on them, and some seek to avoid any direct involvement in its use. Most are ready to employ IT if they see an advantage in terms of efficiency for 'their' department. Again IT personnel may easily fail to appreciate managers' apprehensions or ignorance and consequently fail to win them over.

Employees, whether or not they are unionized, are still the people who will normally have to implement systems in the most literal sense. Their cooperation is therefore vital and must be won, not assumed. Again different kinds of employees may well react in different ways:

- unskilled vs. skilled
- young vs. old
- technical vs. clerical or sales.

The idea of 'stakeholders' in companies has recently been popularized by Will Self and taken up by Tony Blair as a prescription for changing the culture of British industry. Their ideas are somewhat broader and more controversial than the limited interpretation given to the concept here, which is derived from earlier, more technical, government publications.

Conflicts in organizations: informal factors

So far we have been considering 'stakeholders' in fairly formal organizational terms as those who have a more or less legitimate interest in the outcome of the project/strategy. In real life we must also consider both the informal organization at work and the motivations of the people on the ground ('players' as they are often termed in the literature). We shall then briefly consider some of the dirtier 'political' tactics that people resort to in relation to projects.

The 'informal' organization of a firm or institution is often vital to its operations – it is by no means always a disadvantage to project managers. The most obvious example is 'the grapevine' – the informal patterns of communication, by which, in many cases, most useful information is received! This may work through car pools, secretarial gatherings at the photocopier, canteen and corridor conversations, etc. Less obviously, there may be a whole hidden system of 'patronage' with certain key players building coalitions, rewarding friends and penalizing enemies with exile to remote and undesirable branch locations. There may be obvious categories of interacting employees; for example, if there has been a takeover, those from the predator organization, those from the 'victim' organization and those from a neutral group recruited since the amalgamation.

Another very important aspect of informal organization, which we have already discussed, is the concept of organizational 'culture' – that is, established informal ways of doing things and expectations (e.g. about who gets promotion).

Block (1983) also recommends that as the project manager you should write one-page 'profiles' of each of the major 'players' in a project, so important does he regard individual performance and motivation in achieving successful implementation. Another writer, Ian Mangham (1979), points to the importance of what he calls 'altercasting' in organizations – that is, individuals are primarily concerned to play a particular role within the organization (e.g. the promising young executive) with career objectives in mind. To many, what matters is their public record not the implementation of the project.

In the interests of balancing the somewhat formal accounts of system development given earlier, we can consider Block's list of less formal tactics often employed for and against IT projects (see Box 5.2).

One final point which Block's excellent text emphasizes, from a potential project manager's point of view, is the desirability of assessing the political viability of a proposed project in advance. If it is not viable, it should be refused or, at the very least, its objectives renegotiated downwards or the resources allocated to it renegotiated upwards. Some projects may actually be designed to fail: it makes sense not to be associated with them!

Box 5.2 **Informal political tactics in organizations**

- The lie direct
- Smear tactics
- Expert witness
- Bluff
- Inaction

- Deadline pressure
- Appeasement
- Ignoring orders
- Hanging tough
- Issue confrontation

Source: Block (1983, section 11.4)

Exercise 5.2 **Stakeholding and IT**

1 Prepare a table (on the lines of Table 5.1) illustrating the main 'stakeholders' concerned with the three scenarios below.
2 Consider the likely political problems in implementing the projects.

Scenario 1

The organization

Jim's Crisp Company is an old established Walsall private company marketing its products mainly through several Midlands breweries and as 'own brand' supermarket items. The Yetsan Corporation of Tokyo has recently bought an 80 per cent interest in the company from the Moore family on the retirement of James Moore as Managing Director. (The remaining 20 per cent are held by Agatha Moore, aged 83, who could not be persuaded to sell.) Financial returns to date have been adequate but declining.

The new Managing Director, Mr Tokaido, is planning a considerable expansion of the company, possibly transferring to a greenfield site at the new town of Telford a few miles away. Most of the workforce is composed of unskilled female process workers, some of whom are members of the Transport and General Workers Union. The maintenance and engineering craftsmen, are, however members of the ETU. Managerial, sales, and administrative staff are not unionized.

The project

One production line of automated processing equipment has been purchased and is to be installed. To obtain an adequate financial return on such expensive equipment, 24-hour shift work is necessary. In return, much higher levels of quality control can be achieved, fewer crisps need to be 'given away' to ensure minimum weights are achieved, and the new production line can produce more crisps in one 24-hour period than the two existing lines can produce in a week. The new line is staffed by two process workers and one (specially trained) technician/supervisor per shift, compared with the ten process workers, one forewoman and a mechanic per production line on the old system.

Scenario 2

The organization

The Piddle Water Company is a privatized water authority striving to achieve higher levels of efficiency and service in a new environment.

It has a strong data processing department, which uses an IBM mainframe to maintain financial controls, process customer accounts and model water collection and distribution systems. It has instituted a system of district general managers to increase its responsiveness to local needs. As an ex-public sector organization it is strongly unionized through appropriate clerical, manual and craft unions.

The project
In one district a successful experiment has taken place in applying a database on a microcomputer network to the cataloguing of public complaints about water quality and supply in individual streets and using this information to control the allocation of manual staff to rectifying the problems. (This often involves digging up roads etc.) It is now proposed to extend this system to all districts.

Scenario 3

The organization
The National Association of Citizens' Advice Bureaux (NACAB) is a national voluntary organization controlled by a council representing its member bureaux. They, in turn, are staffed largely by volunteers, although with some full and part-time employees. Local CAB are largely financed by local councils (plus donations from satisfied clients and charitable trusts), whilst NACAB obtains most of its income from central government. Local CABs depend for their success on the quality of the information distributed from NACAB and the willingness and capacity of their volunteers to make use of this – they go through an initial training programme and periodic refresher and supplementary training courses.

The project
The proposal from NACAB's Information Department is that an on-line information system replaces the existing largely hard-copy information system. The present system having numerous defects including (1) updates are normally only possible monthly; (2) only one advice worker can access a given paper file at a time, but several may require it; (3) the system requires a considerable local effort in weeding and amending out-of-date files when updates arrive.

These scenarios are discussed later in this chapter (pp. 172–3).

The future of IT and organizations

Flatter management structures?

A number of authors (particularly Peter Drucker in the *Harvard Business Review*, January 1988) have argued that IT has and will have a revolutionary impact on the role of managers in organizations, and consequently on the numbers of layers of structure in the organization. He writes:

> Whole layers of management neither take decisions nor lead. Instead their main, if not only function, is to serve as relays – human boosters for the faint unfocussed signals that pass for communication in the traditional pre-information organisation.
>
> (Drucker, 1988)

Since other research suggests that the most financially successful companies have four fewer layers of organization than the least successful, the implications for restructuring seem obvious! With electronic communication systems salesmen or production line workers can be directly provided with more information than ever before, whilst top-level staff can obtain immediate summaries of their performance and be alerted to units performing below par through executive information system's 'exception reporting' facilities. What need of middle management?

Greater management integration?

Another argument is that integrated information systems will enable previously separate functions like accounting and clerical processing to all be brought together under one integrated management, thus enabling (for instance) a particular class of customer only to be dealt with by one office rather than several. Hence a much more flexible and competitive service can be given to individual customers.

Hybrid managers?

The implications of all this for managers are quite radical. Fewer of them may be needed – but those who remain will increasingly be responsible for sophisticated and integrated information systems, and for using them in an imaginative manner to acquire more customers. This presupposes an increasingly highly trained flexible and IT-literate body of managers – the so-called 'hybrid manager' we discuss in the next chapter.

Discussion of stakeholder exercises (see pp. 169–70)

The first two examples are hypothetical. The Piddle valley in Dorset is, in fact, too small to a have its own water company! NACAB is, of course, a genuine UK non-governmental organization, which has now started to implement an on-line information system after many years of attempting to do so.

Scenario 1 (Jim's Crisp)

Agatha Moore can be easily outvoted should she attend a Shareholders' Annual or Special General Meeting to discuss these issues, but Mr Tokaido might wish to convince her of the wisdom of his plans in case she and the family retain influence with employees, managers and customers.

TGWU members may not wish to move to Telford but they can probably be easily replaced. ETU members are probably more difficult to replace and therefore it might be a plausible tactic for the ETU to be offered sole negotiating rights at the new plant, together with relocation grants, retraining and upgrading for many of its members. Non-union staff, including existing managers, also have to be persuaded of the desirability of the move or offered early retirement, if the move is to go smoothly.

Sales staff will have to find new customers to take the expanded production, which will involve negotiation with existing and new customers.

Walsall's local council and MPs may well wish to dissuade the firm from moving, but there is little they can do except offer an alternative site on favourable terms – which might well be an acceptable outcome. Conversely Telford would need to give planning permission for construction of the new factory, but would probably be happy to do so.

Scenario 2 (Piddle Water Company)

Who has proposed the extension of this new system? If it was not the data processing department then they may resent an encroachment on their territory and argue that integrating a customer relationship system with their finance system would be a better plan. The new district managers might also resent any new systems if they are imposed upon them, given that they have just been given the responsibility to manage relationships with local customers.

Unions representing clerical workers may argue that they need training, upgrading and a guarantee against redundancy. Manual workers may fear they will have less idle time, but it is difficult to translate this into a respectable grievance!

Customers will be affected after the event by the success or failure of the scheme, but are unlikely to be influential on its implementation. Similarly, the scheme involves too little financial commitment to be likely to worry shareholders.

Public authorities who could be affected include local councils (responsible for roads), OFWAT and the National Environmental Agency.

Scenario 3 (NACAB)

As with the other scenarios, there are no great technical problems to implementing such a project.

A major problem here is one of finance since both the national government departments who fund NACAB, and the hundreds of independent local authorities who fund local CABs, would have to, more or less simultaneously, fund the project. Otherwise some local CABs will be left with paper-based systems which would have to be expensively supported at national level or collapse.

Another problem with a voluntary organization is whether the (mostly elderly) volunteer advisers are ready to be retrained in new 'high tech' procedures. The financial and organizational strain of this retraining effort would also be considerable. Hence the long delay in implementing this scheme.

Recommended reading

Block, Robert (1983) *The Politics of Projects*, New York, Yourdon Press. Out of print and elderly, but still very relevant and readable.

Cadle, J. and Yeates, D. (2001) *Project Management for Information Systems* (3rd edn), London, Prentice-Hall. Good practical guide to management of IS projects.

Weaver, P.L., Lambru, N. and Walkley, M. (1998) *Practical SSADM V4+: A Complete Tutorial Guide* (2nd edn), London, Financial Times/Pitman Publishing. Useful and up-to-date guide to most important formal systems development methodology.

6 IT and jobs

Topics

- IT and the quality of jobs
- Ergonomics and IT
- The design of jobs with IT
- Industrial relations and IT
- Teleworking
- Gender and IT
- Management skills and IT

We saw in Chapter 2 that it is too easily assumed that the adoption of IT must lead to job losses – the reality is shown to be much more complex. In this chapter we focus upon how the quality rather than the quantity of jobs is affected by IT. The nature of jobs with an IT content is shown to depend as much upon management attitudes to technology and human relations as upon any inherent tendency to 'deskilling' or 'empowerment'.

Some specific human relation issues illustrate the scope for managerial choice in managing IT, including the implementation of teleworking within organizations, relations with the workforce, issues relating to gender and race. Finally we consider in more detail the impact which IT has on the jobs of managers themselves.

IT and the quality of jobs

In addition to the question of whether IT is removing jobs, we also have to consider what kind of jobs will be created or transformed by this new technology. (For a good summary see Burgess, 1986, 1–20.)

Pessimists may suggest that IT is like previous mass production technology in deskilling the average worker. Jobs are analysed into a series of algorithms by relatively skilled systems analysts. The role of programmers may be seen as likely to be rendered redundant by CASE tools (computer-aided software engineering), plus code generators and by fourth-generation languages (let alone fifth-generation computing). After which most tasks become mere routine computer-minding with middle management largely eliminated since top management are now in touch with worker/machine activities in an unprecedentedly direct fashion. Thus, as ever, heavy capital investment cuts labour costs by requiring less labour, and less-skilled labour at that.

Such deskilling and concentration of creativity and responsibility at the top is seen as leading to lack of job satisfaction – or even 'alienation' (as Marx would have described it) – below the thin layer of truly skilled and creative managers and systems developers.

Conversely, optimists have argued that automation in fact makes possible the mechanization of all routine and repetitive operations leaving human beings with the interesting, exceptional and non-routine parts of operations. (Thus a more highly skilled and leisured workforce will be created – hence, on both counts, the need for higher standards of education than ever before.)

Manufacturing being increasingly automated, and information-based service industries and teleworking in the workers' own homes becoming increasingly common, the urban factory (or even office) will cease to be the normal locale for work – thus redefining the nature of jobs and their satisfactions.

IT and jobs: case studies

So far, as discussed above, in Britain there has been a limited application of IT in practice so that the evidence does not support either extreme proposition. But some limited suggestions about the sort of impact IT might have on the nature of work can be gleaned from some observations about how IT has affected particular categories of industry and occupation, where it has been applied.

In banking roughly the same number of staff initially dealt with a greatly expanded number of customers and transactions, with the aid of ATMs (automated till machines), automated processing of cheque transactions, and the introduction of centralized and automated debit and credit card operations. Not only was the number of routine clerical operations reduced but staff could, therefore, spend more time on customer service enquiries, selling insurance, arranging loans, etc. From the point of view of the ordinary branch bank clerk, however, the job did not seem to have greatly changed, despite higher profitability for the banks. It may not be coincidental that banks have become more strongly unionized latterly. In recent years, however, with bank financial losses overseas and a domestic recession, a number of banks have announced fairly large-scale redundancies explicitly justified by a reduced need for labour, given better use of IT.

In the newspaper industry a much more drastic pattern of change can be observed in which a traditional number of craft skills (typesetting etc.)

have largely disappeared, along with a radical weakening of their corresponding unions who had previously operated highly successful and remunerative closed shops. Instead, much more of the production process is now integrated in the hands of journalists.

Another case of quite radical change and integration of previously separate processes is in engineering and architectural design offices, where CAD (computer-aided design) software has eliminated vast amounts of routine copying, adapting and redrawing of designs which involved, none the less, some considerable skill. The professionals involved can now work much more rapidly and creatively, and do not have to spend so long as 'apprentices' mastering graphics skills.

A combination of improved flexibility resulting from the CAD techniques and that resulting from the employment of CAM (computer-aided manufacturing) has resulted in a transformation in the nature of a number of highly automated plants. Instead of relying on the standard production line techniques which were pioneered by Henry Ford – which produce mainly 'deskilled' repetitive jobs – the product range has been transformed, with a much wider choice available to customers. Hence the plant has moved towards 'batch' and made-to-order production involving much more flexibility and skill on the part of employees.

What these examples suggest is the wide range of impacts that IT may have on the skill and satisfaction levels of the average employee in different industries. However, there is some rather disturbing evidence that, in a proportion of cases, working with IT, especially where workers sit for much of the day in front of a visual display unit (VDU) hitting keyboard keys, is so unsatisfactory that it is positively bad for the health of those concerned.

Is IT a health hazard?

Complaints reported in a number of studies of the use of VDUs include those indicated in Box 6.1.

The problem with these reports is that not all users report the same problems, nor are rates of incidence constant. It is possible in some cases that disease outbreaks attributed to VDUs may be the effects of 'sick-building syndrome', perhaps related to Legionnaires' disease. To analyse this problem more precisely it may be more useful to draw upon insights from the discipline of ergonomics, which is concerned with such matters.

Ergonomics and IT

Some readers may have seen advertisements claiming that chairs, computer keyboards and other equipment are 'ergonomically designed' or 'ergonomically tested'. Others may be aware that ergonomics (see Box 6.2)

***Box 6.1* Health problems with VDUs**

Visual problems

Repetitive strain injuries
- tenosynovitis, lower back strain, etc.

Stress related(?)
- stomach, heart complaints, etc.
- reduced resistance to infectious diseases
- emotional disturbance (depression, palpitations, etc.)

Radiation related(?)
- pregnancy problems
- skin rashes

***Box 6.2* Definitions of ergonomics**

1 The laws (*nomos*) of work (*ergon*).
2 'Good fit between tools and work' (Gater, 1987).
3 Physiological and psychological behaviour in interaction with working environment.

is a general approach to the use of tools in a work environment. Since computers are the dominant tool used in the modern workplace any such study should have much to contribute to an understanding of the way information technology is used in business and its possible ill-effects.

The first definition in Box 6.2 is derived from the Greek origins of the word and suggests that ergonomists attempt a scientific approach to an analysis of work. Correct though this deduction is, it may suggest a slightly broader concern than most writers in the area adopt. Few ergonomists consider at length relationships of supply and demand, industrial structures and the broader questions of what is today meant by 'economics' which, paradoxically, is derived from the Greek meaning 'laws of the household'.

Traditionally, ergonomics has focused on the area indicated by the second (Gater's) definition in Box 6.2 – relationships between tools and people. Considerations of design – particularly fitting tools to the measured size and capabilities of people using them ('anthropometry') – have tended to be uppermost.

However, as psychologists and designers have studied the use people make of tools they have increasingly come to see that the conditions within which a tool is used modify profoundly the efficiency and effectiveness with which tools can be used. For instance, there is no ideal spade – one used for weeding a garden in England may need to be very different from one used for shovelling cocoa beans in Ghana. Similarly a professional user may react completely differently to an amateur one, so that the psychological characteristics of users must be explored in depth if the best results are to be achieved.

Initially the emphasis was on the physical characteristics of users: how long are people's arms? How much power can a normal pair of biceps be expected to exert? But as tools have become supplied with their own power sources the main emphasis today is on the control system: the interaction between the human being operating the tool and the way it behaves: the human/machine interface illustrated in Figure 6.1. Or, to put it in more general and formal terms, as illustrated in Figure 6.2. Here

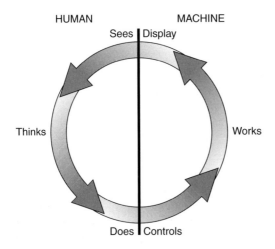

Figure 6.1 The human/machine interface 1

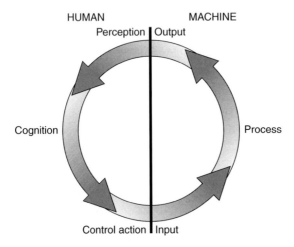

Figure 6.2 The human/machine interface 2

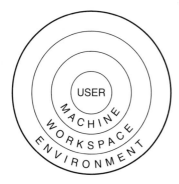

Figure 6.3 Ergonomics as a multi-factor study

we have another variety of system at work. As we saw in Chapter 1 it is often helpful to consider system with their environment and to analyse the relationships between the two. This may be summarized in a further simple diagram (see Figure 6.3).

Again, following Gater (1987), we can summarize the ergonomic approach as covering the aspects shown in Box 6.3. We shall review each of these factors in turn and apply them to the use of IT, especially in the case of the VDU/keyboard user introduced earlier.

The design of an effective human–machine system must begin with a consideration of the physical, psychological and biological characteristics of the human beings concerned. Any workstation should be able to accommodate the vast majority of human beings without strain. Designers

---

Box 6.3 **Key aspects of the ergonomic approach**

The user
- physical anthropometry
- psychology
- biology

User/machine interface
- physical
- cognitive

Workplace
- design/layout

Environment
- physical
- psychological

Job design, selection and training

customarily aim to accommodate at least 90 per cent of the population – although in these days of equal opportunity legislation it may be increasingly necessary to aim at 100 per cent in many circumstances.

Problems will probably centre around the relative height of the chair and the work surface upon which the keyboard rests, but it is also necessary to ensure that the VDU screen is at an approximate level with the user's eyes and at a sensible distance from them. Use of fixed-height chairs and tables, and placing computers on the same work surface as the keyboard, may result in neck and eye strain, unsupported feet, and arms being held at uncomfortable angles to the body. The only real solution is to ensure that relative heights and distances can be adjusted to suit the actual individuals employed.

Psychological issues surrounding computer use are many and varied. We discuss at a later point the possibility of 'computer phobia' and possible gender differences in attitude to IT. But it is worth suggesting that much of the variation in reaction to computers will depend upon the attitude of the user to the technology. This may be partly a matter of inherited or acquired temperament, but it may well also be a function of the social role of the individual in the organization and the purposes for which this general purpose tool is being employed by the particular employee and thus influenced by broader organizational factors. In effect, does the user see the computer as a useful tool enabling them to achieve their objectives or as a remorseless taskmaster with built-in surveillance facilities? Clearly the psychological reaction will differ radically in these two extreme cases.

Biological factors that affect human capacity to use tools include a maximum human capacity for steady effort of about 0.2 horsepower – which was formerly of great importance. Today a capacity, conversely, to sit for long periods without strain is a severe limiting factor in this and many other cases. A simple issue, which can nevertheless be of great importance, is the requirement to see VDU screens clearly. Eye tests are desirable to establish normal vision or arrange for defects to be corrected. With many modern screen presentations colour vision is a requirement, and thus colour blindness a source of additional strain for some workers.

The design of the user/machine interface may be of crucial importance for the health and well-being of users. We have already referred to the case when thoughtless use of screen colour by interface designers may reduce understanding of the message. The background colour of the screen itself may possibly also cause strain with some users. A serious possibility, which may lead to illness, is the possibility of excessive radiation emissions (although these have been reduced radically with most modern designs when in good working order). A good-quality screen display with an appropriate level of resolution and minimal flicker is also necessary.

Keyboard design is another interesting issue. It is clear that modern computer keyboards are direct descendants of the conventional (QWERTY) typewriter keyboard (Figure 6.4), which is mainly the way it is for engineering reasons rather than to suit human beings. Thus the keys are laid out in straight lines, although the fingers which use them are splayed out in two arcs from the wrists. Neither are the most frequently used keys in English text those upon which the fingers naturally rest: this is achieved in the Dvorak layout illustrated (Figure 6.4). Conversion to a Dvorak-type keyboard is unlikely, although logically desirable, because of the problems of conversion to such a new standard when so many existing users are habituated to using the conventional layout.

On the psychological (cognitive) level there is a need for an appropriate interface for the users envisaged. Most readers will be familiar with a GUI (graphical user interface) of the WIMP (Windows, icon, mouse, pointer) variety on their computer screen. This type of interface, first popularized by Apple, and now found on standard Microsoft Windows PCs,

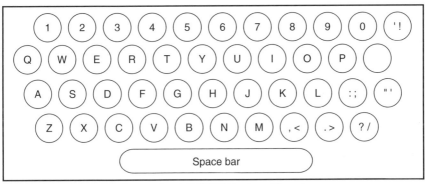

Conventional QWERTY keyboard layout

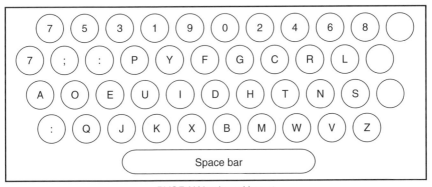

DVORAK keyboard layout

Figure 6.4 Alternative typewriter keyboards

Source: Gater (1987: Figures 5.6, 5.7)

enables users to point at small pictures (icons) of 'objects' such as files or programs on the VDU screen by moving a mechanical 'mouse' around a mat on their desk and clicking once or twice the button(s) on the mouse to indicate selection or activation of the object. A description in words of the use of the interface may serve to remind readers that even such a 'user-friendly' interface is a rather artificial psychological metaphor for the underlying activities. Total beginners to computing may find this a problem to understand until it is explained and practised. Consequently, for uses in which the general public is required to use computers (such as public information displays in shopping centres), 'touch screen' displays have been developed which do not require a mouse or keyboard in order for the user to request specific information. Instead, the part of the display of interest to the user reacts to a touch by displaying further details. At the extreme a voice-activated telephone system might fool a very naïve user into thinking they were talking to a slow-witted and extremely pedantic human being!

Problems with interfaces include that the easier an interface is to use, generally speaking, the bigger the investment it represents, and the narrower the options it presents to the user. Most computer applications today present the user with a series of menus from which to make choices – but this may limit the user to a choice of the alternatives the designer of the menus envisaged. Poor design of interfaces may force a frustrated user to pick their way through several layers of menus when they are already quite clear what they wish to do.

A good application design, like many of the sophisticated databases now on the market, will actually present alternative interfaces to different categories of user. Thus, a routine clerical user can permanently be using one 'form' to enter the same kind of data into the database; a manager will be able to use pre-formatted 'report' facilities to extract and present standard statistics about how the database is being used; a researcher will be able to enter complex queries in Standard Query Language; while the database manager can program in sequences of activities using a third-generation control language. A simpler example is that of word processors, which usually combine the facility to select options by pull-down menus with the option of using a key sequence (say Control + Alt + a letter) to achieve the same result. Whilst student and lecturer, perhaps both occasional users of the program, may prefer menus, secretaries, who use the program constantly, may prefer an option which enables them to keep their fingers flying across the keyboard.

An understanding of how people perform at work cannot be separated from the design of the workplace itself. In some cases problems attributed to the introduction of computers have much more to do with accompanying changes in the layout of the workplace. For instance, secretaries might be moved from operating typewriters in attractive offices next to 'bosses' with whom they personally identify, to windowless word-processing factories with 20 other people in a 'pool'. The consequent unhappiness might have much more to do with the lack of potted plants and sunlight, loss of control over their own environment, feelings that status has been diminished, and perceived reduced opportunities for promotion than with the new machinery. Even very limited changes in physical layout – being placed in a 'dead-end' rather than adjacent to a space through which a variety of people move from time to time, for example – may have a large psychological effect.

The classic Hawthorne experiments on workplace psychology started as an investigation of the impact of physical conditions, such as heating and lighting (together with the frequency of rest breaks). It was found in this case that morale rose largely regardless of the changes introduced in the experiment merely because the workers concerned were so pleased at an interest being taken in their behaviour! Such a positive experience may have a negative counterpart in some cases of RSI (repetitive strain injury) 'epidemics'. The same equipment introduced into different workplaces can lead to very different rates of illness thereafter. The thoughtless and insensitive introduction of new technology, perhaps in an atmosphere of worker/management confrontation, can lead to a much higher sensitivity on the part of the workforce to the physical and psychological demands of the new equipment. This is not to say that RSI is a purely psychological condition – nor should it be thought that in some sense psychological illnesses are less real 'than' physical ones.

Another dimension of the relationship between human beings and machines is the question of which human being has been selected to interact with which machine and how well have they been prepared for the experience. As discussed later in the chapter (p. 200), it may well be that certain personality types are more amenable to particular categories of work with IT. It is certainly clear that, in practice, some people have a more positive attitude to innovation in technology than others. Appropriate selection of personnel for IT-related roles will therefore minimize the problems involved. Still more certainly, asking anyone to operate new complex procedures (including the use of sophisticated computer programs) without appropriate training will inevitably lead to stress and a high probability of failure. As we saw in the previous chapter, however, it is frequently the case that projects involving new information technology are introduced over-budget and late. The temptation to skimp on training for financial and operational reasons seems, alas, to be avoided but rarely.

One conclusion which does seem to be strongly supported by most of the studies of the use of IT equipment is that jobs which are 100 per cent composed of sitting in front of VDU screens are a potential health hazard. Ideally managers should avoid creating such posts, enabling employees to alternate such tasks with others which will build into the work process some physical exercise and opportunities for social interaction with other workers and/or customers. In cases where posts are predominantly

Box 6.4 **Legislative guidelines for the use of VDU equipment**

UK regulations made under the Health and Safety at Work Act 1974, to implement EU directive with effect from 1.1.93, include:

- regular breaks or changes of activity for staff using VDUs;
- entitlement to eye-tests and appropriate corrective equipment;
- minimum requirements for workstations (size of screen, lighting, etc.).

concerned with the use of such equipment there are now clear legislative guidelines, which are not only legal requirements but incorporate much common sense from the point of view of maximizing long-term productivity (see Box 6.4).

The design of jobs with IT

In our earlier discussion of the impact of IT on jobs in particular industries we did not emphasize, at that stage, that the changes described were not necessarily inevitable. In the newspaper industry, for instance, management faced major industrial problems in implementing the new pattern. Perhaps more interestingly a comparison of motor manufacturers shows that, even using information technology, work organization can actually vary radically. Some manufacturers (e.g. Saab) have moved towards creating cooperative work groups in which there is an interchange of roles and collective responsibility for quality; Ford, on the other hand, have continued to use more or less conventional 'production line' techniques whilst seeking to raise quality through increased use of robots and to cut stock-holding costs and increase flexibility by just-in-time logistic techniques.

Similarly, we have already discussed the uses to which word processing and networking technology can be put in an office environment: with the same technology all typing can be centralized in a pool in the interests of maximizing the throughput of documents with minimum personnel being employed; or the emphasis may be laid upon making documents available to all through the organization, encouraging executives to develop keyboard skills and upgrading secretaries to personal assistants.

Hence given new technological possibilities it will generally be possible to *design* new work patterns. For instance Wilcocks and Mason (1987) discuss CNC lathes and show that the programming of these machines can be reserved to IT staff and managers, regarded as a supervisor's function, or allowed by the operators with radically different consequences for the skill level and interest of the jobs concerned.

What sort of objectives can/should the designers of new work patterns pursue? These can include:

1 Elimination or reduction in numbers of a specific job category – e.g. a particular type of scientific or technical personnel cannot be recruited in the area. Hence automatic test routines, or expert systems are introduced to substitute for skilled personnel. (This may also be a union-busting strategy, as in the newspaper industry.)

2 Cost reduction by automating – the 'traditional' replacement of semi-skilled personnel by machines – may not be worth it in a low wage and relatively static economy.

3 Quality control is an increasingly important objective from a competitive point of view. (Japanese success has been based on a 'zero defects' philosophy.) This may be done, however, in a variety of ways (see pp. 187–8).

4 Achieving a more flexible product range by greater integration of the productive process (e.g. CAD/CAM, DTP).

5 Achieving greater management knowledge of, and control over, the production process.

However, these objectives may conflict and they will have different impacts on the nature of the jobs created. Eliminating specific job categories and greater management control are less likely to have a direct impact on a firm's profitability and may a have greater potential for creating conflicts with the workforce than the other objectives – although they may be tempting to managers.

Achieving job satisfaction with IT

Let us examine how IT is likely to affect the way people feel about work, whether this matters to managers, and if so what can be done to improve matters in terms of improving job satisfaction in IT-related work.

Broadly speaking it can be argued that two major schools of thought exist among managers about how workers feel about jobs. They can be summed up in what the American writer James McGregor has called 'Theory X' (see Box 6.5) and 'Theory Y'. Theories (explicit or implicit) (see Box 6.6) about what makes your workforce tick will inevitably hugely influence how you try to motivate, monitor and control them.

Theory X can be regarded as a common-sense, or as a rather cynical, approach to working life. From a 'common-sense' angle it could be

---

Box 6.5 **McGregor's 'Theory X'**

Theory X (extrinsic rewards)
'They only do it for the money, they won't do it unless watched'
   → emphasis on financial incentives, managerial controls

pointed out that if people generally did not prefer leisure to work they would not have to be paid to do it. Our whole economic system is based on economic incentives and their efficacy. This being so we should not be surprised if the rewards of bonuses and the threat of dismissal inherent in management surveillance of workers' activities are the most potent tools in the manager's armoury. Certainly the earliest writers on 'scientific management' assumed this was so and some of them, such as Frederick Winslow Taylor, put great faith in managers scientifically monitoring the way tasks were performed (i.e. maximizing management information) and motivating workers by paying them on a 'piece-work' basis or through other financial devices.

However, it is worth noting that many studies have shown that there is actually a very loose relationship between how hard people work and payment systems. Millions of people actually work for nothing as volunteers for organizations like the Red Cross and Médicins sans Frontières. There are many cases where low-paid workers would actually be better off on social security when travel and other work costs are taken into account. Nor are the jobs with the worst conditions necessarily the best paid, as this approach might suggest. There are also many cases of workers failing to respond to the financial incentives offered by piece-work schemes.

Even if it is accepted that workers are doing the job for financial reward it is a cynical assumption that they will wish to renege on the bargain by not doing a fair day's work for a fair day's pay. It is curious, too, that managers are assumed to pursue rationally the organization's best interests in monitoring workers' performance but that workers are assumed to have no such commitment. In short, Theory X is not quite so commonsensical as it first appears to be – indeed, it owes quite a lot to some rather ideological thinking by long-dead economists.

In contrast 'Theory Y' (Box 6.6) appears at first to be a rather idealistic, if not a positively overoptimistic, approach. It suggests that managers try to win consent from the workforce for the goals in hand and largely relies upon the intrinsic rewards which will naturally be generated from a successful joint endeavour to motivate those concerned. It does not assume that managers necessarily know better than the workforce how things can be achieved, or that the workforce will stop working the moment managers, backs are turned.

However, it is worth pointing out that most workers in a competitive

---

Box 6.6 **McGregor's 'Theory Y'**

Theory Y (intrinsic rewards of work)
'Give people a challenge and they will respond'
  → emphasis on involving and empowering workforce

> **Box 6.7 Maslow's hierarchy of needs**
>
> 1 Self-actualization
> 2 Esteem
> 3 Social
> 4 Safety
> 5 Physiological

economy are aware that if their organization does not succeed their jobs may well be lost. It is also clear that everyone – not just managers – likes to be rewarded by the respect of other people within the organization that can follow from a job well done.

In practice it is realistic to see everyone within an organization as pursuing a variety of objectives, which include obtaining economic advantage, social respect, and even the satisfaction achieved from doing the right thing. This has been formally expressed in Maslow's (1943) concept of a hierarchy of needs met by work and other social activities, as shown in Box 6.7. Maslow sees these needs as being in a hierarchy, with the basic needs at the bottom of the list requiring satisfaction before people can ascend to the higher levels. However, in most modern industrial or post-industrial societies, basic needs can be satisfied through the social security system, and in all societies there are many instances of people putting moral ('self-actualization') imperatives ahead of 'physiological' needs such as those for food, drink, warmth and medicine.

Designing a new work process: rival approaches

These two rival approaches to the motivation of the workforce imply different approaches to the employment of IT in the redesign of jobs. 'Theory X' would imply an emphasis on the goal we referred to earlier, of achieving greater management knowledge of, and control over, the production process, while a 'Theory Y' strategy for designing a new work process involving IT would seek to maximize the intrinsic rewards of work. The application of Theory Y to job redesign was attempted in general terms by Herzberg *et al.* (1959) in their theory of job enrichment.

In relation to IT a similar dichotomy of approach has been observed by Shoshana Zuboff (1988) who also relates this to the more general questions of organizational culture and information technology strategy discussed earlier. In *In the Age of the Smart Machine*, Zuboff, on the basis of a number of detailed case studies, suggests two polar types of IT implementation: an 'automating' approach (Box 6.8) which corresponds to 'Theory X' assumptions and an 'informating' approach (Box 6.9) which employs 'Theory Y' assumptions.

Box 6.8 Zuboff's automating approach

Computerize existing processes preserving existing hierarchy of power

In this approach the managerial role is seen as essentially one of control. Existing processes are transformed into equivalent computerized processes and the opportunity is taken to reinforce managerial surveillance and control over subordinates – particularly the 'shop floor'. Thus tendencies to central control and planning within the organization are reinforced. The numbers of intermediate managers and supervisors may well be reduced, whilst 'shop floor' activities are likely to be further routinized and deskilled.

Box 6.9 Zuboff's informating approach

Empower ordinary working people with information about the whole productive process, enabling new methods of working and improved service/production to evolve

In this approach the opportunity is taken to rethink the activities of the organization and to adopt a more participative approach to the redesign of processes adopted – with ideas from middle management and the shop floor being considered. Hierarchy is modified by making information available to all concerned so that decisions tend to be increasingly made by discussion. Fewer staff are likely to be employed, but these staff are given greater powers of decision and need to be more highly trained and flexible.

The approach outlined in Box 6.9 should allow people to win esteem and realize themselves by developing new skills; to contribute to efficiency by using new information resources; to offer built-in promotion opportunities; to mobilize desire for social solidarity by encouraging group responsibility; to recognize safety and physiological needs by good design of system and environment; and to avoid boredom and low morale by job rotation.

Overall a balance must be sought between the challenge offered by the job, the capacities of the individuals concerned, and the rewards offered by it.

Assessing job redesign schemes

How do we know when the right balance has been struck? One approach to evaluating jobs is to ask people by means of questionnaires or structured interviews. However, something to watch for here is the type of satisfaction achieved – if work is a pleasant place to go and chat to your mates, pick up a pay packet and have a bit of fun, this may be a sort of 'job satisfaction' – though not the sort that managers are looking for!

Perhaps more useful in assessing the success of such schemes are 'behavioural indices' such as:

- production rates;
- quality indices (e.g. numbers of customer complaints/compliments, and/or percentage of production returned by quality inspection);
- staff turnover;
- sickness/absenteeism rates;
- days lost through industrial action;
- incidence of accidents;
- extent of use of equipment.

In all these cases, absolute targets may be difficult to establish, but variations up or down are likely to be highly significant. Comparisons can be made with national statistics and, better still, similar production groups within the plant or other plants within or possibly without the firm.

Research suggests that all these indices are likely to be linked to morale, although not always in obvious ways – for instance, before a strike, production is likely to drop; afterwards it often rises quite sharply.

The use of quality and production indices underlines the fact that seeking job satisfaction for employees is not mere woolly minded liberalism but a rational strategy for achieving profitability. Naturally, in the end, an evaluation of such schemes must consider the 'bottom line' – high morale and even high productivity can be bought at too high a cost in capital investment and training. However, it is important to observe that a major benefit from the 'informating' approach raised by Zuboff is the possibility that such an approach may generate new and more profitable approaches to the work process. These can generate new products, services and ideas which, in turn, can generate intellectual property to be exploited outside the original workplace.

Following Zuboff we may conclude there is no 'inevitable' impact of IT on jobs – much will depend upon the strategy employed for using the technology. Imaginative and participative strategies for redesigning work may lead not only to greater job satisfaction but also to higher-quality results and new products and services (and hence competitive edge for the organization concerned). Conversely, unimaginative and authoritarian cost-cutting strategies may lead to job dissatisfaction, industrial conflict, low quality and business failure. Still more disastrous, however, will be a do-nothing 'strategy' which will almost certainly lead to no jobs (or profits) for anyone as (possibly overseas) competitors, using the technology, produce better products and services at lower cost!

Exercise 6.1 **Job design and IT**

Scenario

The Yetsan Corporation has recently taken over JM Sales & Personnel and is now planning to install a modern management information and communication system. To generate ideas and discussion, it has appointed two project teams to carry out a feasibility study of the idea. Group A is asked to explore a conventional ('automating') approach to the problem, whilst Group B is asked to consider as unconventional ('informating') an approach as possible, utilizing the same technology.

The corporation is particularly concerned to explore the impact such a system would have on work organization, job descriptions and satisfaction in the branches.

The organization

JM Sales & Personnel is a small group of 20 offices in the South of England working mainly as an employment agency specializing in sales staff. With the recent slump in staff recruitment, however, they have diversified into (a) telephone sales on an agency basis for other organizations, (b) sales of computer software relevant to the sales and personnel areas.

At present the branches are organized on the basis of a branch manager (paid on a fixed salary plus a share of the profits); one or two secretary/receptionists (on hourly wages); several recruitment consultants (on monthly salaries plus an annual bonus related to branch profitability) who interview and place clients seeking employment (numbers depending on the recruitment business the branch does); a variable number of telephone salesmen/women (who are paid relatively low weekly wages and may be on temporary contracts – but who can earn large sums on commission either selling software, or obtaining job vacancies to fill, or selling goods for other companies); an assistant manager normally controls the sales team (paid on a similar basis to the recruitment consultants).

The technology

Each branch already has at least one PC used for word-processing purposes by the secretary/receptionist(s), and some branch managers already employ spreadsheets and have built up databases of some classes of customer. It is envisaged that all branches will be connected via modems to a mini at headquarters, which will host a central corporate database and an electronic mail facility.

Task

Sketch out a report from each project team which should discuss (a) the objectives of the proposed work reorganization, (b) how the members of the work group should be rewarded, (c) the anticipated levels of satisfaction for each job, and (d) the defects of the rival project group's proposal.

Some of the issues you will need to consider include:

- What information will go on the central database?
- Who will have access to the database?
- Should data processing clerks be employed to input data?
- What sort of messages are expected to be sent by electronic mail, and to whom?
- How many terminals? Who will use them?
- Can the system be used to create competitive advantage for the firm?
- Should payment systems and roles be integrated?

Industrial relations and IT

Background: industrial relations and trade unions

The author, as the former chairman of a trade union branch, should perhaps make a declaration of possible bias on this topic.

It is worth observing that not all workplaces are unionized, but all have industrial relations: managers and the workforce must relate to and communicate with each other. However 99 per cent of all UK public sector workplaces are unionized and 54 per cent of larger (25+ employees) plants were still unionized in 1990 despite a decline from 71 per cent in 1984.

Non-union plants have strikes (see Patterson [1960] for a vivid account of an unofficial strike in such an environment); conversely some unionized plants do not. The hosiery industry did not have an official strike for 20 years after the Second World War despite being strongly unionized. The former ETU pioneered non-strike agreements with Nissan and other Japanese employers with UK subsidiaries in which union recognition and equal working conditions for all workers were granted in return for long contracts and compulsory arbitration of disputes.

We need to distinguish between 'shop stewards', or other locally elected workers, holding office in democratic branch organizations and employed officials of national unions. The former are seldom rabid troublemakers and are regarded by most managements as helpful; the latter are much more likely to know and feel the need to attempt to implement national union policy.

The British practice is to have multiple unions in the same workplace ('craft' unions). In the USA and Germany unions are usually organized on an industry-wide basis, whilst in Japan unions frequently organize specific firms. (In the UK in 1990 the average was 2.5 unions active per workplace – Dept of Employment Workplace Industrial Surveys, 1980, 1984, 1991.)

Trades unions and IT: new technology agreements

Despite natural anxieties about possible job losses, no UK trade unions are officially 'against' information technology. Trade unions realize that modernization is inevitable if international competitiveness is to be retained. A number of TU leaders have expressed anxiety about the *lack* of investment in IT by UK industry.

Where unions are strong enough they will attempt to ensure that they are negotiated with (or at least consulted) about changes in working conditions, job security and remuneration affecting their members resulting from the implementation of new technology. They will also have a particular interest in issues affecting union *recognition* by employers.

In some cases formal new technology agreements (NTAs) have been negotiated, either with particular employers or with groups of employers on an industry-wide basis. A national agreement between the TUC and CBI was negotiated by representatives of each, but not agreed to by the members of the CBI. However, existing NTAs are often similar to this draft national agreement.

The sort of issues that these agreements cover, and the likely union objectives relating to them, are summarized in Box 6.10. In practice the extent to which such agreements are implemented is subject to both the relative bargaining strength of the local parties on the ground and recognition by both parties that the changes taking place are such as to merit a formal agreement; for example, local line managers may not realize the implications for industrial relations of what they see as purely technical changes in the production process.

'Closed shops' and 'restrictive practices'?

Despite what the tabloids say, closed shops are quite rare in British industry – ordinary British workers are not as good at this as professionals such as solicitors. A closed shop may aid the introduction of IT by allowing a clear negotiation of the issues with representatives capable of 'delivering'

***Box 6.10* New technology agreements**

Area	*Objective*
Consultation	Involvement of shop stewards/local officials in changes resulting from new technology *in advance* of implementation.
Job security	Guarantee of no compulsory redundancies, compensation for early retirement or voluntary redundancy (in addition to statutory entitlements).
	Retraining opportunities for existing staff and arrangements for redeployment to be agreed.
Manning levels	Maintenance of existing job opportunities, including promotion opportunities.
Safety and conditions	Improvement in physical conditions safeguarding health (e.g. breaks and rotation of jobs to avoid repetitive strain injury etc.).
Pay	Increased reward for greater productivity and responsibility.
Job descriptions/recognition	Where new jobs are created, or existing jobs altered, exactly what are the responsibilities of each worker and clarification of which union is to represent them? (Conflict between unions possible here.)

their members' cooperation. 'Restrictive practices' – narrow and exclusive job definitions, with different jobs organized by different unions and 'make-work' restrictions (unnecessary mates, etc.) – are however clearly incompatible with the flexibility and higher productivity sought through new technology. In such circumstances employers may either have to 'buy out' the existing workforce rather expensively or resort to confrontation – as at Wapping when Rupert Murdoch and the management of the News International group, which publishes *The Times* and other titles, in effect fired and replaced all the members of the craft unions who manned their print shop when they introduced new methods of production. A policy of 'divide and rule', in which one union is offered exclusive negotiating rights in return for cooperation (and perhaps a 'no strike' agreement), may be resorted to.

Winning over the workforce to IT

As suggested above, a sensible trade union organization in a plant, and a formal new technology agreement, may be a positive asset in winning consent for changes involving new technology. This will enable natural fears to be met and a clear picture of what is happening to be communicated to the workforce.

In any case, the workforce will have to operate the new system and its cooperation will be vital to its success so that, regardless of unionization, industrial relations aspects of change must be addressed. Thus the issues referred to above need to be thought through by management and their decisions on them clearly communicated to the workforce if morale is to be maintained.

Hence it may well be wise to trumpet loudly a 'no redundancies' guarantee even in a non-union situation – natural wastage, redeployment and early retirement will often mean that manning levels can be quite swiftly reduced even with such a policy in place.

The problems of designing new job specifications and work group structures have already been discussed – their implications for the future of industrial relations should be obvious. In the short run people need to be reassured on the impact the new arrangements will have on their status and their capacity to do the (new) job – as well as on pay issues. If no communication takes place, rumour (informal networks) will supply (probably unsettling and inaccurate) answers.

Most modern systems methodologies stress the importance of consulting 'the user' in the specification, design, testing and implementation of new systems. This ought to help the acceptance of the new system, providing 'the user' is not thought of merely as the manager of the end-user department rather than the work group which will be created to run the new system.

Ideally, from an industrial relations point of view, the new users should be encouraged to develop a sense of ownership over the new system to see it as the answer to their current problems and to look forward to its implementation. In such circumstances it may even be possible that the user group itself will propose that all the jobs in the new structure be put up for competitive application within the group – as happened with the Commercial Department at Avery Hardoll (a subsidiary of GEC, which makes petrol pumps) (Stowell, n.d.).

Teleworking

With the availability of WANs and high power cheap workstations many and increasing numbers of jobs can be carried out at home. Of 1,000 employers surveyed by Huws (1993) 11.3 per cent employed people who work at home (5.8 per cent 'teleworkers'), and a further 8.4 per cent were considering introducing teleworking. Two main groups of teleworkers exist:

1 A number of small schemes for professional and managerial staff who typically are fully integrated into the company culture, participate in staff training and development, and spend one or two days a week at the main site. Occupations included consultancy, telephone counselling, programming.
2 In contrast a small number of schemes with much larger numbers of staff employed in such areas as data entry, typing, translation, or editorial and research work. These staff were less integrated into the company culture.

Both management and teleworkers were highly satisfied with the arrangement, except for a minority of the second group referred to. However, it should be borne in mind that this was a small largely self-selected group who usually regarded the arrangement as a temporary one.

In the longer run this could be seen as a reversal of the first Industrial Revolution (which led to concentration of workers in urban factories) by the second. It could be seen as likely to undermine existing large communities and values of worker solidarity and to make worse existing trends towards the isolation of people in passive consuming households. Conversely it could be seen as increasing choice and reducing the threat to the environment involved in urbanization and mass commuting.

Gender and IT

Views on sexual inequalities in modern Britain

Almost all jobs in Britain and most developed countries are still predominantly staffed by one sex; with higher paid and higher status jobs done by men. Despite some increases in female representation at the 1997 General Election, this still applies to political positions such as MPs and cabinet ministers. Anglican bishops and Roman Catholic priests are still exclusively male. Figures quoted by Davidson and Cooper (1992) show that whilst the number of women managers has increased in recent years from 20 per cent to 25 per cent, these posts are concentrated at lower levels and in traditionally female areas such as retailing and personnel. Of the million or so *senior* managers only 4 per cent are women, and women represent less than 1 per cent of chief executives.

It is still possible to take the conservative attitude that such inequalities are both natural and desirable – reflecting biological imperatives or even fulfilling God's 'master-plan' for 'mankind'. However, an organization (private or public) which explicitly (or, more likely, implicitly by its inaction) adopts policies reflecting this view will run the risk of antagonizing not only what is still probably a relatively small minority of radical feminists but a majority of moderates on the gender issue who believe that women have a right to decide on their own way of life and to equal treatment in the provision of public services. (For more detailed discussion and references see Tansey, 2000, Ch. 4.) Most private organizations will need to consider that a majority of consumers are female; all public organizations must realize that a majority of the electorate is female. If recruitment to organizational positions is based on sexual discrimination, then logically the best person for the job is not being appointed and efficiency suffers.

Gender and IT as it is

Brosnan and Davidson (1994) found that about a quarter of all people are to some degree 'computerphobic', about 5 per cent severely so – manifesting physiological symptoms such as nausea, dizziness and high blood pressure. Women are more likely than men to show some degree of computer anxiety and much less likely to enrol on computer courses (peak enrolment of women on UK university computer courses was 25 per cent in 1979 declining to 7 per cent in 1990) or know much about them.

Research seems to indicate that this has little to do with physical sexual differences but is associated with socially learned perceptions of masculinity and femininity. Thus in co-educational schools computing is widely regarded as a masculine activity, but this attitude is absent in single-sex schools. It has been suggested that boys tend to 'hog' computer equipment in co-educational schools, and it is clear that aggressive 'zap the alien' computer games are much more popular as a recreation with boys than girls.

Where women do enrol on computer courses they often perform better than men and states of computer anxiety do not seem to translate automatically into worse performance. On the contrary, some researchers have found that in a number of respects women may have a more positive and user-oriented view of computers when they do experience their use.

One potential problem is that computer skills are becoming increasingly essential for managerial positions in society, so that if girls are left to opt out of computer education and training they may be undermining women's chances of achieving equality in society.

Research for the Women Into IT Foundation (Skills & Enterprise Briefing, 1993), based upon 200 women and 200 men working in IT in 43 public and private sector organizations, found that women were in a minority – with only one in seven graduates recruited in 1992.

Recruitment patterns for men and women were similar – but externally recruited men were more likely to have been 'head-hunted', while internally recruited women were more likely to have been approached by their new manager than men but less likely to have been nominated by their old boss.

Four out of five respondents had received some training in the last year (averaging ten days), but although women had less technical backgrounds than men (e.g. only 6 per cent had an engineering background versus 21 per cent of men), fewer of them were receiving further technical training (32 per cent versus 42 per cent).

Most respondents were positive about the career opportunities offered by their organizations, but significantly fewer women felt they had a large say in career decisions made about them (46 per cent compared to 54 per cent).

Organizations appeared to promote science graduates with long service, but women were less likely to be science graduates (61 per cent compared to 74 per cent) and to be long-serving (18 per cent versus 24 per cent).

Management, IT and gender

Women in university IT departments average £2,000 p.a. less in pay, accounting for 18 per cent of all jobs but only 10 per cent of top-graded ones. Digital employ 30 per cent women, but only 14 per cent in management positions (November 1992). They have responded by announcing that they wish to have all job categories with women proportionally represented – including three on the nine-member board (there are none at present). Deborah Higgins (an MBA researcher) attributed under-representation at higher levels to women's exclusion from informal but influential staff circles. At ICL Wendy Mason, personnel manager of the Local Government and Health Division, reports the deliberate creation of a network for women in middle and senior management. She is also the founder of the Women Into IT Foundation (Watkins, 1993).

In the survey reported above (Skills & Enterprise Briefing, 1993), most organizations claimed to have initiatives designed to help women, including:

- women-only training schemes;
- home-based working;
- schemes for returners;
- positive encouragement to apply for training and promotion.

The same source advocated the need for all organizations to consider career development strategies designed to enable men and women to realize their potential, such as:

Access for women
- involve more women IT managers in careers/publicity
- recruitment and promotion criteria should not work against women
- reduce emphasis on science/engineering

Equality of opportunity
- more opportunity for high profile assignments for women
- investigate limited technical training of women
- check organization's reaction to different managerial styles

Getting on
- nominations for promotion should be more open
- improved access to information about career planning, training and promotion
- opportunities for part-timers
- work shadowing of managers' opportunities for women

Retaining high-quality staff
- organizations should consider work/leisure balance
- recognition of career development within jobs.

Management skills and IT

IT personnel as managers

As in all other specialist areas of organizations only a limited amount of promotion is possible by exhibiting technical expertise. Simply being better at writing programs or having greater technical knowledge and expertise may lead to promotion to posts which are primarily concerned with managing human and budgetary resources and with communicating with other parts of the organization. The 'Peter Principle' may prevail – people are promoted up to the point at which they do not perform effectively and are then left marooned in these posts. Arguably IT managers require much the same personality and skills as other managers – but recruiting initially for IT skills may make it unlikely they will have the required characteristics (see p. 199).

Arguably managers of data processing-type departments, employing large numbers of relatively unskilled personnel in more or less routine jobs, may be more like ordinary line managers than those in system-type departments where fellow professionals may respond positively to the perceived technical expertise.

However, the growth of on-line and distributed patterns of working clearly calls for more skills in terms of communication and people management – not to mention organizational politics!

As we saw earlier, the stress for top-level information system managers is increasingly upon delivering a strategic vision in which IT serves the business objectives of the organization. Hence the more senior the IT manager the more he will have in common with the rest of the management team of the organization.

As IT becomes more central to more and more 'line' management jobs, then the list of capabilities which IT and other managers have in common of necessity must grow.

The concept of the 'hybrid manager'

Earl (1989) and the British Computer Society developed the idea of the need for 'hybrid' managers who combined IT and managerial expertise to such a degree that they could ensure the development of an organization which makes best use of the technology. Whilst such managers can be seen as an urgent need in the short term to manage the transformation of organizations with IT, in the long term, given the pervasiveness of the technology, it could be argued that all managers will have to be 'hybrids'.

Briefly the hybrid manager can be seen as combining:

- business knowledge
- IT skills
- organizational leadership capability.

A survey by the British Computer Society found that 82 per cent of their executive members held the view that IT could only be effectively exploited if hybrid managers were in place (Skyrme and Earl, 1990).

Table 6.1 Key competencies for hybrid managers

Competence	Comprising	Critical
Business knowledge	Business fundamentals Functional knowledge Understanding specific firm's business	Business instinct to spot opportunities
Organization-specific knowledge	Familiarity with organization's culture structure and processes Knowing key people and their motivations	Knowing how things are done
IT knowledge and experience	Project management experience Awareness of applications portfolio IT fundamentals Methods and providers	Confidence to ask and challenge
Management	Motivation and communications skills Interpersonal and group skills Change management skills Cognitive skills	Ability to get things done

Source: Earl and Skyrme (1992, 174)

Recruiting hybrid managers

The psychological component

Some thought should be given to the psychological make-up desirable for different types of IT and managerial role. Awad (1988) quotes a study by Lyons (1985) which divides employees on four psychological dimensions:

- Extraversion (E) / Intraversion (I) (i.e. outward looking/inward looking)
- Sensing (S) / Intuitive (N) (i.e. practical and realistic versus creative)
- Thinking (T) / Feeling (F)
- Judging (J) / Perceiving (P) (i.e. planned and orderly versus flexible and adaptive).

Lyons concludes we should appoint:

- Is not Es for programming
- Ss not Ns for maintenance posts
- Ts and Is make good programmers but poor organizers
- Ns and Fs for direct user-contact.

A problem in trying to develop hybrids from IT roles is that recruitment to those roles may have followed explicitly or implicitly the policy of recruiting Ts and Is for programming, then attempting to make managers of them.

The financial/risk component

Real hybrids who have successfully demonstrated the rare combination of qualities required in other organizations are likely to come expensive and are liable to be 'poached' in turn by other organizations. The costs of recruitment may include not only high salaries and possibly frequent recruitment costs but disruption to existing pay relativities within the organization.

Developing hybrid managers

Rather than attempting to import hybrids from outside, a programme to develop them within the organization seems a more promising approach. The great advantage of this is that it may impact upon the general culture and structure of the organization, encouraging cross-fertilization of ideas. The BCS survey quoted above found that 95 per cent of respondents acknowledged that training hybrids must be accompanied by cultural and organizational changes. Other advantages include that it is easier to judge people's suitability for such roles from their everyday performance than at interview.

Such a programme would involve a deliberate assessment of candidates, redeployment of suitable personnel from IT departments to line posts and vice versa, training and education programmes, and rewards and encouragement to initiatives across conventional dividing lines, etc. Clearly this involves the concept of 'career planning' in which alternative career paths must be made available from, say, a programming entry point, satisfactory lines of development being open to those with predominantly technical orientation – perhaps towards a technical consultant status. But where the eventual deployment envisaged is in a 'hybrid' role then recruiters must look for something more like the typical graduate management trainee – extroverts with communication skills.

Robson (1994) is interesting on the risks to the organization and to the individual involved in attempting to develop such policies – but the negative risk of being competitively outflanked must also be borne in mind.

Recommended reading

Bailey, John (1993) *Managing People and Technological Change*, London, Pitman. Good short introduction to the area, with some very relevant case studies.

Braun, Ernest (1998) *Technology in Context: Technology Assessment for Managers*, London, Routledge. Good short guide to the problems of assessing the impact of a new technology on a firm and managing its introduction.

Chmiel, Nik (1998) *Jobs, Technology and People*, London, Routledge. A psychological perspective, strong on team working and safety.

Part III
IT and the environment

7   IT and society

The need for choice

Topics

- The social implications of an information society
- Leisure and the home
- Education and information technology
- Culture and cyberspace
- IT and divisions in society
- Communities and IT
- The physical environment and IT
- Democracy, government and IT
- Information technology in a democratic society

The social implications of an information society

The development of technology is difficult to predict – but how it will be used and what the impact of it will be on society are almost impossible to forecast. As we have seen, it is easy to assume over-optimistically that the most desirable possible scenario will inevitably come about. In the absence of government intervention, the most likely outcome is that market forces will largely determine the use society makes of IT and the impact IT has on society. Inevitably, on this basis, there will be a tendency for the most affluent societies (such as the United States), and the most affluent members of societies (the prosperous and the powerful), to make most use of the technology for their own benefit. Under the impact of market forces such changes – responding to individual consumer demand fostered by profit-maximizing multinational corporations – may have unanticipated effects which affect society as a whole and may cost it dear in terms of environmental effects or the impact on social stability. This chapter attempts to consider some possible effects of this sort and the extent to which they can and should be controlled by government on behalf of the community as a whole in a democratic society.

In this new century it is clear that these problems will not be containable within national boundaries – given the impact of a global economy and global communication networks – so that any action required will inevitably have an international aspect if it is to be effective.

Leisure and the home

In many ways, especially economically, the biggest impact of new information and communication technologies has been in the entertainment industry. Conventional cinema and broadcasting has gradually made increasing use of digital techniques in the preparation of special effects, cartoon features, the processing of news and the like. The net effects of all this, however, are arguably quite small compared with the massive impact of television and similar products on home life and the pattern of leisure activities.

Television, beside creating a multi-billion pound new global industry, has had a massive impact – making the family consumption of leisure industry products in their own home a central feature of social life.

More recently massive investments have been made in the delivery of entertainment to the home, often using digital techniques. Digital CD-ROM has replaced older analogue recording technologies for music, necessitating the wholesale replacement of domestic collections of records and gramophones with hi-fis, Walkmans, and the like. The development of video recorders has enabled families and individuals to decide what entertainment products to consume, and when, to a much greater extent. The provision of cable television, the development of satellite broadcasting, and the conversion of terrestrial, cable and satellite broadcasting to digital technology have all made available a greater choice of television channels at the cost of massive expenditure on infrastructure by the companies concerned (satellites, cables, etc.) and on new receiving equipment by the families concerned.

The reducing real cost of reception equipment, the mushrooming availability of myriads of recordings and multiple broadcast channels, the development of specialist interactive multi-media products such as 'zap it' computer games – appealing to small boys of all ages – has led to a further change: a move from family-group home consumption of entertainment products to individual consumption on different consoles at different times in different rooms (or even on the move).

It is easy to jump to conclusions as to what the social impact of such technological changes must be. Thus critics of television and other home entertainments have decried the decline of community life and creativity implicit in the abandonment of collective and relatively spontaneous local activities such as football clubs, pub sing-songs, allotments and local produce shows in favour of the passive viewing of professional sports, pop-videos and gardening programmes. More recently teenage violence has been blamed upon inappropriate role models offered by pop songs, violent video games and horror films consumed by children unsupervised by their over-indulgent parents. Alternatively (and paradoxically some-times simultaneously), a vision of a new generation of passive, isolated and socially inadequate 'couch potatoes' or 'geeks' has been painted.

There has been much serious research on these issues (e.g. Silverstone and Hirsch, 1994), some of which is much less pessimistic and certainly more complicated in its conclusions than that of the critics referred to above. What is perhaps cheering and fits in with one of the themes of this book is the diversity of use to which domestic technologies are put in dif-ferent homes. Rather than a picture of passive and uniform consumption of pre-digested experiences, much research (for instance that by Ang, Haddon and Wheelock, in Silverstone and Hirsch, 1994) suggests that televisions, microwaves or personal computers can all be used to support radically different lifestyles. The same television programme may be treated as a background filler, the subject of derision, a source of a useful minor piece of information on a topic far removed from its main theme, or as a spur to developing a new interest outside the home. With a sophisticated and multi-purpose piece of technology such as a personal computer, it is almost impossible to predict how it will be treated – as an educational resource for a child, as father's new hobby, or as a business tool for mother.

Education and information technology

In the educational sphere it is clear that the potential for a radical trans-formation of learning using the new technology is as yet unrealized, even in countries such as the United States and the United Kingdom where the use of these technologies is most advanced. In many poorer countries it is possible that the use of IT could help to bridge the educational gap between them and richer areas of the world; but such a project would require an imaginative use of resources by the world community, which is perhaps unlikely in current circumstances. In this section we shall examine the potential use of IT in education and then consider the prob-lems of moving from the present restricted use of the technology to a more full-blooded employment of these resources. Finally we shall con-sider the potentially disruptive effects of such a development.

Modern IT offers the possibility of a learner's paradise in which not only can exciting multi-media educational materials be created, but they can be made to interact with the learner and be available just when and where the learner requires them – anytime, anywhere in the world. The very best teachers can design materials and be available to tutor students anywhere in the world – in person if required. For more advanced students and teachers the resources of the world's libraries could be available elec-tronically on-line and global seminars held to discuss work in progress.

The technical systems already exist to implement such a vision. Con-sider the quality and interest of CD-ROMs already available, such as the

Encarta Encyclopedia, and imagine greater and more coordinated efforts applied to all the basic areas of the curriculum. Materials are already constructed linking text, pictures and video and presented on CD-ROM or websites. Hypertext links can be made available to enable any part of the text to be further explained. Batteries of objective test questions can be made available with which learners can assess themselves (or be assessed by third parties). The British Open University, as we saw in an earlier chapter, already has decades of experience of constructing high-quality learning materials which, in this case, combine written learning modules, broadcast or videoed television programmes, computer-marked objective test questions and, in some cases, on-line tuition and conferencing facilities as well as more conventional methods (Eisenstadt and Vincent, 2000). Already global groups of scholars discuss issues on-line – at present mainly in text-based forums – but videoconferencing facilities are technically possible and used from time to time. Project Gutenberg is steadily making available the texts of more and more classics of world literature and philosophy available on-line, whilst increasingly the contents of museums, archives and specialist libraries are available on the World Wide Web. (The catalogues of all the major academic libraries are already accessible – the texts to which they refer could also technically be made available.)

The advantages of making massive quantities of educational material available globally over the web and reorganizing educational systems so that individual learners can access it more or less as required seem obvious to the author. Much evidence shows that the optimum conditions for learning are when the learner perceives the need for the required information or skill and can use or practise his or her knowledge immediately (Illich, 1976). Global productivity should soar as the latest innovations and techniques become available more rapidly and can be utilized by a better-educated workforce. Hopefully the spread of mutual knowledge and increased communication will enhance international understanding.

A further possibility raised by these uses of technology is that most of such learning could take place in learners' own homes or workplaces. Schools and universities could exist largely as meeting places for such activities as sports and laboratory sessions which require physical contact, and as administrative centres for staff who would, however, largely work from home, like the students.

It is instructive to consider why such developments have been slow to materialize – and may never do so! The obvious barriers to such developments are economic, but in the long run the major barriers may well be social, organizational and political.

The economic barriers include, of course, the need for a massive communications infrastructure linking all educational institutions (or homes), investment in hardware and software for each student and in the development of appropriate educational materials (including scanning the contents of libraries into databases). Although appearing to be an enormous proposition, certainly entailing the expenditure of billions of pounds worldwide, this does not appear to be a major problem in the long term. As we have seen, the infrastructure is likely to be created for entertainment and commercial purposes in any event and, if desired, specific educational expenditure could be justified out of cost savings on premises and staff (fewer should be required since much duplication of effort in course-development and delivery could be saved) and in terms of the greater cost-effectiveness of new-style learning compared with outmoded chalk and talk 'school' methods of learning.

Social barriers are much more likely to be a problem. In particular the 'baby-sitting' functions of the schools system might come to the fore if it was seriously proposed to go over in whole or in part to a system of home learning. Millions of working parents would not be enthused by the prospect of arranging supervision for their children's learning sessions – even though remote surveillance of the children's input to the computer could be set up! From an educational point of view, the ability to work and live in a group is something that is difficult to build into individual distance learning programmes. Another social barrier to the effective implementation of such learning systems is, of course, teachers' concepts of their role and their technical competence to operate such new systems. One reason for the slow adoption of IT in schools and universities is that IT has been seen by most teachers as a technical area to be taught and employed by someone else. Most teachers graduated before computers were seen as an essential learning tool for all students, and relatively little in-service training has been provided in most school systems to remedy this attitude.

Organizational barriers to such a scheme are perhaps too many to list, but they include the important consideration that whilst from a learner's point of view it might be highly desirable to be taught electronically by the best institution in the world – every business student might aspire to an MBA awarded by the Harvard Business School, every classics student might seek an Oxford MA – the rest of the educational world might be less than overjoyed at the prospect of redundancy. Furthermore, elite institutions may wish to retain an exclusive posture and status and to concentrate on research rather than teaching. Legal and financial issues such as copyright and the need to levy fees to finance activities also restrict institutions' willingness to make their learning materials available on the World Wide Web.

Political barriers have been left to last, but they are far from least. We have already seen the resistance which parents, teachers and educational institutions might raise to the changes outlined; these may pale into insignificance to those which politicians and nationalists might endorse. Although it has been suggested that the economic resource problem should not be too large, it is clear that politicians frequently find it difficult to make large expenditures on public facilities. Extra expenditure

Exercise 7.1 **Educational reform**

Before reading on, can you anticipate what problems there might be in realizing the educational 'vision' laid out above?

might involve additional taxes or borrowing – even if, in the longer run, such expenditure may more than justify itself. If the justification involves closing local schools and making some teachers redundant, then the problem would be reinforced.

Still more serious, from the point of view of many politicians, is the loss of control over the curriculum, which the concept of a global educational network involves. Whilst there may be a measure of consensus over the mathematics and physics curriculum worldwide, would fundamentalist politicians in Alabama or Iran be happy to see their biology students learning about evolution in a course from Cambridge or MIT? Still more controversial are matters of history and geography in which a Russian, a Serbian or a Chinese perspective might differ radically from that of a US or a British course.

Finally in this brief consideration of the impact of IT on education we return to the issue of the role of IT in education in poorer countries. Here the case for implementing modern IT-based systems for learning is, if anything, stronger because most (but not all) of these countries have a severe shortage of skilled and knowledgeable teachers, lack adequate conventional educational institutions and could probably achieve a higher benefit from the same expenditure on such resources.

The problems of implementation are, however, much greater, a fundamental problem clearly being the lack of financial resources to make the investment required. Even if the technical kit was directly donated by richer countries, the recipients may lack adequate electricity supplies, and the technical and managerial know-how, to install and maintain such systems. There is a danger that expensive equipment will rust idly away when technologically simpler solutions (e.g. subsidizing school textbook production) might be much more effective. Thus considerable thought needs to be given to ensuring that any information technology introduced is accompanied by skills training and the provision of an adequate supporting infrastructure. However, telecommunications companies from richer countries might be induced to collaborate with donor governments in developing potentially enormous markets in these areas.

As in richer countries political problems may be the biggest obstacle to the use of IT in education. Many politicians may well see proposals to give all their schoolchildren access to the web as a plot to subvert national or religious values. The predominance of English as a language on the web is not only a barrier for users in non-English-speaking countries but may also be seen as a device to undermine a national linguistic, literary and historical heritage. Last, but not least, amongst the perhaps unspoken political objections to the web may be resistance to the democratic values predominant upon the web and the opportunities it presents for free discussion and social and political activism.

Culture and cyberspace

The issues raised in the previous section about the impact of the web on national cultures deserve some further exploration and may perhaps be presented more bluntly. For optimists, the net represents a new stage in the development of human culture. This global culture, existing in 'cyberspace', enables human beings across the planet to share and invent new 'virtual realities', to be free and to communicate via new forms of art, and to collaborate in the development of scientific understanding and new technological developments. For pessimists, the net is one more part of a process whereby American capitalism imposes a commercialized and vulgarized English-speaking culture of pop songs, pornography, block-buster films, jeans, hamburgers and commercial profiteering on a previously much more diverse and culturally sophisticated world. Each side of this argument will be presented and some attempt made to arbitrate, but the final judgement must be left to the reader.

The concept of global civilization, in which 'cyberspace' (the hypothetical electronic reality within which understanding, communication and activity on a global electronic net takes place) is the dominant feature of human culture, was probably first popularized by the science fiction writer William Gibson. He described it as:

> A consensual hallucination experienced daily by billions of legitimate operators, in every nation, by children being taught mathematical concepts ... A graphic representation of data abstracted from the banks of every computer in the human system. Unthinkable complexity ...
>
> (Gibson, 1984, 67)

His novels are interesting in being far from 'computopias' (see p. 225). The future society dominated by the net is, in some respects, far from ideal, being still full of conflict, inequality, violence and subject to the power of large corporations. But it is a future in which technical knowledge and competence leads to personal power and effectiveness: the individual can make a difference. It is also a future in which national boundaries and geography seem of very limited importance.

In the future it seems likely that most people (in the richer parts of the world at least) will spend most of their day learning or working at a computer and also spend much of their leisure time interacting with computers or television monitors. If all these monitors are basically part of a global net using similar software and drawing upon a more or less common pool of data, then the social and cultural implications of all this seem both undeniably large and difficult to predict.

Commentators such as Rheinghold (1992) have stressed the potential importance of 'virtual reality' technologies. Three-dimensional graphic depictions of reality can be made to interact with one or more human participants, perhaps through specially designed helmets (which enable the display to respond to the participant's angle of vision) and gloves, or a joystick which enables participants to manipulate imaginary objects in the display. Most readers will have played computer games, which work on similar principles. At their most realistic such technologies have been used to train firemen, astronauts and pilots to respond to life-like emergencies on simulations of actual equipment. (Viewers of *Star Trek* will be familiar with the 'Holodeck' in which the crew interact with computer holograms indistinguishable from reality – perhaps the ultimate expression of this idea.) The more interactive and realistic computer data is, arguably the more addictive it becomes, and the less easy it is for participants in the system to distinguish 'reality' from the contents of the screens before them. Conversely this type of presentation of data is undoubtedly effective in conveying an understanding of alien situations or the principles behind dynamic models.

In the arts 'video installations' have already sold for large sums in art galleries. Computer-generated graphics and special effects play an increasing role in the presentation of films and television programmes. Just as photography became accepted as an art form and immensely influenced other graphic arts in the nineteenth century, so it is to be expected that computer-generated displays will both influence art and be seen as a legitimate and major form of artistic expression in the twenty-first century. The use of mathematically generated 'fractal' displays has already proved influential. Already electronically generated music is seen as a legitimate part of both popular and serious music. There have been suggestions that the great artists of the twenty-first century will be computer 'games' designers. Indeed the distinction between film and computer game may well disappear as the century progresses, and each member of the 'audience' will be able to 'customize' many imaginative interactive audio-visual presentations by (for instance) language, background, desired main characters, and preferred outcome. (Already DVD film tracks are produced in multiple language versions and can be indexed and accessed in various ways rather than merely played straight through.)

The use of the net in academic enquiry and debate has already been referred to. It can also be used to generate collaborative research teams (perhaps dispersed across the globe) to mount new enquiries, and to publicize new scientific discoveries and technological innovations. For that matter there are many 'alt.' (=alternative) discussion groups which seek to discuss and perhaps develop new forms of social cooperation. Hence it is possible enthusiastically to endorse the development of cyberspace as the herald of a new global society in which enlightened individuals from across the globe cooperate in a democratic (if not anarchic) fashion to build a better life for all. The academic origins of the Internet and its growth in the hands of well-intentioned private hobbyists has helped to generate an individualistic and optimistic 'net-culture' to which we referred earlier (Chapter 4). It is natural to envisage the growth of the net as bringing about more of the same – individualism and creativity thriving across the globe.

However, it is possible to be much less optimistic about the likely future of the net if we consider that it is now moving into a new era of commercialization. As we have seen, the driver towards a massive expansion of the net in the twenty-first century is likely to be the prospect of profit from e-commerce. Particularly as far as ordinary individuals are concerned, they are likely to be interactive users only in the sense of using the net for electronic shopping and downloading entertainment (which may be interactive in a rather pre-programmed sense). Already the most visited site on the Internet has been said to be *Playboy* magazine's. In the future it seems likely that supermarket sites, such as the one Britain's huge Tesco chain is already operating, will be the most used on the web, perhaps contributing to the downfall of small 'craft' producers and retailers.

The great majority of Internet users and sites are, at present, American. This dominance seems unlikely to change in the foreseeable future. The slickest and often most useful and entertaining websites tend to be commercial US enterprises selling US-branded consumer goods and US cultural goods – videos, films, books. As with the worldwide film industry, the US industry can invest larger sums in development than any other because of the size of their home market, and then export at virtually zero additional cost. In the sphere of information goods the US is at a considerable advantage over most European countries and Japan because (US) English is the world's leading second language and the language of aerospace, computing, pop music and international commerce.

Consider the USA's success in dominating broadcast media, publishing, and international finance, in dictating world teenage fashions and lifestyles, as well as its diplomatic and military predominance. It is easy to see why intellectuals in France, Islamic clerics in Iran, and any number of Third World dictators should suspect that the Internet is a tool of American cultural imperialism. To many, the freedom, individualism and increasing commercialism of the net seem to indicate not so much an indication of a new world order but the export of characteristically American values to an unwilling world.

Summarizing the likely cultural impact of the Internet and IT in general is a difficult task. In line with a frequent theme within this book, however, it is worth emphasizing that no outcome of technical change is inevitable or totally predictable. The policy decisions of governments and the ingenuity of groups and individuals may discover undreamed of opportunities latent in current technologies. New technological advances may easily undo the many assumptions behind the preceding discussion. What is clear is that IT will inevitably change how people all over the world understand reality and create opportunities to change that reality. The more individuals and organizations grasp the nature of the technology and its possibilities, the greater the probability they can influence the direction of change. A modest hope is that increased communication and a greater pooling of information should in the long run make it easier for people, organizations and states to reach, if not a consensus on what should be done, at least informed compromises on how to live together.

IT and divisions in society

One aspect of the impact of IT on communities which raises some controversial issues is the extent to which it can be seen as promoting or reducing existing divisions in society. These include economic divisions between rich and poor and social divisions between genders, ethnic groups (e.g. people of different national origins or religion) and races.

An optimistic view of this is that information technology, by definition, promotes communication between people and must therefore help to spread social and international understanding. People who are thousands of miles apart, either literally or socially speaking, can communicate through 'chat' groups, bulletin boards or e-mail; they can obtain information on different ways of life through World Wide Web sites and even experience the 'virtual reality' of other ways of life through interactive programs. More efficient production using IT creates more wealth which can be shared amongst all the groups concerned. It can thus be argued that the technology has a built-in bias in favour of reducing social and economic divisions.

Until recently, most communication using IT has been through the exchange of text unaccompanied by images of the senders, so that it has been possible for dialogues frequently to take place between individuals unaware of the race, national origin, religion or gender of the other participants. Indeed it has been a fairly frequent practice in some contexts for participants to misrepresent their age, sex or other social characteristics and thus to some extent experience the world (or cyberspace at any rate) from a radically different perspective to their own. While such behaviour may or may not be justifiable, it certainly enhances the idea that the web is open to everyone regardless of social background!

This rosy view of technology superseding social divisions must, alas, be seriously modified on further reflection. In particular it should not be assumed without question that the exchange of information must necessarily promote understanding. The proliferation of racist websites and the use of the web to organize extremist political action illustrate the possibilities for the use of the technology to make social divisions worse rather than less significant. As multi-media methods of communication replace text (e.g. videoconferencing rather than bulletin boards), the social anonymity of exchanges may well be severely reduced.

The apparent degree of democratic interaction on the web should not mislead us into thinking that everyone can participate equally in using IT. It has to be understood that access to modern technologies is at present restricted to a relatively small minority of the earth's inhabitants – what sociologists would term an 'elite'. Tables 7.1 and 7.2 illustrate the point graphically in global terms.

From Table 7.1 we can see that a Finn or an American is much more likely to have access to the web (and similar technologies) than a Chinese or a Nigerian. In global terms citizens of rich technologically advanced countries are at an advantage over those of the 'South'. Even within richer countries there may well be areas and groups with conspicuously different access to information technology. Thus whilst roughly 90 per cent of UK households have telephones, access to this fairly elementary form of communication technology falls to less than 50 per cent in many urban working class 'council estate' areas. More affluent households – especially those containing younger graduates – are much more likely to own a computer and/or have web access.

Table 7.1 Web users, by language

Language	Numbers with Internet access (millions)	World on-line Population (%)	Percentage of language speakers on-line
English	218	45	43
Non-English	266	55	5
Chinese	41	8	5
Finnish	2	Negligible	45

Source: Global Reach (June 2001)

Table 7.2 Net users on-line by area, December 2000

Area	Net users (millions)	Users as approximate % of population
World	419	7
Africa	3	0.005
Asia/Pacific	105	3
Europe	114	16
Middle East	2	1
USA and Canada	178	62
Latin America	16	5

Sources: NUA Internet Surveys (2001); col. 3, author's calculations

Whilst the increasing wealth brought about by the use of information technology can be used to reduce economic and social divisions, in contemporary capitalism, however, this seems unlikely to occur by the operation of market forces. In the absence of state intervention it seems likely, as we have seen earlier, that the 'winners' in a process of economic competition based upon technological innovation will be highly educated entrepreneurial figures like Bill Gates or existing large multinational corporations. Affluent, technologically advanced areas like the 'silicon valleys' of California and south-east England, may find themselves in a situation of almost continuous boom and full employment whilst less fortunate former heavy industrial areas in the same economy are still frequently in the depths of recession.

The extent to which the government should intervene to ensure that the gap between the 'information rich' and 'information poor' is reduced, if not eliminated, is to some extent a matter of political ideology. If, however, we assume some commitment to ideas of equality of opportunity, then as IT becomes more and more important to education it seems reasonable to advocate that the government should at least ensure that all school children have good access to this important educational resource. This might mean not only provision of substantial Internet access and computing facilities at school but the availability of these for homework – perhaps through supervised evening sessions at schools in less affluent areas, or free computing facilities for children in public libraries or community centres.

If, as the UK government has now pledged to do, all public services are made freely available on the net, then it would seem undemocratic not to make the means of access to taxpayer-financed services available to all taxpayers. This would imply a considerable expansion in the availability of net access – again through public libraries and community centres, and perhaps bank ATMs and special terminals in shopping malls and other public areas.

Of course it is possible that the expansion of cheap digital television on a commercial basis may make some of these measures unnecessary in the medium term.

Communities and IT

In Chapter 6 we discussed teleworking from the point of view of firms and, to some extent, individual employees. Earlier still we saw how the impact of IT on the geographical distribution of employment could be seen as a reversal of the first Industrial Revolution (which led to concentration of workers in urban factories) by the second. In this section we consider the cumulative impact which teleworking and the concentration of educational and leisure activities in the home might have on community life, and whether there are more positive ways in which IT can be used to develop, rather than destroy, the lives of local communities.

IT could be seen as likely to undermine existing local communities (especially cities) and older values of worker solidarity and to make worse existing trends towards the isolation of people in passive consuming households. Conversely they could be seen as increasing choice and offering a technology which enables more people to cooperate and interact in ways previously unthought of.

The increasing availability of sophisticated (including interactive multimedia) entertainment and education (and a blend of the two) is arguably of enormous social importance. Current cases of a minority of adolescents addicted to video-games may pale into insignificance compared with the possible future implications. A combination of more attractive home entertainment, the conversion of school learning to home learning, and perceived violence and danger outside the home (possibly also lower levels of employment and shorter working hours for most workers and higher energy costs discouraging travel) may lead to still further 'privatization' of communal life with unpredictable consequences for future social behaviour.

On a more positive note it has been suggested that, rather than being a threat to local communities, the creation of electronic links between households and/or local organizations and creating public access points in libraries, shopping and community centres, could revitalize rather than undermine local communities. Morino Institute (1994), Schuler (1996) and others in the Community Networking movement in the USA suggest a number of objectives to which local community networks (LCN) may contribute positively.

Community cohesion may actually be enhanced by facilitating communications between individuals within the community through local bulletin boards and e-mail facilities and encouraging the development of voluntary associations by publicizing their activities. Public access terminals may make resources available to deprived neighbourhoods.

Health information – including on-line advice – can be provided through electronic media. Support can be given to the ill and the disabled and their carers by matching volunteers to those in need and enabling those affected by particular conditions to form self-help groups (Box 7.1).

Local educational provision can be improved by the provision of databases of educational and training opportunities, publicizing the catchment areas of schools and organizing on-line tuition, seminars and information sources. Local archives can be placed on-line. The use of such systems may increase employability through familiarizing older residents with IT.

Citizen information and participation is an important objective of many of these systems giving information on government activities and sources through bulletin boards, discussion forums, and providing e-mail facilities to contact elected representatives.

In addition a number of municipal initiatives in the UK and elsewhere

Case Study 7.1 Spinal muscular atrophy: self-help on the web

Spinal muscular atrophy

Spinal muscular atrophy is an inherited neuromuscular condition causing weakness of the muscles. Approximately 1 in 50 people are carriers of the defective gene which can bring about the disease. Since both parents of a child must be carriers, and, even then, there is only a 1 in 4 chance of a child being affected, the incidence of the disease is about 1 in every 10,000 births. In the most serious cases of the condition (type 1) babies affected do not usually survive their first birthday as they develop breathing difficulties which undermine their capacity to resist respiratory diseases. However, those less severely affected may be able to walk and attain a normal lifespan.

Since the condition is relatively uncommon, many general practitioners and hospital staff are unfamiliar with it. Equally, the parents of an affected baby are unlikely to meet other parents in their local community in the same position.

In this situation the websites run by voluntary associations composed mainly of relatives of sufferers from the condition perform an invaluable role. In Britain the Jennifer Trust for Spinal Muscular Atrophy (http://www.jtsma.org.uk) and in the United States Families of SMA (http://www.fsma.org) have constructed informative sites which contain detailed information and case histories which can help to inform and, in some cases, reassure families and those affected. Both organizations can then put affected families in touch with each other to provide mutual aid and comfort, as well as offering telephone counselling and a library of loan equipment, including suction machines and suitable toys.

Through the websites information on ongoing research into the condition is available, and news of fund-raising activities to finance research and the associations' support activities is disseminated.

On a local level, websites have been constructed to publicize and organize fund-raising events. For instance, the illustrated site (Box 7.1) http://www.onyerbikes.co.uk was constructed in July/August 2001 to publicize and organize a sponsored bike ride through the picturesque New Forest in the South of England. Knowledge of the site was spread by e-mails to friends and friends of friends and through a number of large local employers' intranets. Over £12,000 was raised for the JTSMA and consciousness of the condition was raised amongst the general public. A follow-up event is likely to be organized from the same site in 2002.

Box 7.1 OnyerBikes: fund-raising through the web

have emphasized the possible employment objectives of such systems. Provision of a sophisticated information infrastructure has been shown to attract inward investment to areas. Many municipal websites concentrate on advertising the attractions of the area to external potential investors; they may also be used to encourage tourism – thus increasing local employment.

As we shall discuss in more detail later, local-government-sponsored systems are increasingly stressing improved public service delivery.

A study by Schuler (1996) shows that most community networks are sponsored by local authorities; in a few cases universities have sponsored local community networks alone, but more frequently they are important co-sponsors with local government, bringing technical expertise and web access. Various national and international voluntary associations are also important sources of advice and ideas. British Telecom has recently launched a local trial of a series of added value resources (including video-on-demand), which also included some local information. A number of 'virtual city' websites are basically commercial ventures sponsored by companies with varying degrees of support from local authorities. Bristol has had five separate 'virtual Bristols', only one of which is municipal in origin!

Within local authorities different departments or power centres may manifest different degrees of enthusiasm. At one extreme an education or library department may mount a virtually solo effort – which may then be likely to be a passive database of (perhaps ageing) data. At the other extreme a project may represent a high-level political initiative to improve and decentralize customer service for all citizens or inhabitants of a key development area. The latter seems rare to date, with most schemes being of an intermediate type involving a keen project champion from one departmental home-base seeking alliances across and without the organization.

Clearly financial issues loom large in determining the shape and extent of such a system. If they are heavily involved in delivering large-scale public services they may involve large capital expenditure, require high-level political support in the area and have to be justified in today's political climate by cost savings or clear political and social benefits. Other approaches may be relatively inexpensive but can generate unacceptable levels of demand for expensive services.

In principle such networks can be financed in a wide variety of ways – but some of these might work against the objectives of such systems. Cisler (1993) and others suggest that the main sources are general local government revenue, local educational/health/training funds, European/national/federal grants, business sponsorship, advertising revenue and user charges. (The national lottery might be an additional source in the UK.)

The case for public funding is obviously that local community networks are attempting to realize many conventional public sector objectives which are otherwise financed from revenue; avoiding user charges encourages all sections of the community to access the system, which is clearly necessary for building links to deprived sections of the community; educating children who may not have independent financial resources, etc. Commercial sponsorship and advertising may lessen the credibility of independent advice on the system and/or bias the content in the direction of entertainment or consumption.

It is possible, however, to combine free access from public libraries, schools, council offices and even shopping malls with paid-for access from private homes and business. Similarly publicly available databases can be sold commercially in different formats (e.g. CD-ROM or print).

Given the continuing constraints on public sector investment and the trend towards 'enabling authorities' who commission and monitor services on behalf of the public, a likely route for the development of local community networks may be for authorities to bargain with commercial information providers to provide the services they require on a PFI (pay as you go)/public relations basis. In the USA, state and local government may be in a stronger position to bargain in that they may be in a regulatory position *vis-à-vis* the commercial providers (e.g. 'You can dig up our streets in return for free services to libraries and schools'). Unfortunately, in recent years the UK central government has given little attention to these issues in its relationships with BT and the cable companies.

Case Study 7.2 **Some unusual US local community networks**

1 Community Memory of Berkeley California is notable for its creative approach to funding with many public access terminals which are free to read but cost 25 cents to contribute to a forum, or a dollar to start a new one. It stresses open access and community training schemes. The 'Almeda County Veterans' Memorial Project' contains information upon every deceased local veteran.

2 Big Sky Telegraph in Montana is a university-sponsored effort to use low-cost modern technology to overcome the problems of the isolation of small schools in a sparsely populated rural area. Over 600 lesson plans are available through a 'telecurricular clearing house'.

3 Electronic Café International in Santa Monica, California has linked a variety of restaurants for cultural events. Using slow-scan television over voice-grade telephone lines a shared video, audio, text and 'sketch' area has been created.

Source: Schuler (1996)

Case Study 7.3 **Digital Amsterdam**

Digital Amsterdam has adopted the practice pioneered by US Free-Nets of adopting a city metaphor to orient users. Operating in Dutch and English on the Internet, it has attracted over 100,000 registered virtual inhabitants from all over the world, as well as thousands of visitors a day. About 200 mostly non-profit providers arranged in a variety of 'squares' offer mainly cultural, travel and political information.

Initially government-financed, digital Amsterdam is now run by a non-profit foundation and supports itself largely by charging information providers. 'Citizenship', including the hosting of a house or homepage and e-mail facilities, is free to anyone.

The digital city offers a variety of opportunities for interaction, including the hosting of over a hundred discussion groups on cultural, leisure and civic affairs.

There are 50 public terminals available, whilst the claim is that a high proportion of Amsterdam inhabitants have access to modems at home or at work. However, surveys indicate that 'inhabitants' are predominantly young, male and relatively affluent.

Source: Francissen and Brants,
in Tsagarousianou *et al.* (1998)

The variety of such networks is difficult to convey. A good international selection of case studies is to be found in Tsagarousianou *et al.* (1998) which includes a description of several European examples. Readers are urged to log on for themselves!

The physical environment and IT

A consideration of the impact of information technology on the physical environment is particularly relevant to two of the themes of this book: the first is the interaction of systems of different kinds; the second is the need to manage such interactions by making appropriate strategic choices.

In many systems theories 'the environment' is simply everything outside the group of objects that it has been decided to analyse as an interacting group (e.g. Easton, 1979, Ch. 1); in this section, however, we mean something nearer common usage in that we are concerned with what may perhaps be best described as the biosphere – that is, the other animals, plants, atmosphere, oceans and major physical features of the planet. One is tempted to say those parts of our collective existence which are not man-made – but this would be to underestimate humanity's previous impact on the planet. The landscape of the United Kingdom, for instance, is largely an artefact in that virtually all features are the products of human intervention (hedges and fields, and even forests and heaths). Even such an apparently 'wild' landscape as the Sahara is thought to be as it is because of human activity – it is largely the dustbowl product of attempts in Roman times to grow unsuitable cereal crops. The Sahara is expanding still because of the greenhouse effect of excessive consumption of fossil fuels. The animal population of the planet consists of those remnants of the original species which have survived the changes in environment wrought by humans, and have not been hunted or fished to destruction. There are theorists who regard the biosphere 'Gaia' as a homeostatic (self-righting) system (Lovelock, 1979), but these are a minority of optimists.

In considering the environmental impact of a product, service, or technology it is necessary to consider all stages of its employment. In this case we should consider the manufacture and distribution of the hardware and software; the installation of the required infrastructure; the direct and indirect consequences of use, and the costs of disposal.

The direct costs of manufacture are probably the least significant of these factors. Certainly producing software seems one of the most environmentally harmless activities imaginable since it is mainly done by sitting and thinking and can be done almost anywhere. The product is embodied in a disk composed of some of the commoner materials on the planet in very small quantities. Any direct environmental impact of manufacturing is a small part of that of using the technology generally – mainly the use of electrical energy and hardware. (Electrical energy is still mainly obtained from fossil fuels and is therefore potentially a contributor to the greenhouse effect.)

The production of hardware is, on the whole, similar to most manufacturing operations. The production of chips is somewhat exceptional in that it takes place in an ultra-clean, purpose-designed factory usually built on a greenfield site with global production concentrated in one place which is, at the time of construction, presumably the most cost-effective location on earth. Ultra-clean factory environments are paradoxically rather environmentally destructive since air conditioning and similar measures use a lot of energy. Since these factories often have a life of only a year or two they are certainly conducted on the opposite of the 'green' principles of long-term sustainability. The major problem with hardware production is the global pattern of production described in earlier chapters. There is much air-freighting of components from one continent to another. (Sending some components by ship would mean they would be obsolete on arrival!) This, in turn, involves consuming much fossil fuel, leading to atmospheric pollution. However, to be fair, many of the air-freighted components are not very bulky.

Probably the major direct environmental costs of IT involve the installation of network infrastructure. Cables involve the use of large quantities of metals, which have to be mined and refined, and the digging up of millions of miles of trenches. The energy cost of the digging is high. In many cities large numbers of tree roots have been damaged by hasty TV cabling activity – reducing the absorption of carbon dioxide and the attractiveness of previously tree-lined avenues. Broadcast systems may be less costly in energy, but may involve the erection of many unsightly (and possibly unhealthy) masts, or the launching of satellites with unknown risks to the stratosphere and huge fuel costs per launch.

Most discussion of the environmental impact of IT has focused upon possible unhealthy electromagnetic emissions and the energy costs of monitors. Certainly, as we have seen, the safety of monitors should be investigated by users, and the habit of leaving machines always switched on discouraged; but these are probably minor issues compared with the indirect effects of IT.

The indirect effects are undoubtedly important but difficult to estimate. For instance, is IT contributing to a high-consumption, throw-away society by spreading the values of the globe's most wasteful society (the USA) more widely? An industry in which obsolescence is normal after a year or two seems to encourage a throw-away approach to consumer goods. However, the messages about the possibility and desirability of affluence, carried worldwide by the technology, may be even more potent in promoting such attitudes. Alternatively, IT might help to reduce wasteful consumption by offering low-cost and superior substitutes for environmentally suspect activities such as tourism and commuting, and by reducing the threat to the environment involved in urbanization and mass commuting.

Democracy, government and IT

Most people in Britain have only the vaguest idea of what is meant by democracy. Some may vaguely remember President Lincoln's definition – 'Government of the people, by the people, for the people' – but would be amazed to learn that even the old-style communists in the former Soviet Union claimed to be practising democracy in this sense of government by, and in the interests of, the majority!

Without trying to define formally what democracy means, or to establish its desirability, I am going to assume it is a 'good thing' and that it involves not just majority rule but, among other things, two key principles: government by discussion and respect for individual rights. To illustrate this, suppose a lecturer proposed that one member of the class be thrown under a car, and the majority of the class, disliking him or her, immediately did so – few would accept that, desirable or not, the action had at least been democratic!

Information and democracy

If the two principles suggested are accepted, then it follows there is a very strong relationship between a government's attitudes to information and whether it is democratic or not.

In terms of 'government by discussion', this can only make sense if people are free to obtain the information upon which decisions are based, and know about decisions which are taken which affect them in time to do something about the decision. You could also reasonably argue that discussion can only be effective if people have been educated to assess the information and arguments that are offered to them. (This idea of a right to education is, in fact, embodied in the United Nations Declaration of Human Rights.)

A number of writers on information science argue that there is a hierarchy of 'data, information, knowledge, wisdom'. This implies that not only do the facts have to be available, but that they must be debated and interpreted to be useful.

In terms of 'respect for individual rights' many of the same ideas apply. We can particularly pick out, in terms of information, people's right to express their own ideas and, conversely, to have their privacy respected.

Thus most democracies have some sort of constitutional statement of the rights of the individual (including freedom of speech), and democracies such as the United States and Sweden go further by accepting the idea of freedom of information as central to democracy. In both these countries the statutory principle is that a citizen has the right to know what his or her government is doing and that all government documents will normally be open for inspection. (Exceptions to this have to be justified.)

In contrast, in Britain the principle relating to government documents traditionally has been that everything is an official secret unless it is cleared for release. A non-statutory Code of Practice on Access to Government Information, introduced by the Conservatives in April 1994, rather half-heartedly moved the UK in the open government direction. The Code allowed for numerous exceptions – including advice to ministers and anything that could be the subject of a public enquiry. Much controversy has surrounded the New Labour government's Freedom of Information Act (2000), which was heavily criticized as little, if at all, stronger than the Code. At least the statutory basis of the new arrangement makes access to government information a right of the citizen, rather than a concession by the executive, although, at the time of writing, it seems the government is likely to postpone its implementation to the last possible date.

Information technology and the state

Fundamentally, as Youeji Masuda points out in an article on 'Computopia', governments and societies can use the potential of information technology either to liberate or control the individuals within it (Forester, 1985). Thus with everyone offered free access to sophisticated information acquisition and processing systems, a democratic 'Computopia' may be established in which ordinary individuals possess more information than the most sophisticated Prime Ministers could have twenty or thirty years ago.

The opposite possibility – what Masuda calls the 'automated state' – is to mobilize the power of IT on behalf of state control and surveillance of its citizens. In 1948, George Orwell's idea of television sets in every household which could also monitor every household's activities (in the novel *Nineteen Eighty-Four*) seemed like a fantasy. Now that GCHQ is apparently monitoring all satellite-based international telephone calls, virtually all domestic financial transactions are recorded in banks' computer systems (from which they could, at least, be extracted), whilst developments in road traffic control may well mean individual vehicle movements will also become centrally available over the next few years. The potential for central monitoring and control is disturbing to say the least.

The possible relationships between IT and types of government can be illustrated in another way: why were PCs a rarity in the former Soviet Union? Partly for the same reason that all duplicators and Xerox machines were registered with the KGB: individual citizens were not trusted by the Party with such information processing power. Decentralized information technology is a powerful force for democracy. But it can be argued that centralized information technology is as potentially destructive (literally in the case of the sort of 'Star Wars' technology deployed in the Gulf).

Information technology and democratic government

The argument is, then, that IT is a powerful tool which must be harnessed by, rather than against, democratic government. But, as has also been said, the price of liberty is eternal vigilance.

The sinister possibilities of the use of IT in the surveillance of the population and for warfare (always described as 'defence' when employed by our side!) have been already touched upon. Two other major uses of IT in government will be briefly considered. The first is IT's relevance to the process of electing and controlling a government, the second is its use in administering large-scale programmes such as social security or taxation.

As far as electing and controlling governments are concerned, information technology has already made a large contribution, but a still greater impact is entirely possible.

Already in many parts of the USA complicated multi-candidate elections are routinely conducted using 'voting machines' which should (despite the unfortunate example of the presidential election of 2000!) enable a speedy and accurate tally of the result to be made. More significantly, the whole electoral process has been transformed by the nationwide availability of information on television. Not only are presidential elections arguably decided by debates between the major candidates, but most US electoral campaigns now are basically electronic media events – with slick ten-second paid TV advertisements currently figuring largely in most successful candidates' strategies. In addition the selective-mailshot (also the product of IT) has come to figure largely in the financing and tailoring of campaigns to particular constituencies of voters. The strategy and tactics of campaigns are also largely conditioned by computerized statistical analysis based upon opinion surveys (which also would be virtually impossible to conduct without computers). Finally, of course, the results of campaigns will be announced in advance with computerized graphics on television as the result of exit polls made possible by the same technology. These phenomena are clearly spreading to the rest of the democratic world. (Just as competitive party democracy is also, hopefully, spreading across the world as never before.)

It can be argued that opinion polls are also making a contribution to controlling the actions of governments by making them aware of public reactions to their policies with greater accuracy and rapidity.

Potentially the impact of IT on democratic procedures goes much further than this since, in principle, the technology exists to enable the issues to be explained to all voters over television and for them to respond in a series of 'electronic referenda'. This has already been tried on a local level in the United States, whilst the UK readers will all be familiar with similar techniques used to vote for pop songs, films or talent show contestants.

The question arises, however, as to whether all this constitutes the development of a modern 'super-democracy' (re-enacting the old Greek idea of democracy in which all citizens vote directly on the issues), or whether, in practice, this enables the forms of democracy to be combined with a manipulation of public opinion by the rich and powerful in society. If access to the mass media is open only to those who can pay for it (along with a similar control over the technology of campaigning), then a superficial popular 'chat-show' style of pretend participation may hide a failure to expose the real issues critically.

Turning now to the government's output of services to citizens, similar problems may also apply. IT has already been extensively employed by the public services, although less by the civilian parts of the government than by the armed forces (and to some extent the police). Relatively well-known examples include DVLA at Swansea, the payment of child allowances, and, at present in progress, massive projects relating to the computerization of social security and income tax.

Again it can be argued that computerization is highly desirable in ensuring an efficient, economical, fast and fair service to clients of the public agency concerned. With a computerized system, like cases can be treated alike, right across the country. Data on millions of people in the National Insurance or tax system seem an obvious candidate for treatment via an automated database. Just as private insurance companies and accountants are now extensively computerized, the same might be expected for public insurance or accounts systems. In their evidence to a Select Committee enquiry, IBM argued that the public sector is behind equivalent private employers in these respects (House of Commons Industry Committee, 1988–9).

Is this process of computerization a politically neutral one? IBM in their evidence criticized the way in which, so far, the Civil Service has merely attempted to do the same thing more economically with computers. Insufficient attention has been given to the possibility of giving better service using the potential of the technology. One of the problems then becomes that from an industrial point of view such exercises look to be merely concerned with job cutting – and this has certainly caused problems with the social security project. It also seems that an obsession with cost-cutting computerization has led to some of the recent reforms in social security which have reduced the flexibility with which clients are dealt with. Such an approach may end in alienating both workforce and clients by reducing the whole process to a soulless and remote form-processing operation.

However, a more imaginative use of IT could, in contrast, help to humanize and improve administrative processes. For instance, there is much evidence that current social security decisions are frequently wrong in terms of the statutes because the regulations are very complicated, the workforce overstretched and the clients ill-informed. The use of intelligent systems, in which clients interacted direct with a user-friendly terminal, could well help to give a better service (but probably it would cost more because more clients would get the benefits they are entitled to).

Similarly it has been suggested that a 'negative income tax' scheme could only be implemented when both social security and income tax have been computerized – but that it would result in a much fairer benefits/tax system.

Another potential benefit from the imaginative use of IT would be the establishment of 'one-stop' service points from which all government agencies could be interacted with. The Highlands and Islands Council LAMDA project (50 per cent financed by the EU) is a pilot for this sort of operation. It provides a database of information, including video clips, on-screen completion of appropriate forms, and a videophone link with various government agencies.

In summary a democratic welfare state can be improved – or dehumanized – with the aid of information technology.

Information technology in a democratic society

There are many broader issues relating to what might be termed the democratic social use of information technology. A common theme in relation to these issues might, however, be that in a democracy ordinary people should, as Apple Macintosh computers would put it, be 'empowered' by the technology rather than being its passive objects or victims.

Not being a victim involves not only data protection in the rather narrow sense current UK law gives to it, but also rights to privacy and freedom of information (briefly referred to on pp. 224–5), and possibly some sort of right to reply in the increasingly varied media.

More positively, if people are to have access to the power made possible by the technology, then positive steps to this end seem necessary. First and foremost in this respect is a requirement to ensure that everyone has the educational and training opportunities to enable them to use IT. After this, imaginative government initiatives may help to create a mass understanding of, and market for, the technology. A good example of the sort of thing that can be done is the French initiative in using an electronic database (Minitel) as the standard telephone directory facility. Compare the UK approach which has led to the wasting away of Prestel (a similar electronic database system provided by British Telecom) and 'commercial' charging for directory enquiries.

It seems a paradox that the UK should have the largest home micro market in the world, but that all this individual interest, knowledge and enthusiasm is not being channelled into economically and socially constructive channels. Without offering any 'solution' at this stage, it does seem that there must be scope for imaginative policy-making in this respect.

Unfortunately in recent years in the UK a (correct) understanding of the crucial economic and competitive importance of information has led to the (incorrect) idea that information is a commodity to be charged for at the maximum possible price, like any other. This fails to appreciate that, particularly from the point of view of society as a whole, information is a 'public good' (like a bridge) – that is, one person 'consuming' it does not prevent someone else from doing so, and that the cost of producing it is best capitalized upon by encouraging its consumption for the public benefit.

Conclusion

The conclusion, therefore, is that information technology will neither automatically ensure democracy nor undermine it. However, this does not mean that as democrats we can safely ignore IT. The impact of IT on democracy will depend on the choices that are made as to how such technology is employed.

These 'choices' may be made by big business or individuals in ignorance of, or ignoring, their impact on the rest of society. It may simply be that no one will make a conscious choice on some issues, but that as a result of choice, or failure to consider alternatives, one future for democracy rather than another equally possible future will be established.

The author's preference for a future in which many individuals have access to information technology, and in which democracy is a participatory reality, has been made clear. The most likely alternative future seems to be one in which all are nominally free to use IT (as to enter the Ritz), but few have the actual resources and know-how to take full advantage of the opportunities. The most unhappy possible future in this respect is one in which the extensive powers of surveillance and manipulation offered by this technology are used, ultimately, to undermine even the fiction of democracy.

Recommended reading

Eisenstadt, M. and Vincent, T. (2000) *The Knowledge Web: Learning and Collaborating on the Net*, London, Kogan Page. Draws upon research and practice at Britain's Open University.

Jackson, Paul and Van Der Weilen, Jos M. (eds) (1998) *Teleworking: International Perspectives*, London, Routledge. Stimulating collection of research papers on teleworking, including discussion of the concept of virtual organizations.

Rheingold, Howard (1992) *Virtual Reality* (2nd edn), London, Mandarin. Interesting treatment of VR which considers the industrial, cultural and psychological dimensions of 'grasping reality through illusion'.

Schuler, Douglas (1996) *Community Networks*, Harlow, ACM Press and Addison-Wesley Longman. Comprehensive treatment of US scene with interesting case studies and many website references.

Silverstone, Roger and Hirsch, Eric (eds) (1994) *Consuming Technologies*, London, Routledge. Excellent collection of research papers on the impact of information technology and the media on the family and consumers.

Glossary
Including acronyms and abbreviations

Words or acronyms in *italics* are explained in a separate entry.

AI   Artificial Intelligence.

Analogue   Prior to digital technology, electronic transmission was limited to analogue technology, which conveys data as electronic signals of varying frequency or amplitude that are added to carrier waves of a given frequency. Broadcast and telephone transmission originally used analogue technology (cf. *digital*).

Applications   Programs other than an *operating system* are called applications.

ASCII   American Standard Code for Information Interchange – standard method of translating alphabetical and numerical characters and other symbols into binary numbers.

ASP   Application Service Provider – is a company that hosts and manages business applications on behalf of a client. These applications can vary from basic e-mail to extremely complex and demanding applications such as *ERP* and *CRM*.

Availability   The percentage of time a system is operating efficiently.

Backbone   The major artery of a distributed system. At the local level, a backbone is a line or set of lines that local area networks connect to. On a wide area network, a backbone is a set of paths that local or regional networks connect to for long-distance interconnection.

Bandwidth   The bandwidth of a transmitted communications signal is a measure of the range of frequencies the signal occupies. Animated videos, large sound files, and some computer programs require a great deal of bandwidth, and can sometimes cause the system to slowdown in performance.

Banners   Can either be an image that announces the name or identity of a site (and often is spread across the width of the web page) or an advertising image. Advertisers sometimes count banner 'views', or the number of times a banner graphic image was downloaded over a period of time.

BASIC   Beginners All-purpose Symbolic Instruction Code (computer language).

BEAB British Electrical Approvals Board.

Bit The smallest data element of a *digital* information system, corresponding to either 0 or 1.

BPR Business Process Re-engineering – the complete redesign of business processes to make best use of new technology (see Chapter 5).

Browser A software program used to locate and display information on web pages.

BT British Telecom. Major UK *PTO*.

Byte A group of eight *bits* often used to represent a number or character in a *digital* information system.

B2B Business-to-Business commerce. Using electronic interactions to conduct business among enterprises, typically as a result of formal, contractual arrangements.

B2C Business-to-Consumer commerce. Using electronic interactions to conduct business with consumers. B2C may include formal relationships (e.g. customers with assets under care or with subscription services or content) and real-time relationships to enable a new user to buy, sell or access information.

CAD Computer-Aided design.

CAM Computer-Aided Manufacturing/management.

CBI Confederation of British Industries – employers' lobby group.

CCIT International Telephone & Telegraphic Consultative Committee.

CCTA Central Computing and Telecommunications Agency – UK government executive agency.

CD-ROM Compact Disk-Read-Only Memory.

CEN Pan European Committee for Standardization.

CENLEC Pan European Committee for Electrotechnical Standardization.

CEPT Conference of European Postal & Telecommunication Administrations – covers all Europe, including EU.

Client-server Configuration of networked computers in which a central server provides much of the software and data storage for satellite 'client' PCs.

CNC Computer Numerically Controlled (of machines and tools).

COBOL Common Business Oriented Language – computer language mainly used on older mainframe-based business systems.

COCOMO Estimating technique used in project planning.

.com Appearing on the end of a *URL*, this indicates that the host computer is run by a commercial organization (often in the United States). The phrase 'dot.com' has now been widely accepted as a term for an Internet-based enterprise.

Content provider A firm whose products are information-based (content), including services to access and manage the content.

Cookie Information that a website puts on your hard disk so that it can remember something about you at a later time. Cookies are able to record likes, dislikes and preferences so that it can present a user with information and offers specific to the individual user. Cookies create great opportunities for advertisers and direct marketers. Web users must agree to let cookies be saved for them but, in general, it helps websites to serve users better.

CPU   Central Processor Unit.

CRM   Customer Relationship Management – a technology enabled strategy to convert data-driven decisions into business actions in response to, and in anticipation of, actual customer behaviour. From a strategy perspective, it represents a process to measure and allocate organizational resources to those activities that have the greatest return and impact on profitable customer relationships. From a technology perspective, CRM represents the systems and infrastructure required to capture, analyse and share all facets of the customer's relationship with the enterprise.

CSP   Commerce Service Providers – they specialize in web-enabled e-commerce services, as well as those offering specific software or outsourcing support for these services.

Datamining   The analysis of large quantities of data for relationships that have not previously been discovered.

Data warehousing   Centralized storage of all, or significant parts of, the data that an enterprise's various systems collect to facilitate business analysis.

Decryption   See *encryption*.

DES/DfEE   Department of Education and Skills, Department for Education and Science, Department for Education and Employment – UK Ministry variously titled over time.

Digital   An electronic technology that generates, stores, and processes data in binary form (i.e. two states: positive and non-positive). Data transmitted or stored with digital technology is expressed as a string of 0s and 1s. Each of these state digits is referred to as a 'bit' (cf. *analogue*).

DIP   Document Image Processing. Software which facilitates the storage, classification and use of paper documents. Images of original documents are scanned into database systems.

DoD   Department of Defense – USA Federal Department.

Domain   Domains are the Internet's method of allocating a place in the naming hierarchy to Internet server sites. An Internet domain name consists of a sequence of names (labels) separated by periods (dots) e.g. www.bournemouth.ac.uk

DNS   Domain Name System – the way that Internet domain names are located and translated into IP (Internet Protocol) addresses. A domain name is a meaningful and easy-to-remember 'handle' for an Internet address. Because maintaining a central list of domain name/IP address correspondences would be impractical, the lists of domain names and IP addresses are distributed throughout the Internet in a hierarchy of authority.

DOS Disk Operating System – formerly the dominant *operating system* for *PCs*.

Downtime Measures the amount of time the system is not available for use. Unlike 'uptime', downtime is measured in physical time rather than as a percentage.

DTI Department of Trade and Industry – UK Ministry which sponsors and regulates the information technology industry.

E-business A business which has transformed its business processes, distribution channels and organizational structures to maximize performance using Internet technology.

E-commerce (EC) The use of modern communication technologies to transmit business information and transact business.

EC European Community (older name for *European Union*).

ECU European currency units (£0.78 December 1994) replaced by the Euro, of roughly similar value, in January 1999.

EDI Electronic Document Interchange – standardized form of e-mail for commercial transactions.

E-market maker Intermediaries that develop a *B2B* e-marketplace of buyers and sellers within an industry, geographic region or affinity group. They enter supply chains introducing new efficiencies and new ways of selling and purchasing products and services by providing content, value-added services, and often e-commerce capabilities. A third party within a trading community generally manages them.

E-marketplace A website that enables buyers to select from many suppliers. E-marketplaces are buying environments that put together supplier content and provide decision support tools that enable a buyer to make a more informed decision.

Encryption The conversion of data into a form, called a cipher, that cannot be easily understood by unauthorized people. Decryption is the process of converting encrypted data back into its original form, so it can be understood by the recipient.

ENVIAC Pioneer US computer.

E-procurement The business-to-business purchase and sale of supplies and services over the Internet.

ERP Enterprise Resource Planning. The process of integrating personnel, sales, manufacturing and financial functions into a single unified system.

ESPRIT European Strategic Programme for Research & Development in Information Technology.

ETSI European Telecommunications Standards Institute.

EU European Union.

EWOS European Workshop on Open Systems.

Extranet A collaborative, Internet-based network to link an enterprise with its suppliers, customers or other external business partners and to facilitate intercompany relationships.

Firewall A system that connects a local network to the Internet but acts as a security perimeter between internal and external data or systems.

FSP Full Service Provider. Extends the *ASP* model by offering full business process 'out-sourcing'.

FTP File Transfer Protocol. A standard Internet *protocol*, it is the simplest way to exchange files between computers on the Internet.

GB Gigabytes (memory capacity in approximately billion-*byte* units).

GUI Graphical User Interface. Enables relatively unskilled users to program computers by manipulating *icons*.

HDTV High-definition television.

Heritage/legacy applications Those that have been inherited from languages, platforms, and techniques earlier than current technology.

Homepage The 'starter' page of a website, usually the main page of a company, organization or person.

Host The primary computer in a multiple computer installation network – especially one that accommodates an ISP's web pages.

HTML HyperText Markup Language – main computer language used in constructing World Wide Web pages.

HTTP Hypertext Transfer Protocol. The set of rules for exchanging files (text, graphic images, sound, video, and other multi-media files) on the World Wide Web. HTTP is an application protocol.

IBM International Business Machines – American 'multinational' IT company.

Icon Symbolic representation of an object in a program (e.g. a small picture on the screen).

ICTs Information and communication technologies – often used as this book uses *IT*, with stress on convergence through use of *digital* techniques.

Intelligent agent Software that acts as an intermediary for a person by performing some activity. Agents can 'learn' an individual's preferences and act in the person's best interest, and may even negotiate and complete transactions.

Internet A huge network of computers, where, potentially, any one computer can get information from any other computer. The most used part of the Internet is the *World Wide Web*. Its distinctive feature is the use of *protocols* called *TCP/IP*.

Intranet A closed corporate version of the Internet that runs via Internet protocols and tools.

IP/TCP Internet Protocols/Transmission Control Protocols – the rules which ensure that World Wide Web applications can intercommunicate.

IPO Input–Process–Output model of thinking.

ISDN Integrated Services Digital Network – standard format for digital telephones.

ISO International Standards Organization.

ISP Internet Service Provider. A company that provides access to the Internet. For a monthly fee, or a percentage of telephone call charges, the service provider supplies users with a software package, username, password and access phone number. ISPs are also called IAPs (Internet Access Providers).

IT Information technology – see Introduction and Chapter 1.

JANET Joint Academic Network (Linked UK universities, replaced by SUPERJANET).

Java Object-oriented programming language which allows different computers to communicate with each other across networks.

JIT Just-In-Time. A manufacturing technique which minimizes stock-holdings, and maximizes flexibility of production, by organizing production of goods to order on the basis of the last-minute deliveries from suppliers. Requires use of *WAN* and *EDI*.

KB Kilobyte – memory capacity in approximately a thousand *bytes*. Strictly, 1 kilobyte = 1,024 (2 to the power of 10) *bytes*.

Knowledge management (KM) A business process that manages a firm's intellectual assets. It promotes a collaborative and integrative approach to the creation, capture, organization, access and use of information assets, including the tacit, uncaptured knowledge of people.

LAMDA A European local government networking project.

LAN Local Area Network. A relatively small network of computers operating without *modems* or *leased lines* and hence usually at higher bandwidths than *WANs*.

Lead-time The amount of time it takes for a product to be delivered from the inception of the original order. The pressure is always on to reduce lead-times, particularly with the speed of ordering created by the Internet.

Leased line A leased line is a telephone line that has been leased for private use. In some contexts it's called a dedicated line. A leased line is usually contrasted with a switched line or dial-up line.

Market spoilers or killers Web-based businesses that collect information about a market and its suppliers, present the aggregated information to consumers via a website, and increasingly offer decision support to allow customers to choose between competitors' services and features.

MB Megabytes – memory capacity in approximately millions of 'bytes' of 8 binary digits. Technically 1 megabyte equals 1,048,576 (2 to the power of 20) *bytes*.

M-commerce Mobile commerce – using a mobile device to transact business over the Internet.

MHz Megahertz. Speed of (e.g.) *central processor units* in millions of clock cycles.

MI5 Military Intelligence section 5 (UK counter-espionage organization).

MIS Management Information Systems.

MIPS Millions of Instructions per Second. An alternative measure of processor speed.

Mission critical A mission critical application is one that, for operational reasons, cannot be allowed to fail. An example is an air traffic control system. High availability can be achieved through 'clustering', when if one system fails another can take over.

Modem Modulator–demodulator. Converts digital language from a device such as a computer into analogue signals for transmission across the telephone network, and then demodulates the incoming analogue signal converting it back into a signal for the digital device.

NAP Network Access Points. Connect *ISP*s together.

NIC Newly Industrialized Countries.

NREN US Internet.

NSA National Security Administration – USA government body coordinating intelligence advice to the President.

NSFNET National Science Foundation Network – US academic Internet.

OEM Original Equipment Manufacturers. Computer hardware production firms.

OFTEL Office of Telecommunications. UK regulator.

ONP Open Network Provision. EU policy for telephone services.

OS Operating System. The program, such as Unix or Windows, that manages all the other programs in a computer.

OSI Open Systems Interconnection. Set of international standards for the interconnection of computing devices.

Out-sourcing Out-sourcing is an arrangement in which one company provides services for another company that could have been provided in-house.

PBS Product Breakdown Structure. An early stage in the project planning process (see Chapter 5).

PBX A *digital* telephone exchange.

PC Personal Computer.

PDA Personal Digital Assistants. A small mobile hand-held computing device for personal or business use. Often allows Internet access.

Personalization Using continually adjusted 'user profiles' to match content or services to individuals. Profiles are based on user preferences or behaviour. Personalization involves constructing business rules to select relevant content and presenting the content to the user in a coherent format.

PGP Pretty Good Privacy. Encryption system.

PID Project Initiation Document (see pp. 158–64).

Portal A website with a wide range of content, services and links intended to be the first point of entry to the *Internet*. It acts as a value-added middleman by selecting the content sources and assembling them together in a simple-to-navigate interface for presentation to the user. Portals typically include services such as search engines, e-mail, community information and chat rooms.

PRINCE Projects IN Controlled Environments – UK government project control system.

Protocols A formal description of messages to be exchanged and rules to be followed for two or more systems to exchange information.

PTO Public Telecommunications Operators.

QUANGOs Quasi-Autonomous Non- [or National] Governmental Organizations.

RAM Random Access Memory. Silicon chip which temporarily holds data and programs being worked upon by a computer.

ROM Read-Only Memory. Silicon chip which permanently holds part of computer operating system instructions.

Scalability The ability of your systems to grow with a company's needs and expected utilization.

SCM Supply Chain Management. The process of optimizing delivery of goods, services and information from supplier to customer. SCM is a set of business processes that encompass a trading-partner community engaged in a common goal of satisfying the end customer.

Server system A system that supplies services to other computers (clients) on a network.

Service provider Service providers host another company's software applications, e-mail and Internet connections leaving the client company to concentrate on their own core business skills.

SSADM Structured Systems Analysis and Design Method – UK government standard systems development methodology.

SSM Soft Systems Methodology – approach to system development pioneered by Checkland.

TB Terabytes – approximately 1 trillion *bytes.*

TCP/IP Transport Control Protocol/Internet Protocol. The default protocol suite originally developed for the Internet.

TUC Trades Union Congress. UK employees lobby group.

Uptime Measure of the time the computer system is running and available for use.

URL Uniform Resource Locator. The address of a file (resource) accessible on the Internet (e.g. http://www.bournemouth.ac.uk/business-school/staff/stansey/businessITsociety) is a URL.

Value chain An analysis of where in the supply chain the company can add value to the customer.

VAT Value added tax. EU sales tax.

VDU Visual Display Unit. A computer monitor.

VLSI Very Large Scale Integration. Technology enabling complex electronic circuits to be embodied in a small silicon chip.

WAN Wide Area Network connects users together over several locations using either *leased lines* or the *Internet*. Usually connects many *LANs* together.

WAP   Wireless Application Protocol. A secure specification that allows users to access information instantly via hand-held wireless devices such as mobile phones, pagers, two-way radios, smart-phones and communicators. It defines a connection *protocol* and mark-up language, similar to a reduced version of *HTML*.

WBS   Work breakdown structure. Early step in the project planning process (see Chapter 5).

WIMP   Windows, icon, mouse, pointer. Type of user interface.

Wintel   (Microsoft) Windows (operating system) Intel (CPU) – 1990s standard PC.

World Wide Web   An *Internet* service whereby users can gain access to millions of pages of information throughout the globe.

X25   International standard for data transmission over telephone circuits.

On-line resources

The following is only a very small list of web sites not referred to in the bibliography. A more complete and systematic list is available online at www.bournemouth.ac.uk/businessschool/staff/stansey/businessITsociety

Please feel free to email the author with queries or comments on this book at stansey@bournemouth.ac.uk and/or steve@thetanseyfamily.org

Business Education Resources: www.biz.ed.ac.uk

BPR Online Learning Center: www.prosci.com
(indexes many articles on Business Process Reengineering and Change Management)

British Government Information Portal: www.ukonline.gov.uk
(also indexes local government sites)

British Association for Open Learning: www.baol.co.uk

Business On Line (UK Government: site including 100 case studies of business use of IT): www.ukonlineforbusiness.gov.uk

Confederation of British Industry: www.cbi.org.uk

Daily technology news on-line: www.vnunet.com

European Union: www.europa.eu.int

Families of SMA (United States): www.fsma.org

Information Commissioner (Data Protection and Freedom of Information in the UK): www.dataprotection.gov.uk

Internet news service: www.internetworld.com

Jennifer Trust for Spinal Muscular Atrophy (Britain): www.jtsma.org.uk

Guardian Newspaper: www.guardian.co.uk

London School of Economics and University College London research on British Government use of the web: www.governmentontheweb.org

Open University (UK) research and practice to illuminate the theme of e-learning: www.kmi.open.ac.uk/knowledgeweb

Silicon ebusiness news service: www.silicon.com

THOMAS: US legislative information: thomas.loc.gov/

Virtual Amsterdam: www.dds.nl/dds/info/english

Washington Post: www.washingtonpost.com

Organizations for Business and IS Academics and Professionals:

UK Academy for Information Systems: www.ukais.org
(useful list of relevant journals)

Association for Computing Machinery: www.acm.org
(see material on computing and public policy)

British Computer Society: www.bcs.org

Institute of Management: www.inst-mgt.org.uk

Bibliography

Adair, J. (1991) *Not Bosses But Leaders*, London, Kogan Page.

Ang, Ien (1994) 'Living Room Wars', in Roger Silverstone and Eric Hirsch (eds) *Consuming Technologies*, London, Routledge.

Angell, Ian (2000) *The New Barbarian Manifesto: How to Survive the Information Age*, London, Kogan Page.

Armistead, Colin and Kiely, J. (eds) (1997) *Effective Organisations: New Directions and Perspectives*, London, Cassell.

Arterton, C.F. (1987) *Teledemocracy*, London, Sage.

Awad, Elias (1988) *Management Information Systems*, Merlo Park, Calif., Benjamin/ Cummings.

Bailey, John (1993) *Managing People and Technological Change*, London, Pitman.

BBC2 (1995) *The Money Programme:* 'The Information Superhighway'.

Beer, S. (1985) *Diagnosing the System for Organization: The Managerial Cybernetics of Organization*, Chichester, John Wiley & Sons.

Bell, Daniel (1973) *The Coming of Post-Industrial Society*, New York, Basic Books.

Bertalanffy, L. von (1968) *General System Theory*, New York, George Braziller.

Bird, Emma (1980) *Information Technology in the Office: The Impact on Women*, Manchester, Equal Opportunities Commission.

Block, Robert (1983) *The Politics of Projects*, New York, Yourdon Press.

Boddy, David and Buchanan, David A. (1987) *Management of Technology: The Technical Change Audit*, Sheffield, Manpower Services Commission.

Brady, Tim and Liff, Sonia (1983) *Monitoring New Technology and Employment*, Sheffield, Manpower Services Commission.

Braun, Ernest (1998) *Technology in Context: Technology Assessment for Managers*, London, Routledge.

Brosnan, Mark and Davidson, M.J. (1994) 'Computerphobia – Is it a Particularly Female Phenomenon?', *The Psychologist*, 7 (2), 73–8.

Bryson, Valerie (1992) *Feminist Political Theory*, Basingstoke, Macmillan.

Buckley, W. (1967) *Sociology and Modern Systems Theory*, Englewood Cliffs, N.J., Prentice-Hall.

Burgess, Charles (1986) *The Impact of New Technology on Skills in Manufacturing and Services*, R & D Series 28, Sheffield, Manpower Services Commission.

Burns, Tom and Stalker, G.M. (1966) *The Management of Innovation* (2nd edn), London, Tavistock.

Campbell, Duncan (2001) 'How US Plotters Escaped the Net', *Guardian Online*, 27 September, 1–3.

Cash, J., Eccles, R.G., Hohria, N. and Nolan, R.L. (1994) *Building the Information Age Organization*, Burr Ridge, Ill., Richard Irwin.

CBI (Confederation of British Industries) (1985) *Managing Change*, London, CBI.

Chalton, Simon and Gaskill, Shelagh (eds) (1988 and Supplements) *Encyclopedia of Data Protection*, London, Sweet & Maxwell.

Checkland, Peter (1981) *Systems Thinking, Systems Practice*, Chichester, John Wiley & Sons.

Checkland, P. and Holwell, S. (1998) *Information, Systems, and Information Systems*, Chichester, John Wiley & Sons.

Checkland, P. and Scholes, J. (1990) *Soft Systems Methodology in Action*, Chichester, John Wiley & Sons.

Chmiel, Nik (1998) *Jobs, Technology and People*, London, Routledge.

Cisler, S. (1993) 'Community Computer Networks' in A. Bishop, *Emerging Communities*, Champaign-Urbana, University of Illinois.

Clement, Bernard *et al.* (2001) 'Cyber-Security Issues', *The ITPS Report, Seville*, vol. 57, 2–8.

Cockfield, Lord (1995) *Network Europe and the Information Society*, London, Federal Trust.

Collier, Harry (1988) *Information Flow Across Frontiers*, Oxford, Learned Information.

Comptroller and Auditor General (1993) *Data Protection Controls & Safeguards*, London, HMSO.

Computer Law and Security Report (recent issues).

Conner-Sax, Kiersten and Krol, Ed (1999) *The Whole Internet: The Next Generation*, Sebastapol, Calif., O'Reilly & Associates.

Cornish, W.R. (1999) *Intellectual Property, Patents, Copyright, Trade Marks and Allied Rights* (4th edn), London, Sweet & Maxwell.

Coutsoukis, Photius (1999) 'Singapore Economy', http://www.photius.com (1 March).

Dahrendorf, Ralf (1959) *Class and Class Conflict in Industrial Society*, London, Routledge & Kegan Paul.

Dainhoff, M.J. and Dainhoff, M.H. (1987) *A Manager's Guide to Ergonomics in the Electronic Office*, Chichester, John Wiley.

Daniel, W.W. (1987) *Workplace Industrial Relations and Technical Change*, London, Frances Pinter/Policy Studies Inst.

Darnton, G. and Giacoletto, S. (1992) *Information in the Enterprise: It's More Than Technology*, Burlington, Mass., Digital Press (now available from the first author ISBN 1-902755-01-4).

Data Protection Registrar (1993–) *Annual Reports* 9, Wilmslow, Cheshire, HMSO.

Data Protection Registrar (1995) *Student Information*, Wilmslow, Cheshire, Data Protection Registrar.

Dauncey, Hugh (1996) 'France and the Information Superhighway', *Politics*, 16 (2), 87–94.

Davidson, M.J. and Cooper, G.L. (1992) *Shattering the Glass Ceiling*, London, Paul Chapman.

De Woot, Philipe (1990) *High Technology Europe*, Oxford, Basil Blackwell.

Dean, Phyllis (1965) *The First Industrial Revolution*, Cambridge, Cambridge University Press.

DeLamarter, Richard T. (1987) *Big Blue: IBM's Abuse of Power*, London, Macmillan.

Dennis, A. and Wixom, B.H. (2000) *Systems Analysis and Design: An Applied Approach*, New York, John Wiley & Sons.

Drucker, Peter F. (1985) *Innovation and Entrepreneurship: Practice and Principles*, London, Heinemann.

Drucker, Peter F. (1988) *Harvard Business Review*, 88 (1).

Drucker, Peter F. (1993) *Post Capitalist Society*, Oxford, Butterworth-Heinemann.

Dunning, John H. (1988) *Multinationals, Technology and Competitiveness*, London, Unwin Hyman.

Earl, Michael J. (1989) *Management Strategies for Information Technology*, New York, Prentice-Hall.

Earl, Michael (1994) 'Viewpoint: The New and the Old of Business Process Redesign', *Journal of Strategic Information Systems*, 3 (1), 5–22.

Earl, Michael J. and Skyrme, D.J. (1992) 'Hybrid Managers – What Do We Know About Them?', *Journal of Information Systems*, 2, 169–87.

Easton, David (1979) *A Framework for Political Analysis*, Chicago, University of Chicago Press.

Economist Intelligence Unit (1991) *European Trends* (3), London, EIU.

Eisenstadt, M. and Vincent, T. (2000) *The Knowledge Web: Learning and Collaborating on the Net*, London, Kogan Page.

European Commission (1995a) 'Directive 95/46/EC of the European Parliament and of the Council on the Protection of Individuals with Regard to the Processing of Personal Data and on the Free Movement of Such Data', *Official Journal EC*, 38 (1) L, 281/32, 24 October.

European Commission (1995b) *European Integration*, Brussels, European Commission.

Ferguson, Marjorie (ed.) (1986) *New Communication Technologies and the Public Interest*, London, Sage.

Financial Times (1999) *Mastering Global Business*, London, Financial Times.

Financial Times (2001) 'Survey Singapore', *Financial Times*, 11 April.

Financial Times Survey (1992) 'Information Technology in Europe', *Financial Times*, 17 March.

Finn, Dan (1984) *The Employment Effects of the New Technologies*, London, Unemployment Unit.

Flaherty, M. Therese (1996) *Global Operations Management*, London, McGraw-Hill.

Flowers, Stephen (1988) *Success in Information Processing*, London, John Murray.

Forester, Tom (ed.) (1985) *The Information Technology Revolution*, Oxford, Blackwell.

Forrester, J.W. (1961) *Industrial Dynamics*, Cambridge, Mass., MIT Press.

Forrester, J.W. (1969) *Urban Dynamics*, Cambridge, Mass., MIT Press.

Forrester, J.W. (1971) *World Dynamics*, Cambridge, Mass., Wright-Allen Press.

Foxall, Gordon R. (1984) *Corporate Innovation: Marketing and Strategy*, Beckenham, Croom Helm.

Francissen, Letty and Brants, Kees (1998) 'Virtually Going Places: Square Hopping in Amsterdam's Digital City', in R. Tsagarousianou *et al.*, *Cyberdemocracy: Technology, Cities and Civic Networks*, London, Routledge.

Frankel, Maurice (1995) 'State's Open Secrets', *Guardian*, 2, 24/1, 17.

Freeman, Christopher (1982) *The Economics of Industrial Innovation* (2nd edn), London, Frances Pinter.

Garnham, Nicholas (1990) *Telecommunications in the UK: a Policy for the 1990s*, London, Fabian Society.

Gater, Ian (1987) *Applied Ergonomics Handbook*, London, Butterworth.

Gerth, H. and Mills, C.W. (1948) *From Max Weber*, London, Routledge.

Gibson, C.F. and Nolan, R.L. (1974) 'Managing The Four stages of EDP Growth', *Harvard Business Review*, January–February.

Gibson, William (1984) *Neuromancer*, London, Victor Gollancz.

Gilster, Paul (1994) *The Internet Navigator* (2nd edn), Chichester, Wiley.

Global Reach (2001) Global Internet Statistics, www.glreach.co/globstats/index.php3, revised June 2001, accessed 29 September 2001.

Goodridge, J.M. and Twiss, B. (1988) *Technology Management and Change*, Sheffield, Manpower Services Commission, MC 100.

Graves, John (1986) *Liberating Technology*, London, Peter Owen.

Gross, N., Giacquanta, J.B. and Bernstein, M. (1971) *Implementing Organisational Innovations*, London, Harper & Row.

Hadden, Lelic (1994) 'Explaining ICT Consumption', in Roger Silverstone and Erich Hirsch (eds) *Consuming Technologies*, London, Routledge.

Hammer, M. and Champy, J. (1995) *Re-engineering the Corporation: A Manifesto for a Business Revolution* (revised edn), London, Nicholas Brearley.

Handy, Charles (1982) *Understanding Organisations*, Harmondsworth, Middlesex, Penguin.

Harvard Business Review (1991) *The Information Infrastructure*, Cambridge, Mass., Harvard Business Review Paperback 90078.

Heap, N., Thomas, R., Einon, G., Mason, R. and Mackay, H. (eds) (1995) *Information Technology and Society: A Reader*, London, Sage.

Herzberg, F., Mausner, B. and Bloch Snyderman, B. (1959) *The Motivation to Work*, Chichester, Wiley.

Hills, Jill, with Papathanassopoulos, Stylianos (1991) *The Democracy Gap: The Politics of Information and Communication Technologies in the United States and Europe*, London, Greenwood Press.

House of Commons Industry Committee (1988/9) *First Report: Information Technology (HC 25)*, London, HMSO.

Huczynski, Andrzej (2001) *Organisational Behaviour* (4th edn), Harlow, Financial Times/Prentice-Hall.

Huws, U. (1993) *Teleworking in Britain*, London, Employment Department Research Series, 18.

Hyman, Richard and Streeck, Wolfgang (1988) *New Technology & Industrial Relations*, Oxford, Basil Blackwell.

Illich, Ivan (1976) *De-Schooling Society*, Harmondsworth, Middlesex, Penguin.

Industrial Relations Services (1988) *Industrial Relations in Britain*, London, Industrial Relations Services.

International Business Intelligence (1989) *1992 – Planning for the Information Technology*, London, International Business Intelligence.

Jackson, Paul and van der Weilen, Jos M. (eds) (1998) *Teleworking: International Perspectives*, London, Routledge.

Jenkins, Clive and Sherman, Barrie (1979) *The Collapse of Work*, London, Eyre Methuen.

JFIT News (1993) 'European R&D', *JFIT News*, 4, May.

Johnston, Nicholas and McCarthy, Ellen (2001) 'After the Tech Implosion, Measuring the Shock Waves', *Washington Post*, 5 November, E01.

Jones, Gwyn (1975) *Agricultural Innovation and Farmer Decision Making*, Milton Keynes, Open University.

Kaye, David (1990) *Game Change: The Impact of Information Technology on Corporate Strategy and Structures*, London, Heinemann.

Keene, Peter G.W. (1991) *Shaping The Future*, Cambridge, Mass., Harvard Business School Press.

Locksley, Gareth (ed.) (1990) *The European Single Market and the Information and Communication Technologies*, London, Bellhaven Press.

Lovelock, James (1979) *Gaia*, Oxford, Oxford University Press.

Lynch, Daniel C. and Rose, Marshall T. (eds) (1993) *Internet System Handbook*, Reading, Mass. and Wokingham, Addison-Wesley.

MacInnes, John (1987) *Thatcherism at Work*, Buckingham, Open University Press.

MANDIT (1986) *Management Development for Information Technology*, Sheffield, Manpower Services Commission.

Mangham, Ian (1979) *The Politics of Organisational Change*, London, Associated Business Press.

Mansell, Robin (1993) *The New Telecommunications*, London, Sage.

Margetts, Helen (1991) 'The Computerization of Social Security: The Way Forward or a Step Back?', *Public Administration*, 69 (3), 325–44.

Maslow, A.H. (1943) 'A Preface to Motivation Theory', *Psychosomatic Medicine*, 5, 85.

Marx, Karl and Engels, F. (1962) *Selected Works*, Moscow, Foreign Languages Publishing House.

Masuda, Youeji (1985) 'Computopia', in Tom Forester (ed.) *The Information Technology Revolution*, Oxford, Blackwell.

McCloughlin, I. and Clark, J. (1988) *Technological Change at Work*, Buckingham, Open University Press.

McFarlane, F. Warren and McKenny, James L. (1992) *Corporate Information Systems Management*, Homestead, Ill., Irwin.

Meadows, D.H., Meadows, D.L., Randers, J. and Behrens III, W.W. (1972) *The Limits to Growth*, London, Earth Island.

Miles, Ian (1990) *Mapping & Measuring the Information Economy*, London, British Library Research & Development Department.

Moore, N. and Steele, J. (1991) *Information Intensive Britain*, London, Policy Studies Institute.

Morino Institute (1994) 'Assessment and Evolution of Community Networking', www.morino.org

Moschella, David (1997) *Waves of Power: Dynamics of Global Technology Leadership 1964–2010*, New York, American Management Association.

Naisbitt, J. and Aburdene, P. (1985) *Re-inventing the Corporation*, London, Macdonald.

Nolan, R.L. (1979) 'Managing The Crises in Data Processing', *Harvard Business Review*, March–April.

Northcott, Jim and Walling Annette (1988) *The Impact of Microelectronics*, London, Policy Studies Institute.

NUA Internet Surveys (2001) 'How Many Online?', Dublin, Computerscope Ltd, www.nae.ie/surveys/how-many-online/index.html

OECD (1986) *Trends in the Information Economy*, Paris, Organization for Economic Cooperation and Development.

OECD (1987) *Information Technology and Economic Prospects*, Paris, Organization for Economic Cooperation and Development.

OECD (1989) *Government Policies and the Diffusion of Microelectronics*, Paris, Organization for Economic Cooperation and Development.

Parker, Barbara (1998) *Globalization and Business Practice*, London, Sage.

Patent Office (1993) *Designs – Basic Facts*, Newport, Gwent, Department of Trade & Industry.

Patent Office (1994a) *Patent Search Service*, Newport, Gwent, Department of Trade & Industry.

Patent Office (1994b) *What Is Intellectual Property?*, Newport, Gwent, Department of Trade & Industry.

Patterson, T.T. (1960) *Glasgow Ltd*, Cambridge, Cambridge University Press.

Peppard, Joe (ed.) (1993) *IT Strategy for Business*, London, Pitman.

Perry, Keith (1994) *Business in the European Community*, Oxford, Butterworth-Heinemann.

Pheasant, Stephen (1988) *Bodyspace: Anthropometry, Ergonomics and Design*, London, Taylor & Francis.

Phlips, L. (1988) *The Economics of Imperfect Information*, Cambridge, Cambridge University Press.

Pickles, Dorothy (1971) *Democracy*, London, Methuen.

Pinto, J.K. and Slevin, D.P. (1988) 'Critical Success Factors Across the Project Life Cycle', *Project Management Journal*, XIX (3), 67–75.

Porter, Michael (1990) *The Competitive Advantage of Nations*, New York, Free Press.

Proddow, Louise (2000) *Heroes.com*, London, Hodder & Stoughton.

Pugh, D.S. (ed.) (1997) *Organization Theory* (4th edn), Harmondsworth, Middlesex, Penguin Books.

Pugh, D.S. and Hickson, D.J. (1996) *Writers on Organizations* (5th edn), Harmondsworth, Middlesex, Penguin Books.

Remenyi, D., Sherwood-Smith, M. and White, T. (1997) *Achieving Maximum Value from Information Systems*, Chichester, John Wiley & Sons.

Rheingold, Howard (1992) *Virtual Reality* (2nd edn), London, Mandarin.

Richardson, L.F. (1960) *Arms and Insecurity: A Mathematical Study of the Causes and Origins of War*, Pittsburgh, Pa., Boxwood Press.

Robson, Wendy (1994) *Strategic Management and Information Systems*, London, Pitman.

Rogers, E.M. (1983) *Diffusion of Innovations* (3rd edn), New York, Free Press.

Rowe, Christopher and Thompson, Jane (1996) *People and Chips* (3rd edn), London, McGraw-Hill.

Rowland, Diane and Macdonald, Elizabeth (2000) *Information Technology Law* (2nd edn), London, Cavendish Publishing.

Samuelson, P.A. (1973) *Economics* (9th edn), Kogakusha, Tokyo, McGraw-Hill.

Schuler, Douglas (1996) *Community Networks*, Harlow, ACM Press and Addison-Wesley Longman.

Self, Will (1995) *The State We're In*, London, Jonathan Cape.

Silverstone, Roger and Hirsch, Eric (eds) (1994) *Consuming Technologies*, London, Routledge.

Sirimanne, Shamika (1996) 'The Information Technology Revolution: What About the Developing Countries?' Summary by Canadian International Development Centre at www.acdi-cida.gc.ca

Skills & Enterprise Briefing (1993) 'New Jobs: Old Prejudices', Skills and Enterprise Briefing, 9/93, March.

Skyrme, D.J. (1999) *Knowledge Networking: Creating the Collaborative Enterprise*, Oxford, Butterworth-Heinemann.

Skyrme, D.J. and Earl, M.J. (1990) *Hybrid Managers: What Should You Do?*, Swindon, British Computer Society.

Springett, Peter (1994) 'Goodbye to Gossip', *Government Communication Information Management*, December, 7.

Stalling, William (2000) *Computer Organization and Architecture* (4th edn), Upper Saddle River, N.J., Prentice-Hall.

Standage, Tom (1996) 'Excalibur Revealed', *Guardian 2*, 8 February, 2–3.

Stone, David (1991) 'Future Directions in Computer-Aided Software Engineering', Taking CASE into the 1990s Symposium, Geneva, Digital Equipment Corporation.

Stowell, Frank (n.d.) Unpublished paper to Bournemouth Polytechnic staff seminar.

Strassman, P.A. (1990) *The Business Value of Computers*, New Canaan, Conn., The Information Economics Press.

Strassman, P.A. (1997) *The Squandered Computer*, New Canaan, Conn., The Information Economics Press.

Tansey, Stephen D. (1991) *The Politics of Information Technology*, Poole, Bournemouth Polytechnic Business Information Systems Working Paper, 01.

Tansey, Stephen D. (1997) 'The Politics of Effective Organisation: the Youth Training Scheme in Dorset and other Cases', in Colin Armistead and J. Kiely (eds) *Effective Organisations: New Directions and Perspectives*, London, Cassell.

Tansey, Stephen D. (2000) *Politics: The Basics* (2nd edn), London, Routledge.

Tapscott, Don and Caston, Art (1993) *Paradigm Shift: The New Promise of Information Technology*, London, McGraw-Hill.

Taylor, John A. and Williams, H. (1991) 'From Public Administration to the Information Polity', *Public Administration*, 69 (2), 171–90.

Teather, David and Cassy, John (1999) 'The Cyber Slickers', *The Guardian*, 4–6 October.

Teather, David and Cassy, John (2001) 'Where Are They Now?', *The Guardian*, 8–9 May.

Thomason, George (1988) *A Textbook of Human Resource Management*, London, Institute of Personnel Management.

Time International (1995) 'Wired Democracy', 23 January.

Tsagarousianou, R., Tambini, D. and Bryan, C. (1998) *Cyberdemocracy: Technology, Cities and Civic Networks*, London, Routledge.

Twiss, Brian (1986) *Managing Technological Innovation* (3rd edn), Harlow, Longman.

Various authors (1994–2001) Guardian On-Line.

Vincent, D.R. (1990) *The Information-Based Corporation*, Homewood Ill., Dow Jones-Irwin.

Waltermann, Jens and Machill, Marcel (eds) (2000) *Protecting Our Children on the Internet*, Gutersloh, Bertelsmann Foundation.

Ward, J. and Griffiths, P. (1996) *Strategic Planning for Information Systems* (2nd edn), Chichester, John Wiley & Sons.

Warr, Alan (1991) *Implementing IS Strategy: An Exploration of Key Issues*, Poole, Bournemouth Polytechnic Business Information Systems Working Paper.

Wateridge, John (1995) 'IT Projects: a Basis for Success', *International Journal of Project Management*, 13 (2), 169–72.

Watkins, Simon (1993) 'Closet Sexism Remains Rife in IT', *Computing*, 25 February.

Wheelock, Jane (1994) 'PCs, Gender and the Institutional Model of the Household', in Roger Silverstone and Eric Hirsch (eds) *Consuming Technologies*, London, Routledge.

Wiener, N. (1948) *Cybernetics: Or Control and Communication in the Animal and the Machine*, New York, John Wiley & Sons.

Wiener, N. (1950) *The Human Use of Human Beings*, Boston, Mass., Houghton Mifflin. (Second edition published in 1954 as *Cybernetics and Society*.)

Wilcocks, Leslie and Mason, D. (1987) *Computerising Work*, London, Paradigm Publications.

Winston, Brian (1998) *Media, Technology and Society. A History: From the Telegraph to the Internet*, London, Routledge.

Wittfogel, Karl (1957) *Oriental Despotism*, New Haven Conn., Yale University Press.

Yolles, M. (1999) *Management Systems: A Viable Approach*, London, Financial Times/Pitman Publishing.

Zerdick, Axel *et al.* (2000) *E-conomics: Strategies for the Digital Marketplace*, Berlin, Springer, for the European Communication Council.

Zuboff, Shoshana (1988) *In the Age of the Smart Machine*, London, Heinemann.

Index